BADGE 112

FOR DEBORAH -
A WESTSIDER -
Pete Alton
BADGE #112
&

PETER STIPE

BADGE 112

Down & Out Books
3959 Van Dyke Road, Suite 265
Lutz, FL 33558
DownAndOutBooks.com

Cover design by Shmael Graphics

ISBN: 1-64396-209-4
ISBN-13: 978-1-64396-209-2

For
My Mom & Dad
Gladys, George, Tyler, Darby, Riley & Brodie

Chapter One
Culver Military Academy

In June of 1970 the film *Catch 22* opened in theaters, The Beatles *Let It Be* album charted at #1, and my dad shipped me off to Culver Military Academy in Indiana. I was fourteen years old. Culver was a turn of the century college prep school with a sprawling campus of ivy-covered halls, enclosed by an imposing wrought-iron fence.

An impressive list of alumni included actors Hal Holbrook, Eugene Pallette (*The Adventures of Robin Hood*), Tim Holt (*The Treasure of the Sierra Madre*), George Steinbrenner, Gene Siskel and Roger Penske. One alumnus was made famous by Steven Ambrose's *Band of Brothers*, Easy Company's Captain Herbert Sobel. I was to meet others like him.

Culver had a fascinating "time warp" quality about it. The whole institution seemed oblivious to the world outside. As the Vietnam War ground on, Culver ignored the diminishing allure the military suffered in the midst of a contentious war. They offered two options for boys my age: a naval academy and a school of horsemanship. My dad's love of horses made cavalry the logical choice.

When I arrived at Culver, I was immediately befriended by a second classman from Bloomington, Indiana. Will Houseman had a folksy twang common to Indiana natives and he was the first kid I'd ever seen with wire-rimmed glasses and a blinkety-blink

1

disorder. I liked him immediately. After my initial check-in, he took me down to the lakeside campus hangout called "The Shack." There he introduced me to Cherry Cokes and the inspired system of charging all your purchases on your ID card. We ate there all the time, and since he always left his card "back at camp," he had the honor of being my guest nearly full-time.

The Culver campus did have an enormous tangible asset: a school for girls. The naval cadets and girls lived in aging, three-story brick dormitories. Those of us in the cavalry spent the summer in seven-by-ten foot wood framed, canvas covered tents. They were stifling in the daytime and leaked when it rained. Two cadets were sardined into each one. Footlockers, shoes and uniforms had to be carefully arranged. Beds were to be made with square corners and a fold from which you could bounce a quarter. Tents were inspected daily, and failure to pass meant "extra duty," usually some wretched chore in the horse stables. I was instantly homesick.

Disputes were settled in "The Ring," an area on the second floor of the creaking gymnasium where the wrestlers and boxers trained. The broiling summer sun and the cramped, squalid quarters brought out the worst in everybody. There was an ongoing rivalry between the naval cadets and the cavalry troopers, but fights within the cavalry squadron were also common. My dad sent me to the Culver Academy to distance me from my older, neighborhood buddies and to instill a sense of discipline and independence. Many other kids were sent there because they were incorrigible troublemakers. Slocum and Krill were two of these guys. Slocum picked fights with everyone else, Krill picked one with me.

As we started to square off on a tent porch, several other troopers separated us and a match was set for the next day at The Ring. Krill was reputed to be a trained boxer and my only qualification was that I had once wrestled in elementary school. Slocum prepped Krill for my annihilation but all the Cherry Cokes and burgers I'd invested in Will Houseman paid off when he offered to coach me. Houseman showed me how to block punches and taught me to focus on Krill's tinsel-toothed mouth but since I also wore braces, this gave me more cause for concern. I also worried about Slocum intervening on Krill's behalf.

"Don't worry about Slocum," said Houseman. "I'll take care of him. Now, let's go down to The Shack..."

The next day, equipped only with boxing gloves and shorts, we threw down at the gym. Krill caught me in the mouth right away. I could taste the blood oozing out of my lips, now impaled on my braces. I could see Houseman standing behind Krill, blinking furiously and beckoning me to let him have it the same way. I popped him over and over again. His mouth swelled like a bloated fish. He looked bad, and I felt great. In the ensuing wrestling match, I pinned him instantly.

Each week, the upperclassmen rotated rank to give them exposure to different levels of command responsibility. At the end of the summer, a final "make" was published, whereby two weeks before going home, top-ranked troopers led us on a one-hundred-mile, week-long horseback hike. We awoke at 4 a.m. and rode dust-covered Indiana back roads until late afternoon.

We pitched pup tents and used slit trenches to relieve ourselves. At night we took turns posting for picket duty watching ninety restless horses until the sound of reveille snapped us back to reality. If one was not careful to secure his gear at twilight, he could be sure it would be lost in the mad, darkened scramble at dawn. As with all situations where we're cast together to endure hardship, friendships are formed and character is molded. Before my last term at Culver was over two summers hence, those friends and my character would be tested beyond imagination.

* * *

3

The Summer of 1971

I returned to Culver the following year a strutting second classman. Underclassmen were required to leap to attention once a second classman stepped onto their tent porch. I spared them the trouble. As noncommissioned officers, we held various command support positions: sergeant major, first sergeant, guide on bearer, etc. Acquiring more responsibility improved my outlook considerably and as my riding skills improved, I began to enjoy even more aspects of our regimented existence.

One morning, while seated in the cavernous mess hall, I had a life-changing experience. I looked up to see a girl who took my breath away. She had golden hair, shimmering green eyes, and a deep, dark complexion. I watched as she turned from the food line and glided to a table across the room. I hadn't been able to read her nametag, but I pledged to find out who she was.

Stephanie Alexis was from Shaker Heights, Ohio, and dating a cavalry first classman. I was so smitten I followed them around all summer, constantly imposing on their privacy. I basked in the glow of her radiant looks and infectious laughter. I could not believe his good luck. He was tolerant of my presence because I made Stephanie laugh and he didn't perceive me as a legitimate threat. After all, he was a first classman. I had fallen in love for the first time. I could not stop thinking about her, even when summer was over and I returned home.

The Eve of Self-Destruction — The Summer of '72

As teenagers, we tested our limits, yearned for answers and sought acceptance. One method of seeking the truth was through the use of marijuana. In the early seventies, smoking marijuana was a routine part of our high school existence. It was an escape from our immediate problems and seemed to enhance sensitivity and cultivate creative thought, forcing us to look at life from a different angle. Whatever it did, we smoked a lot of it. The enlightenment was largely imaginary.

I turned sixteen on May 5, 1972, and took my driver's test before school was out. Around this time, Granger Avenue friends Brad "Tadley" Thompson, Jay Brady and I had procured a small bag of pot and split it three ways. Ignoring all common sense, I stowed my baggie and a small brass pipe among my Culver Academy gear.

When it was time to return to Culver for the summer, I arrived a day early. I was encouraged to see that Red Stuart, a Shaker Heights native and friend of Stephanie's, was already there. With only a handful of cadets on campus, I made Stuart my emissary, prevailing upon him to scout out my chances with Stephanie. I could not believe it when he returned with the good news. "She says you can ask her out... and she'll go." All the anticipation, all the anxiety, all the fantasizing of the past nine months had culminated in a simple answer to a simple question. This was one of those moments in my life when I felt I was on the brink of something truly remarkable. I wanted to be with this girl more than anything else, and I couldn't believe she'd agreed to a date.

When I finally set eyes on Stephanie that summer, she appeared more luminous than the summer before. She had blossomed into a young woman who appeared to be closer to twenty than sixteen. Her hair was a shimmering gold, her emerald eyes always sparkled, and her dark complexion implied she had just emerged from an exotic island. Built like a model as well as being extraordinarily fit, she drew looks from everyone she passed. Were she not so friendly, one might be unable to speak in her presence. She seemed oblivious to her appeal and there was nothing pretentious or aloof about her. Every male cadet and officer eyed her wherever she went. On our first date, we went to see *The Undefeated,* starring John Wayne. Twenty minutes into the film, she was grasping my hand. When we strolled outside afterwards, she whirled around, closed her eyes, and melted into me for a deep, warm kiss. When I asked her if we could go out again, she said maybe we should *only* go out with each other. The sense of relief that surged through my chest pounded my head into a dizzying euphoria. I walked her to her dorm and floated back to the squadron camp on a cloud.

Sixteen years before Timothy Hutton, Tom Cruise and Sean Penn avenged the undignified ouster of George C. Scott in the film *Taps*, Culver cadets in the heart of Indiana also had a commander they admired. Lieutenant Colonel F. W. Townsend, USA, Retired, was the embodiment of a strict academy director. A commanding presence with a soft but raspy voice, he was easy to respect and we always had the feeling he had been there and done everything he asked of us a thousand times. He was not like some of the martinets who returned as officers simply to avenge some past indignity in their Culver experience.

Reveille was sounded by Bugler at 0600 hours sharp, Monday through Saturday, with physical training (PT) formation following ten minutes later. It was scarcely enough time to leap out of bed, dress for calisthenics and pee before forming our lines. Even in the summer, the chilly Indiana dawn tempted one to remain huddled in his square cornered bunk. Like every activity, PT had strict uniform requirements, and those who did not invest in the navy-blue hooded Culver sweatshirt and heavy sweatpants would end up standing and shivering in their T-shirts and shorts. A rigorous workout and run was followed by a quick change into khakis for the long march across campus to the mess hall.

Occasionally, one of our cadre captains would have us assemble in the massive swimming hall. Addressing us in his riding breeches and boots he would swing his riding crop and order us to strip naked and play water polo while he stood by and watched, gleefully. His keen interest in naked boys combined with his flamboyant mannerisms convinced me I should never enter his tent alone.

* * *

Personal tent inspections (PI's) were conducted daily by the upperclassmen, always a stressful morning ritual. On Sunday mornings, the cadre donned white gloves and examined every inch of the tents in a general inspection, or GI. On a typical Sunday, if everything wasn't just so, or sometimes even if it was, they would flip a trunk tray and scatter the laundered clothing to kingdom come.

Before we could ride, troopers were expected to groom the horses. A mounted troop is only as good as its mounts. Culver had one hundred twenty Black Horse Troop warhorses kept in a massive stable with connecting riding hall. They were curried and brushed after inspection every morning.

Because of Stephanie I may have been the most envied guy on campus. She and I spent every spare moment together. She laughed at all my jokes, kissed me constantly and spurned all other offers to go out. We were partners in a senior life-saving class and we splashed and groped each other playfully, all under the weathered, scowling gaze of the magnificently built Ms. Garza. She was young, around thirty, but my constant clowning did little to improve her grumpy disposition.

Fed up with my antics, she ordered me off the dock and into the lake to demonstrate the proper rescue technique. She told me to flail away like a drowning victim while she affected the rescue. She dove off the pier and pulled me under the water by my ankles. She spun me around facing away from her like we had been shown, and reached up and clamped onto my scrotum as tight as she could.

The air gushed out of my lungs and I found myself nearly drowning. She pulled me to the surface all the while maintaining her death grip. I struggled to take shallow breaths and became dizzy and scared. She whispered to me, "Have we learned our lesson?" As I couldn't speak, I nodded my head in the affirmative. She dragged me back to the dock where the rest of the class marveled at the realistic demonstration. Stephanie wrapped a towel around my shoulders as I sat there gasping for breath.

From then on, every time Ms. Garza looked at me, I got a knot in my stomach and a twinge in my privates.

Stephanie's multi-colored, striped bikini contrasted nicely with her bronzed complexion. She was simply a knockout. We found ourselves surrounded by cadets every time we went sunbathing down at the naval pier. I was so high on my romance I had all but forgotten about the stash of marijuana I had brought with me. I'd lost my interest to indulge.

Although a good portion of the troop smoked pot, it was really more trouble than it was worth. There simply was no discreet place to go. The small amount I brought I kept hidden in my civilian clothes. These were hung up, in prescribed fashion, behind my academy blazer.

Alan Baxter was a fellow First Classman from Lansing, Michigan. He was a stocky brute with a mop of blond hair and black, square-rimmed glasses. An extremely sound sleeper, Baxter often dozed through reveille. Attempts to wake him up were likely to find him snapping out of his stupor with his fists flying and he bloused officers on more than one occasion. I found him to be a pain in the ass.

Discretion was not among Baxter's traits. Instead of slyly going across the road into the woods to smoke his pot like everyone else, one night, shortly after taps, he elected to light up on the tent porch next to his own. Cadre Lieutenant Henry was on his way to the latrine when he caught a whiff of the distinctive scent. Baxter, caught in mid-bowl, thereafter set in motion a series of events that would define my remaining time at Culver.

Baxter immediately offered me up as a co-conspirator, and Lieutenant Henry swept into my tent and seized the offensive substance while I sat up in my bed, blinking in bewilderment. I was whisked into the sinister tent of Captain Chase, who paced back and forth wearing a bathrobe he conveniently failed to keep tied. Most of the cadre had been mustered up for my inquisition, and I resisted the temptation to point out Captain Chase was exposing himself. They wanted to know where the dope had come from, who else was involved in the conspiracy to smoke it, and who from the troop may have partaken in marijuana smoking at any time during the summer.

I was frightened by the consequences of my stupid decision to break the rules. Stephanie didn't smoke pot and wasn't even aware that I did. I was ashamed to disgrace her and afraid our brief love affair was about to be over. On top of that, I was petrified by what would happen when my father found out. For all my insistence otherwise, he had extended to me a great deal of independence and now, before I had even enjoyed the benefits of being a licensed driver, the scandal was going to force him to crack down on me in unimaginable ways. Lastly, the three years I had invested in the Black Horse Troop were swirling down the drain as the staff mulled over how to make an example out of me.

Baxter and I had only one brief opportunity to talk to each other. Sarcastically I thanked him for squealing on me and told him that no matter what happened, no one else was to be named. There was going to be no glory in destroying the reputations of our friends, and it looked as if the only dignity remaining was in taking the well-deserved rap by ourselves. I had been stupid enough to bring pot to school and dumb enough to confide in an imbecile.

I was questioned several times. Each time I lied, saying an unknown stranger had given the pot to me during the academy's homecoming weekend. When questioned about the other cadets, I insisted no one else was involved and that I believed Baxter was a first-time user, evidenced by his ill-fated attempt at covert activity. By now, no one was speaking to Baxter, and my own friends were at cross purposes, anxious to know all the juicy details while whispering their support, but not wanting to be caught up in the scandal by virtue of association.

Ultimately, I was summoned before the Commandant of Cadets, Colonel Paule. After a prolonged wait, I was ushered into his dark, wood-paneled office. The colonel was dressed in a khaki U.S. Army uniform and motioned for me to sit down in a huge, red, button-tuck leather chair in which there was no comfortable position. He again wanted to know the source of the marijuana and wanted to clean house by having me name anyone else on campus I believed to be involved with drugs. He reminded me that possession of marijuana was a high court misdemeanor in the state of Indiana.

The commandant said that if I refused to expose others he would be forced to turn me over to the state police. Suddenly, I was no longer scared or intimidated. I'd had an epiphany. Angered at his blackmail proposition, I told him possession of marijuana was not a criminal offense in my home town of Ann Arbor, Michigan. I reminded him I was one of only seven remaining First Class cadets of a class of fifty just two summers before. I also suggested that if parents believed the academy would turn their kids over to the police for such an infraction, they might not send them to Culver at all.

The thought seemed to register as he no doubt considered the current Ann Arbor cadets and the dozen alumni who hailed from there. Military academy attendance in the United States was at an all-time low in 1972. It could easily get worse. The colonel quickly changed tactics. "Stipe, you are guilty of a serious breach of academy regulations. You have, up to now, displayed outstanding citizenship. Your impertinence under these circumstances is surprising, but this may be a learning experience for you. Effective immediately, you will be reduced to the rank of private and will forfeit all permits and privileges until graduation. Consider yourself on citizenship probation." I was dismissed with a wave of his hand, and I traipsed back to the camp.

I had a catalogue of worries. Among them was the impending letter the academy would send to my dad. I called Tadley and Jay Brady to enlist them in a scheme to intercept the letter before George (my group of friends referred to our parents by their first names) could open it. It would be a simple matter during the week since both George and my stepmother Deb worked, and our mailbox was at the entrance to our cul-de-sac, well out of view from the neighbors.

At the academy I was confined to my tent for everything except formations and class. I could see Stephanie only at life-saving class, but her understanding reaction to my story gave me a surge of relief. She had turned down a dozen offers to go out with other cadets thus far. She said she was my girl and she'd stick with me no matter what. When she told me this her loyalty and the culmination of all the anxiety, pressure and fear sent me back to my tent in tears.

A collective sigh of relief blew through the ranks when it was clear no one else was to be named. Baxter was a nearsighted rat, and I became the martyr. With only one or two exceptions, I was well received back into the troop. I was no longer a troop commander, but a first-class private, relieved of his saber and marching at the rear of all formations. I would now be at the mercy of any vindictive second classman but nothing ever happened. My laid-back style of command paid me back for not alienating any of my subordinates and I was treated better than ever. With the exception of Captain Chase and Lieutenant Henry, the cadre cut me slack, and I was able to relax.

By this third summer, I was in an advanced equitation (horsemanship) class that amounted to hell-bent-for-leather trail rides. There were miles of trails on and off campus and we tore down them all. I never lost my mount until the graduation ride. We cut down a narrow, sloping trail with the woods tight on either side. One tree stripped my leg and boot right out of the stirrup and flung it over the horse so I faced backwards on the opposite side. My back hit another tree and down the hill I tumbled. For three years I had posted a spotless riding record, up until that very last ride.

The annual one-hundred-mile troop hike got underway and,

unfortunately for me, Captain Chase was the coordinator. My duties were to ride at the rear of the entire mounted squadron, choking on road dust and horse farts, collecting any items of lost personal property such as hats or ponchos, as well as picking up the litter. As I did this I was to speak only when spoken to. While the other troopers swam their horses in the lakes and streams of our campgrounds, I dug slit trenches for the troops to relieve themselves in. Every hour I was to check the trenches and spread lime over the deposits left by my pals. I stood on night picket duty full-time, guarding the horses while the troop slept, and I pulled daylight KP, cleaning dirty plates, pans and silverware.

The hike was grueling work, and I was exhausted but I knew it was only for a week. I was so intent on ignoring Baxter that his contribution to these demeaning details eludes me. My spirits soared with the arrival of at least two letters from Stephanie with each daily mail call.

The night before the troop headed back to Culver, a number of the girl school cadets were bussed out for a bonfire. I was wrapping up my KP chores when Lieutenant Jensen approached and took me aside. "Your girlfriend's here. She brought a sleeping bag and asked where you were. I told her I'd find out." I had yet to lime the slit trench and was due to report for picket duty. I could feel the tightness in my throat and my membranes welling with tears of self-pity. "You know, Stipe, every guy at this school would like to be in your shoes. To have a girl like that, who *looks* like that, waiting for you, with a sleeping bag no less. Wash up and go to the bonfire. I'll reassign your detail."

I asked, "What about the captain?"

"Go on, I'll take care of it," he responded.

I mumbled an inadequate "thank you" and rushed off to the fire. I had met Stephanie's parents earlier in the summer, and it was evident her dad had bigger things planned for his daughter. Once they found out about my episode, I would surely be persona non grata. Her grandfather had been president of the Boy Scouts of America for crying out loud. But that night, snuggled up together in her sleeping bag, we made plans for her to visit me in Ann Arbor in the fall. She suggested having my step-mother Deb call her mother to ensure her parents' approval. She left no doubt she was coming and I knew whatever I faced going home, it would be tempered by the fact I'd see her again.

When the troop returned from the hike, I called Tad back home for a status check on the academy's letter. He and Jay had checked every day, Monday through Friday, and it hadn't arrived. On Saturday they were in position, but before they could move in, George was on his way down the steps toward the mailbox. They'd done their best, but I was doomed. I was in no hurry to explain the strange Baxter episode, and the role of marijuana in the scandal, to my father when I arrived home.

With five days remaining in the summer session, my rank and privileges were restored, and I was allowed to attend the commencement ball. Stephanie was resplendent in her gown, and for a few dreamlike hours I was able to forget the nightmare I'd created for myself. Colonel Townsend returned my impounded saber to me and, when handing me my diploma at commencement, gave me a hearty handshake and a reassuring "Nice job, Stipe."

Trooper Mac Browning of Toledo, Ohio, had been named squadron commander and, through all my controversy, had stuck by me as a loyal friend. Recognizing my fear of the extended ride home with George after camp, he offered a brief respite, inviting me to go home with him for a few days. We packed our gear into his parents' car and made our way across campus to say our goodbyes.

As anxious as I was to leave Culver, I knew I would miss Stephanie terribly. She vowed to visit and to write me often. After a prolonged embrace, I watched her run off to join her folks. We climbed into the Browning's station wagon and pulled onto the two-lane Indiana highway. I have never been back.

Home From the Rear

George was disappointed in me. It was not the first nor the last time I'd let him down. He insisted on seeing my Culver diploma as he and Deb counseled me on the dangers of drugs. They sat on the edge of their gigantic bed while I was grilled on the summer's events. Deb asked if I wasn't concerned about the possibility someone may spike marijuana with stronger drugs in order to get me hooked. I was relieved when in the end they both seemed satisfied my Culver ordeal had been punishment enough.

They were right in everything they said, and when they understood their son wasn't about to become the neighborhood junkie, Deb and George surprised me with a gift. Deb's father passed away in June, leaving behind a baby blue 1965 Plymouth Belvedere. Deb's dad had kept the car purring through one hundred eighteen thousand miles, and the 318cc V8 engine gave me newfound freedom.

In early fall, plans were finalized for Stephanie's visit. Deb worked out the details with Stephanie's mom, and she was set to arrive the third weekend of September. George and I drove to Detroit City Airport, where she arrived by charter flight. After we got her squared away in one of the downstairs guest rooms, she and I went out to eat. It was a thrill to be with her away from the confines of Culver, and I shuffled her around to show her off to all my friends.

Double dating with Jay Brady and his girlfriend Debbie, we started off at Fraser's Pub, a neighborhood watering hole. Stephanie was surprised we could sip beer so publicly at sixteen. We went to the Scio Drive-in Theater to watch *The Killing of Sister George*. I haven't even a vague recollection of the plot, since Stephanie and I made out constantly in the back seat, but I've heard it was controversial.

The next day we tooled around in the Belvedere and went shopping. I bought her a Seals & Crofts album featuring the single, "Summer Breeze." I showed her all the places I had lived

(George had exquisite taste in architecture), and we enjoyed a glorious afternoon. We had dinner with George and Deb and spent the evening in spirited conversation. Stephanie was not only a knockout, but she impressed them with her magnetic personality. I think they both realized that, despite my mishap at Culver, my summer had been well spent.

After George and Deb went to bed, Stephanie and I watched television. At about midnight, she went to take a shower and get ready for bed. I flipped through the channels looking for something to watch, my stomach churning because I knew the next day she would be gone. But I could feel my head spin and my heart flutter because that night, at that moment, she was still there, just twenty feet away.

I pulled the huge cushions from the easy chairs and laid them on the floor. *The Pawnbroker* with Rod Steiger came on and I gave up flipping channels, letting my mind drift. I heard the bathroom door open behind me as I continued to stare straight ahead. After the movement there was only silence and I was seized with the fear she had gone to bed thinking I had fallen asleep.

I whirled around and there she stood, wearing a nightgown and smiling at my shocked expression. She walked over and looked at me in her own beguiling way. She knelt down and kissed me and I was overwhelmed by the smell of her fresh, clean skin. Stephanie tenderly melted all my anxiety away.

The next morning brought pouring rain. Because Detroit City Airport was in the heart of the homicide capital of the country, I enlisted trusted friend Jimmy Hall to drive down there with us. I watched as Stephanie walked to her plane, not knowing it would be the last time I would ever see her. Had I known how difficult it would be to ever match the serenity of her companionship, I might have tried to leave her with a more memorable farewell. I'd endured some anguished times at Culver but in that one swirling summer, she'd made me feel luckier than anyone I knew.

Stephanie wrote me often throughout high school, and during her early years attending Southern Methodist University. She met and married someone who shared her active lifestyle. Their children became competitive equestrians.

On the drive home, the rain came down so hard several underpasses on Interstate 94 were flooded, and numerous cars stalled, intermittently blocking lanes. When we entered the freeway from the airport, the driver's side windshield wiper flew off the Belvedere and struck the car behind us. Jimmy steered from the passenger side all the way home. The bare wiper arm had etched an arc into the windshield, a lasting reminder of the euphoria of the weekend.

I'd be reminded of my unfortunate episode at Culver at least one more time. One day in late April, 1973, I was sitting in the sunlit recreation room of my parents' home when the phone rang. It was Alan Baxter, the Narc of Culver Academy, and I was both surprised and disgusted to hear his voice come over the line. I couldn't even pretend to be happy he'd called. He told me he was going hunting somewhere in Northern Michigan on my birthday weekend and wanted to know if I'd like to go along.

Baxter had always been a different kind of guy. He was just wired differently from most folks and was about the last person I wanted to spend personal time with. My instincts screamed at me to pass, and I told him no thank you and felt no pangs of guilt or regret.

Six weeks later, thumbing through the June issue of the Culver alumni newsletter, I read where Baxter had died of a self-inflicted gunshot wound while hunting in Northern Michigan on May 5th, the date of my seventeenth birthday. I'd never know the real reason for that final phone call, or what he thought I may have been able to do for him that particular weekend, but I never regretted not accompanying him.

Chapter Two
The Ghosts of War and the Dearly Departed

Suicide survivors. There are many of us. No, we're not the ones snatched from the brink by timely intervention or rational second thought. We are the ones left behind to reconcile unexplainable loss. That the victim meets the end on their own terms is little consolation. Any nobility in their act is lost in the shadow of overwhelming grief left behind.

Alan Baxter's death was not my first experience with someone I'd know who had taken their own life. The first time had been with someone much more dear, much more profound, and affected every aspect of my life.

My mother was a combat nurse in France in World War II. Lt. T. J. Gwin was born in Memphis and raised in Atlanta, the daughter of a Methodist minister. She presided over the Honor Society at Fulton County High School, earning a scholarship to Agnes Scott University. Armed with a nursing degree, she enlisted in the Army Nurse Corps.

She witnessed the grim realities of war firsthand and bore lingering emotional scars for years to come. Leaving her country's enemies behind, she fought depression at home. She'd tended scores of men who never made it back. She didn't speak about the war, but often sang me lullabies about soldiers being far away from home. She combined a refined sensitivity to suffering with a strikingly elegant presence, caring for children at my preschool as well as veterans at the VA hospital.

As the child of a minister and a native of Atlanta, my mother identified closely with the Rev. Martin Luther King, Jr. and the civil rights movement. An eloquent proponent of racial equality, by 1968 she was incensed at the polarizing rhetoric of Governor George Wallace and the violence in the south. Her typically genial nature was brushed aside by her fiery Irish temper.

She began smoking and seemed fazed by her medication. I was scared for her because she had never before appeared so angry and resentful. She held a frequent coffee court in our kitchen with a succession of close friends. When I delivered the news bulletin of Dr. King's assassination on April 4, 1968, she was incensed. That night she composed a letter and sent it to *The Ann Arbor News*. It read:

> Dear Sir,
>
> As a southern white, I want to express to the people of Ann Arbor my appall and shame over the assassination of Dr. Martin Luther King in Memphis tonight.
>
> By coincidence, I was born in the hospital in which he died. Also, I grew up in Atlanta, his hometown.
>
> Let me assure you all that many whites, in the South, do not share the same views of the bigots responsible for his death. And this includes the narrow-minded views of men like George Wallace, too.
>
> It is my hope that this tragic incident will give some pause and reflective thought to those in Ann Arbor and elsewhere, both Negro and white, who have the mistaken idea that violence is the only way to bring about a solution to our problems of today.

Most Sincerely Yours,
Thyra J. Stipe

Her letter was posted on the Letters to the Editor page in the Saturday edition of the *News*. The next morning, Sunday, April 7th, my dad told me to get dressed for church. We weren't going to disturb her. As we crossed the entry courtyard to the garage, we heard the sound of an engine running behind the closed back door.

I opened it and went inside while my dad sprang around to the overhead garage door in front. The closed garage was oppressive with engine heat and choked with exhaust fumes. I entered the passenger-side door of our 1964 T-Bird and climbed across the seat to turn off the ignition key. It was white hot. I looked in the back seat and there was my mom, clad in a white car coat, seated upright with her eyes closed. A hose from our built-in Black & Decker vacuum system was wedged into a rear window.

My dad had opened the garage door and, as fumes billowed outside, he dragged me into the house to call police and rescue personnel. He sent me down the block to guide them in. I'll never forget waving frantically to the patrol car as the officers first drove toward me then inexplicably, turned the wrong way onto a side street. When they finally arrived, they directed me inside the house to anxiously await word. My sister Molly walked home from her University of Michigan dorm and as she entered the living room, my dad sat next to me on the couch and told us our mom was gone.

I cried in his lap while Molly stood in silent shock. It seemed like mere moments before the house began filling with friends and neighbors. For me, it was the death of the world's gentlest, most sensitive soul. It marked the end of the line for the boy I had been. There would be no more singing, no more hugs or reluctant naps. She was gone. I was eleven years old.

Chapter Three
A Sudden Stop On a Darkened Road

My citizenship must have troubled my father. Not only had I nearly been drummed out of a military academy, but by age sixteen I'd been arrested twice for juvenile drinking related offenses by the Ann Arbor police. My grades were marginal at best, and I showed no promise as an athlete. There was only one way for my dad to monitor my behavior: he put me to work in his tire store.

Ann Arbor Tire Company customers relaxed in rocking chairs and sipped fresh coffee while their cars were serviced. That is, until the summer of 1973, when they left their car radios on and listened to the Watergate hearings outside the service bay doors. George B. Stipe began working retail tire stores in 1938. He was drafted into the Army in January of 1941 and earned campaign stars as an infantry commander for action at the Ardennes Counteroffensive and the Battle of the Rhineland from December '44 to into the next spring. Captain Stipe met Lt. T. J. Gwin through a mutual doctor friend the first week of July, 1945 in Marseilles. They dated, fell in love, and married on the 28th of the same month.

Back home, George's boss held his job at the tire company for him for nearly five years of war service. When George bought out Ann Arbor Tire in 1952, he had architect Ted Smith design a Mid-Century Modern service center in 1963. Goodyear Tire Company sponsored an appearance by the Detroit Lions at the grand opening and I've been a fan of the team ever since. A respected Main Street retailer, Dad wore a suit and tie to work every day except Saturday. At the time, I didn't appreciate just how lucky I was to work for him.

After my mother's death, Dad married again, this time to the socialite ex-wife of America's top office furniture manufacturer. She was down to earth but her refined breeding and expensive lifestyle were hard to adapt to. Her own children were gracious and welcoming and together we went on some fun vacations, but the time the newlyweds shared was often interrupted by the active children. The marriage did not last long and my dad and I moved into our own townhouse within a year and a half.

His third wife, Deb, was substantially more grounded but equally refined. He'd found his life companion in my stepmother Deb. They built a four level, five-bedroom house designed for maximum comfort and entertaining. He wouldn't be allowed to enjoy it for long.

During a routine exam, my dad was diagnosed with cancer of the lymph nodes, a condition likely brought on by the smoking he'd begun in the Army. George had been so fit and such a health food fanatic it was hard to believe he could have gotten so sick. He may have been better off had the disease remained undetected. Cobalt treatments had an immediate, detrimental effect on his health. He became winded simply climbing stairs and soon had to retire from his daily basketball games. Every effort was grueling, and his face bore a tired, pained expression whenever he exerted himself.

One Sunday night in late November, George was so stricken with pain Deb called an ambulance for him. As when my mom died, I ran down the street to direct the rescue personnel up to our house. Just as they'd done five years before, they drove right by me and went the wrong way.

George was admitted to St. Joseph Mercy Hospital and underwent an endless battery of tiresome tests. I skipped class every day to visit him. The following Thursday morning, I sat at his bedside and he turned his head toward me and placed his hand on his chest. "I feel so strange inside here," he said. He had such a bewildered look on his face I strained to imagine what he was feeling. He died the next day. I was seventeen years old.

Just two weeks later, on a frigid December night, a drunk driver parked his car on the darkest stretch of Geddes Road, turned off his lights and climbed into the back seat to sleep it off. I slammed into that car with the Belvedere going fifty mph, not seeing it until it was too late. The impact broke my nose and bruised my ribs. It also set the drunk driver's 1974 Impala on fire—I dragged him to the side of the road before it burned up.

I concluded 1973 with a wrecked car and without a father. I had no prospects and little ambition. As part-owner of the tire store, I no longer wanted to work there. It was just an empty place without my dad. I skipped high school commencement and drove out west with my step-brother Bo. The two-week trip revived my spirits but gave me no better sense of direction.

Chapter Four
Some Who Wander Are Lost

Back at home, I worked a series of jobs, which included a stint as a custodian at Michigan State University, and as a "material handler" at Allied Automotive in Ann Arbor. Despite my lack of mechanical aptitude, the owner had been a close friend of my father's and hired me anyway.

I worked hard for very little but was aided by full-time Ann Arbor firefighter and part-time Allied employee Chuck Browning. Chuck offered some good advice. He'd been a firefighter for twenty-eight years and suggested that someone without a college degree could make a good living on the wages and benefits paid to city employees. It was a tip I kept in the back of my mind.

I hadn't entertained a girl since I'd dropped Stephanie off at the airport three years before. A friend arranged a blind double date for us with his girl and her best friend Rhonda. Rhonda was five-foot-two-inches with straight brown hair and blue eyes. I'd been assured she was cute and she certainly was.

Although she was just a high school junior, it was immediately evident she was far more experienced than me. The four of us bought some wine near the University of Michigan and parked in a remote North Campus lot. It had been three years since I'd kissed someone and Rhonda was ripe and ready in that realm. We retired to a townhouse I shared with Tadley and Hunter "Nard" Bernard, two friends also seeking direction. Our unit was situated next to the abandoned Ypsi-Ann Drive-In theater and a McDonald's. As I showed Rhonda our magnificent view, we began kissing again and soon we were thrashing around on Tad's waterbed, where my long romantic drought came to a sizzling conclusion.

I'd been informed by a trusted source that Rhonda was popular with several boys, some who would go into graphic detail about her sexual prowess. I dismissed the report as gossip. To reassure myself I called her and asked her out for Friday night, two days hence. She said yes, and I felt much better. I was naïve in these matters and equated sex with love. I honestly believed that to *be* with someone meant that you *loved* them. I already had strong feelings for her.

To ensure a romantic evening, I arranged with Tad and Nard to have the townhouse to myself and set about grooming myself for the occasion. I drove over to Rhonda's house at the appointed hour and anxiously rang the doorbell. Her mother answered with a most quizzical look on her face—Rhonda was out with someone else.

Her mother assured me she must have been confused about which night she had the date with me and insisted I call the next day to straighten things out. I returned to the townhouse with that sick, empty feeling of betrayal. I sat in the living room feeling sorry for myself while listening to Horace Silver on Tad's state-of-the-art stereo system. It was to be the beginning of a long pattern describing the heartache of my relationship with Rhonda.

Holidays and anniversaries turned into brutal occasions. Every Mother's Day, Father's Day, Christmas—every break where my friends and co-workers would go home to spend time with their parents and families—turned into long periods of sadness and loneliness. Every year my parents' birthdays and the dates of their deaths rolled through like dark clouds. I had no goals, no ambition. I had no idea what I was supposed to do with my life. In July of 1976 I rented my own apartment, composing forgettable poetry and burying myself in books and movies. I was lost.

At Allied Automotive, I was nearly crushed by hoist pistons in a workplace accident set in motion by a recently promoted "efficiency expert." There was a reason we didn't stack racks four high. It was my second and last close call there. Allied gave me a secure job and Chuck Browning instilled an admirable work ethic, but the inherent risks deserved more money. I gave my notice and quit, vowing to find a position more befitting my time.

It was August, 1977, and it turned out to be a memorable month for all the wrong reasons. Elvis died and I was ticketed three times in two weeks—twice for speeding and once for drag racing. I owned a Camaro Z28 and a Pontiac GTO, the car that would "eat anything" on the streets. My insurance rates soared. Not a very auspicious record to present to prospective employers.

I didn't hang out with any girls. I waited patiently for Rhonda, who had enrolled in the Wilma Boyd School for Girls to be trained as a flight attendant. She wrote to me regularly, but she got herself in a jam that convinced me she was still careless in her choice of male companions. Whether self-imposed or not, I was being faithful at home. I saved what money I could, determined to be the first of my friends to own my own home.

Chapter Five
A Civil Servant

In January, 1979, I took Chuck Browning's advice and applied for a job with the City of Ann Arbor Building Department. Despite my shoulder-length hair and informal attire, I was selected as the Ordinance Enforcement Inspector over forty-nine other candidates, charged with enforcing Ann Arbor's restrictive sign ordinance. On my first day of work I pictured myself amid the buzz of a bustling City Hall office, doing important work and accomplishing something significant.

Instead I spent the next couple of weeks reading the sign ordinance and being briefed on various aspects of enforcement. Plan Examiner Jerry Brickell and I hit it off right away, both being aficionados of obscure television, film and music trivia. I did not pretend to understand the compelling need for a strict sign ordinance, but I did know those who willingly obeyed the code were depending on me to ensure their business competitors did the same. I patrolled the streets like a sentinel, noting every sign that didn't comply. I scheduled on-site assessments, where almost every merchant I met told me I sounded much older on the phone.

Building Director Jerome Garner, an architect with a brilliant mind and a Captain Kangaroo's personality, ensured my long-term security by training me in every aspect of building inspection. He budgeted for my position to be adopted full-time which gave me a certain amount of job security. Sadly, his big heart gave out on him one day and after a short leave of absence, he died suddenly. I attended his memorial service, sitting in the back of the church, and listened to his son recount the special time Jerome had set aside for each of his children. If Jerome had been kinder to his kids than he had been to me, they were lucky indeed. I'd miss him a lot.

Assistant Building Director Donald Jackson was given the monumental challenge of replacing him. Jerome had always empowered his staff by helping them draw their own conclusions while making sure you kept on your toes. Don seemed to think the office ran itself. I was conducting housing inspections full-time, handling fifty percent of the housing bureau service requests (five inspectors divided the rest) and was also responsible for sign enforcement. Yet I remained several steps behind on the pay scale. I sent Don memos outlining the inequity but they always seemed to get lost on the mountainous stack of untended paper-work on his desk.

Don enhanced the work environment by hiring attractive women to fill the clerical positions. When he needed to find an office manager, he hired Nena Langston, who had cat-like eyes and flawless, ebony skin. Quiet in manner and private in her thoughts, she nevertheless engaged in playful teasing with me. Every time I saw her she'd greet me with an open-ended "Well?" There were beautiful women all over the building, not just Nena, but I lacked the courage or sophistication to approach any of them.

Faith and Faithfulness

Rhonda was angry a lot and my relationship with her was a volatile one. Our intimacy somehow implied to me that this was the girl I should marry. I hadn't been around much and I could count my partners on one hand but Rhonda'd had lots of boyfriends. I hung in there anyway. Despite the mixed messages and confused feelings, I proposed in mid-1982. The year before I'd purchased a seven-hundred-fifty-square-foot house on Fair Street in Ann Arbor. I'd achieved my goal of being the first of my friends to buy my own home, and I took some pride in that.

The day my offer for the house was accepted, Rhonda and I were at a softball party. We posed for pictures and drank champagne and beer. I called my realtor at the appointed time and got the good news. I ran to find Rhonda to share it with her, only to find her pinned against the side of the house with her pants undone while being mauled by a local disc jockey. She was so trashed I had to carry her to the car. She slept for hours while I agonized about just how sexually active she really was.

One day I found photographs of Rhonda and her karate teacher out on the town in Detroit. I knew he'd been calling her often and even sending flowers. One of the photos showed the two of them with their arms around each other; in another I could see Rhonda's lipstick smeared across her mouth. She was as popular as she was puzzling.

Don Jackson threw a Christmas party at his house in December of 1982 and the entire building department showed up. Nena arrived with another secretary and at the end of the night asked me for a ride home. She was glowing and intoxicated, and I felt a surge of excitement at the prospect of being alone with her. But the pangs of guilt and the obvious implications of our leaving together compelled me to politely decline. I admired Nena immensely but I was getting married in just over a month. I tossed and turned over what I'd done for two nights before returning to work on Monday.

That day I picked up a Christmas card for Nena reading, "I've decided what I want for Christmas... YOU!" I slipped it onto her desk and sweated like a schoolboy on Valentine's Day, waiting for her response. I dealt with a person at the permit counter and returned to my desk. There I found a reply saying, "It will be wrapped and ready!" I nearly exploded from the head rush as I sat there, staring at her note.

I walked up to the front desk to retrieve some blueprints when I sensed her right behind me. She asked me point blank, "Well? What are you going to do about it?" I turned to see her incredibly beautiful face as she arched an eyebrow and stood planted with her arms crossed in front of her. Nena was the most elegant woman I had known since Stephanie Alexis. I wanted her so badly but was bound by some inner sense of restraint that said no.

"I can't, Nena, it isn't right of me."

"What did you send the card for?"

"Because I'm mixed up," I said weakly.

"OK," was all she said as she smiled in an understanding way.

Her reaction emphasized her value as a friend. How could I have turned down such an enticing invitation? It was a pattern on my part: falling for women well out of my league.

Rhonda and I were married the following month in a small ceremony in the First Presbyterian Church. A reception for our friends and relatives followed at Rhonda's parents' house. The whole gang from work was there, including Nena, who leaned against the living room wall sipping drinks and returned my admiring glances.

That was about as good as it got. Rhonda was chronically late and nearly caused us to miss our honeymoon flight to Nassau. On the first day there, we burned in the sun and bickered at dinner like George and Weezy from *The Jeffersons*. I returned to work, she to a life of leisure. There was constant tension. She spent most of her time getting angry.

I forged ahead with my job at the building department though some days were more of a pain in the ass. There were houses that were so filthy I had to strip before entering my own home at night. I inspected some that didn't have running water, where a family of seven would urinate and defecate into an overflowing bathtub. A cleaning contractor motioned me into a bedroom one day where, after removing a sock drawer, he'd found a family of mice.

I decided I needed to refocus on a number of fronts. At twenty-seven, I realized how out of shape I truly was when I went on a run with Jim Hilbert, a friend from work. I pledged myself to fitness, skipping happy hour and running the par course at the U of M North Campus every day after work. eighteen exercise stations spanned a distance of two miles and I timed every run, averaging thirty minutes to complete the course. I'd adopted a faithful dog, Augie, from the Humane Society. He ran with me nearly every day.

Rhonda and I had a son we named William, and I was devoted to him. I played guitar and sang to him and we spent every moment at home in one another's company. I joined a church and cleaned up my act—no more swearing or drinking. In my seventh year with the city, I had uncovered a newfound confidence about life as well as my commitment to public service.

Chapter Six
A Chance Meeting

One day while walking to the bank, I fell in stride with Police Chief Jim Colby. James J. Colby was a retired Detroit Police Department Commander who brought his no-nonsense, spit and polish program to Ann Arbor PD. With ramrod-straight posture and a booming voice, he cut an impressive figure. By odd coincidence, we walked the same way for several blocks. To my surprise, he asked me if I'd ever thought about joining the police department.

When I told him I hadn't, he asked if I'd consider it. I thought he was kidding for a minute but one look at him changed my mind. The words "I don't know" were about all I could summon up on the spot. He looked annoyed. He asked me to fill out an application and I promised I would, hoping he'd forget.

I'd always admired the police officers I'd seen on TV and in the movies, like Steve McQueen in *Bullitt*. Michael Douglas's "Inspector Keller" character on *The Streets of San Francisco* intrigued and impressed me. But it was the portrayal of the uniformed officers in *Adam-12* and *Police Story* that really captured my imagination. These guys were the first to arrive at an emergency and already knew what to do.

I was flattered by Chief Colby's invitation, but I presumed my baggage would come back to haunt me. I'd smoked pot, worn my hair to my shoulders and acquired eight points on my license in less than two weeks. I'd also had several questionable encounters with the AAPD. What was the chief thinking? I had no intention of applying and subjecting myself to such microscopic scrutiny.

For a while I didn't see the chief around much, until the two weeks leading up to the application deadline. Suddenly I saw him everywhere. We'd see each other and he would wave to me and bellow, "Got that application in yet?" To which I would reply in a weak voice, "I'll do it today."

In the end I completed an application but was almost too petrified to turn it in. I thought an in-depth inquisition into my past would be both embarrassing and futile. The day it was due, lo and behold, there was the chief in the lobby of City Hall as I came in for work. Before he could say a thing, I held up the wrinkled form I'd been carrying to and from work every day and told him I was taking it right downstairs to Personnel. I did just that.

The police department held a "packet meeting" in the city council chambers. Two hundred fifty of us crowded onto the long wooden pews and reviewed the thorough background questionnaire with Sergeant Ron Conrad and Officer Sean Randall. They asked for every living address I ever had, every vehicle I'd ever owned (including license plate numbers), and every roommate I ever knew.

Drinking habits, drug use and complete driving history had to be detailed. The packet even required a definitive answer on our willingness to use deadly force. The more I pictured my honest responses, the less likely I thought my chances were of being hired. Only five candidates from those present would be considered. I solicited references from my friends and the parents that had known me best from our old neighborhood. I harbored a faint hope they didn't know me too well.

A Daytime Nightmare

Roscoe Robinson was a housing inspector and my AFSCME union steward. He reminded me of Teddy Wilson from *That's My Mama*. Roscoe wore wide-brimmed Super Fly hats, open-collared shirts with wide lapels and disco era clothes. He spoke so fast he stuttered and was always too busy to take care of business. As my steward, he hadn't done a thing to help me gain parity with the other inspectors and his chronic absenteeism regularly plunged me behind schedule as it doubled my already bulging workload.

The weather for the Fourth of July weekend in 1985 was sweltering and it wasn't a shock to return to work on the 5th to find Roscoe had extended his holiday by calling in sick. The problem for me was that he had been scheduled to inspect several properties owned by a slumlord named Harry Grist and now I had to cover. These buildings were often posted as uninhabitable, shut down for various health and safety violations.

Grist himself was filthy and unshaven, usually found in his trademark oil-stained shirts and greasy pants. He rented to a who's who of lowlifes and criminals and his clientele was responsible for a high percentage of calls to the police on the midnight shift and at that point there had been a number of recent stabbings—not to mention a homicide—committed on his premises. He'd been a notoriously bad mechanic for fifty years and his most notorious rental units were located above his garage. Beat up cars parked every which way littered the yard.

It was nearly one hundred degrees with comparable humidity when I arrived at the first address. Grist sent his asthmatic wife to talk to me, hoping to garner sympathy from the city. She needed to be assisted up each flight of stairs, stopping frequently to allow her wheezing lungs to catch their breath. At her pace, the series of inspections would have taken a month. I took her master set of keys, left her on the catwalk outside the first set of apartments, and checked them alone.

The units above Grist's garage were all single rooms with one common bathroom and kitchen situated at the end of the catwalk. Luckily, the hour I arrived found no one home as I walked over the piles of garbage, clothes and debris. Not one door closer, smoke detector or window was operational.

The air was stagnant, with flies buzzing in and out of the unscreened doors. The bathroom smelled like an outhouse and had not been cleaned in years. The toilet was hopelessly plugged and had been substituted with a bathtub, now brimming with fly-covered feces. The kitchen door was wedged shut, and the windows were too filthy to allow visibility. The iron handrails were solid, however, and the plus-sized Mrs. Grist clung breathlessly to the railing, waiting for me to help her down the rear stairway.

The next building was a wood frame house containing four apartments. I always made a point to look at fire escapes from the bottom up and to check each stair's stability before stepping on the next one. I began climbing the exterior stairs on the house with Mrs. Grist pinching my biceps in a death grip. We were only a few stairs from the bottom when a German shepherd leaped out of a second-story window with torn screen and hovered atop the fire escape barking and baring its teeth like a devil dog. Grist's wife nearly pulled me down the stairs in panic as she suddenly regained command of her invalid legs and ran down the steps.

As an inspector, I became accustomed to dealing with dogs. The objective was to present myself in a non-threatening way. This shepherd seemed more crazed and out of his head than most dogs I'd seen. He continued to growl and bare his teeth in a slobbery, better get lost sort of way. I silently cursed Roscoe Robinson as I crept up the stairs, talking softly to the defiant animal. I called to him to come to me, but he stayed right where he was. I repeated "good boy, good boy" over and over as he let me inch closer to his post still growling as I extended my hand. When my position on the stairs had us at eye level he closed his mouth and sniffed my outstretched hand. I called, "Come on, boy," as I turned to lead him down.

He hesitated a moment, then followed me to the bottom, continuing to sniff my trailing hand. When we reached the foot of the fire escape I said, "Okay boy, come on," and I turned around and headed back up, leaving the terrified Mrs. Grist sitting locked inside her car. The dog stayed right next to me as we climbed the stairs to the landing above. I moved through the open window along with the sentry and proceeded to get on with the inspection. The key to protective dogs, at least in my experience, was to keep them with me at all times. When I was finished I closed the window and exited through the door, leaving my newfound friend behind while taking along streaks of his slobber on my clothes.

The combination of the heat, anger and anxiety had left me drenched in perspiration and dog drool. But the worst was yet to come. At the next inspection, Mrs. Grist joined me at the first-floor apartment. Seated on a heavily stained couch were two guys: one white and one black. The white guy was twenty or so and wore a wool stocking cap, despite the oppressive heat. The windows had no screens, but it didn't matter because they were sealed shut. The other guy was about forty years old, bearing gruesome facial scars and missing several teeth. He sat on the couch, eating or sucking on a triangular slice of water melon. They watched an ancient, black-and-white portable television with rabbit ear antennas clung with aluminum foil. The static-filled picture flickered hypnotically.

It was hard to determine whether the heat or the stench was more oppressive. My head was spinning as I walked into the kitchen. The older guy sprang from his seat and asked, "What are you looking for?"

"Housing code violations."

Wide-eyed with curiosity, he munched his melon and said, "Like what?"

I tried to ignore him as I kneeled on the grime-covered kitchen floor, looking under the sink where the plumbing enters the inside wall. I felt several drips on the back of my neck that rolled down to my throat. I ran my hand through the liquid and looked to see what it was. Two watermelon seeds stuck to my moist fingers, and I looked up to see my toothless shadow standing above me dripping juice and seeds all over my back.

I went silently berserk. I could not believe what a swell job this had become. I often reeked of garbage, urine and feces, but that day my clothes were sopping with sweat, dog slobber and now, watermelon juice. Grist's wife clung to my arm every step I traveled, exhaling the most horrid "near death" breath I'd ever smelled. My hand was cramped from writing down the dozens of code violations I found in each unit. It took me four and a half hours to inspect five buildings and I never spoke to Roscoe Robinson again.

Things carried on at work much like before. But I was shocked to hear back from the police department so soon and be called in for an interview. I met with an oral board comprised of Sergeant Leroy Van Den Bosch, a detective and polygraph operator; Sean Randall, the training officer; and Clark Rowry, from the city's personnel department. The board asked me a series of questions about what I thought qualified me as a police officer: What would I do in this situation or that? I gave them honest answers.

I admitted to frequent marijuana use in my packet and they seemed unconcerned. Randall asked why I'd seen a child psychologist and when I explained my mom's suicide, he looked sorry he had. That was about the extent of the interview. I took a written exam the following Saturday, and I don't think I got a single question wrong—civil service exams are about recognizing the right answer. It seemed way too easy.

To my utter surprise, they offered me a job. They wanted me to report right away. On Friday, December 13, 1985, my building department co-workers held a party in my honor at the office. They had looked after me and helped me grow in a way I never would have on my own. Some of the secretaries wept. They had been my family when I'd had none.

Chapter Seven
Badge 112

Conformity is the key to your indoctrination into police culture. Recruits wore drab khaki uniforms to distinguish us from the sworn officers wearing blue. Three of us were to be sent to the Detroit Metropolitan Police Academy in January, 1986, while one experienced cadet remained behind. Training officers sought some way to keep us occupied in the interim.

On my first morning at the Ann Arbor Police Department, I was assigned to Officer Joe Hazard, a Vietnam veteran who chain-smoked cigarettes and didn't wear his seatbelt. He told me to buckle his belt and toss his cigarette out of the car should he be killed in a crash. That he trusted me to sidestep city vehicle policy violations was a start toward being accepted.

We met Officer Dick Guyer in the 700 block of North Main for coffee. While we sat there, a bundled figure made his way toward the city garage across the street. "See that guy there?" Hazard said. "It will take you and six other cops to get him under control. That is Davey Willis Johnson, and he will kick your ass!" I silently nodded in agreement, but I knew he was wrong. Davey Johnson wouldn't kick my ass. Davey Johnson had saved my life.

When I'd worked at Allied Automotive in the steel parts yard, we stocked and loaded heavy duty hoist-lift pistons, their components and compressors. It was difficult, dangerous work.

We had nearly a dozen old-time dumpsters, wide at the top, narrow at the bottom, with the tiniest wheels to roll them around on. They were always loaded over capacity with steel scrap and were extremely top heavy.

Davey Johnson drove the city garbage truck that serviced Allied once a week. He was a bear of a man with a raspy Southern drawl and Rastaman dreadlocks. We'd help him roll the dumpsters to the back of his truck, where his lift would strain under the weight to dump them inside. It was winter, and the entire parts yard was caked in ice, making footing treacherous. I pulled a particularly heavy dumpster in line to stage it for the truck when the casters spun sideways and wedged against some thick ice.

I had been pulling it by the front lift bar, and when the wheels locked the top kept coming. My feet slipped underneath, and the thousand-pound dumpster tipped over as I fell. I remember thinking how odd it would be to die with a flattened body and my head intact, like a fly at the end of a swatter. I heard a primal, guttural groan and the thunk of heavy metal as the dumpster suddenly popped upright and rattled back and forth. A smiling Davey Johnson extended his hand and helped me, badly shaken, to my feet.

I have no idea how he gained the leverage to thrust that dumpster upright. It is the single most phenomenal feat of strength I have ever witnessed. From that day on, his eyes warmed up the moment he saw me. Almost as if I was a trophy he treated with delicate hands. I would see him downtown, usually drunk, but he would always greet me like a little brother and clasp my hand tightly.

He drank too much and fought often. He was not nearly as delicate with his girlfriend, and when I became an officer, I ran a number of domestic assault calls to Davey's addresses. No matter how drunk or wound up he was, when he saw me his shoulders sank and he became as passive as an old, tired dog. He would turn around and offer his hands behind his back, to the amazement of my veteran partners. I think Davey looked at sparing my life as his greatest achievement. I sure look at it that way. Joe Hazard's assessment of our dynamic was one of the very few things he was ever wrong about.

That first day was the extent of my road experience. Until we had to report to the academy, I worked at the complaint desk. The desk was the bane of all sworn officer positions, a purgatory for injured officers on light duty and it certainly was no picnic. Five telephone lines buzzed constantly, and at peak hours the lobby was lined ten people deep. Citizens taking the trouble to come to City Hall to make a report deserved better. My head was spinning. I even began answering my home phone, "Ann Arbor Police, Officer Stipe."

The Detroit Police Academy — Class 86-H

Three of us took turns driving the hour-long trip for our eighteen weeks at the Detroit Police Academy. Joanie Ellis and Lee Christiansen were seven years younger than me and fresh out of college, while I was twenty-nine and starting over. We would need each other's support to endure the coming weeks. It was a bitter cold January, and the wind knifed through our thin khakis as we hiked the Cass Corridor in midtown Detroit. Inside the academy, an ancient boiler radiated intense heat throughout the building.

Our 86-H Class consisted of thirty-seven Detroit police cadets and thirteen suburban recruits. Our speed-talking tactical officer was the hip and animated Henry Hayden. He would pace back and forth as he dispensed rapid-fire facts for us to absorb, and he would tell us where to be, what to wear, and who to see. Our schedule was tight, but downtime was common. We staged in a remote corner classroom while an outgoing class wrapped up their final week of testing.

Protocol required recruits hug the walls and look straight ahead when moving outside the classroom. You spoke only when spoken to, and any breach of discipline resulted in "flight time" up and down the seven-story stairwell. Officer Hayden singled me out the first day. Pointing to the back of our classroom, he brushed his hand over the top of his head, hinting my haircut was not short enough. I sought out a barber that very night.

We didn't meet our tactical sergeant for a long time, but when we did, we didn't regret the delay. Jack Cooke came on very strong. A veteran narcotics officer, Sergeant Cooke must have been a great performer. He sure put on a show for us. He paced the floor like a caged tiger; speaking in such soft tones I strained to hear him from the back of the room.

Repeating himself for emphasis on key points, he'd uncoil his stocky frame and bellow the name of an inattentive recruit. He'd single them out with a caustic verbal beating, placing the rest of us on pins and needles. I felt fortunate he never got around to me. My seven years with the city had taught me when to listen and when to speak and when I did, my reluctance to utter profanity prompted Sergeant Cooke to nickname me "Father Stipe."

Our seats were aligned in alphabetical order. A female Detroit recruit, Doris Tilley, sat just a seat or two away. She imprudently shined her shoes on the new academy carpet, leaving a black stain on the brown rug. Sgt. Cooke entered the room that morning and bellowed, "On your *feet*, Tilley!" so loudly the entire room jumped. The class often sat and trembled like cold, jittery old dogs, waiting for the next thunderbolt. I was grateful to be left alone.

On January 28, 1986, in our second week at the academy, the Challenger space shuttle exploded. That was followed on the 31st by a rare Michigan earthquake registering 5.4 on the Richter scale. A week of seismic events, real and virtual, grew much worse on February 5, 1986, when two Detroit police officers, one a recent academy graduate, were killed in a freak shootout in a Detroit crack house.

Two uniformed officers had responded to a report of shots

fired at the address. What they didn't know was that plainclothes narcotics officers were already inside, conducting a raid. The exchange of fire resulting from the surprise killed veteran officer Jake Brougher and rookie Mike Gladwin. The incident drove home the fact that police work could get you killed, especially in a city like Detroit.

Two months later, in April, an FBI shootout with bank robbery suspects in Coral Springs, Florida, left two agents and the two suspects dead; seven other agents were also wounded. It was yet another sobering reminder of the violent nature of being a cop. On the brink of graduation, it gave all of us pause.

Our graduation in May was the first event held at the renovated Fox Theatre. Chief Bill Hart handed us our diplomas. Tad Thompson attended the ceremony and took a couple of photographs. He was the only friend or family member who showed up, and he also was one of the few friends who didn't panic over my newfound profession. Typically, my wife Rhonda skipped the event.

Lee, Joanie and I returned to Ann Arbor as graduates to begin an eight-week in-house academy. The three of us joined the already certified Mark Godowsky, who had been working the police desk during our basic academy training. We received our intensive schedule and began to pore over the many policies, rules, regulations and report-writing requirements for our new positions. Compared to the building codes of my last job, I found it fascinating.

Lieutenant Robert LeGrange taught the report writing class. He had an imperious way about him, and reminded me of Colonel Flagg, the over-the-top intelligence officer on television's *MASH*. He would knit his eyebrows, rub his hands together, and give the impression he knew it all. He did know report writing, and he could tell us how to unfold a story in a logical sequence.

This had not always been the case with Detroit Police

Academy instructors. He pounded the cardinal rule of report writing into us: proofreading is key—a tip I use to this day. He was also responsible for the best piece of advice I got in the in-house academy: "Your stock with your fellow officers will rise dramatically if you swing by their traffic stops and stand by until you know they're secure." This sunk in deeply.

We were sworn in as officers at the city clerk's office and "Badge One-Twelve" hit the road in late June, 1986. Charlie James was my first field-training officer (FTO). A seventeen-year road veteran, Charlie was a big, soft-spoken guy with an odd emotional detachment. Charlie said little to me all day. Seemingly seeing nothing, he didn't miss anything. He silently monitored my performance, and lowered the boom on my evaluations. I would have preferred having my shortcomings pointed out when they happened so I wouldn't repeat my mistakes, but that was his way. He taught me a lot though, and helped set my standards. Speeders had to be driving fifteen mph or more over the limit to merit a stop and/or a ticket—a policy I carried on throughout my career.

He advised me to take my time when looking for a suspect. Slow down, look everywhere, don't give up too quickly. That advice paid off over and over. Best of all, he taught me Code One driving: Smooth is fast when running a full signal (lights and siren). Keep going, but stay controlled. I usually got there first, and damaged only one car in my career, but to be fair, that was when my partner accidentally cracked my head with the butt of a shotgun.

I survived four phases of training and on October 5, 1986, I sat in a duty command office with Lieutenant Larry Fiske, Sergeant Dan Beacham and Charlie for my FTO board conference.

Fiske was a petty man. He had ascended the ranks by ticketing every citizen he stopped and exploiting a productivity system designed to keep officers active and accountable for their time. He generated exorbitant numbers that disgusted fellow officers and alienated the public. He lacked tact and warmth and left one wondering what his actual limits were. He had been put in charge of the FTO program, perhaps because the department reasoned if recruits could meet his narrow standards, they could endure anything.

I finished first in my recruit class with a score of ninety-three-point-three percent on twelve weekly exams. Lieutenant Fiske began by citing my intelligence, maturity and respectful nature, but he found my "friendliness" to be a weakness and characterized me as naïve. He thought I lacked awareness and had not developed the sense of "police suspiciousness" that had served him so well. It was his mistrust of every citizen he encountered that had kept him safe. It would be interesting to know just what the next officer encountered after a citizen received the Fiske treatment.

I was a police rookie, but I was thirty years old and had served the city as an inspector since 1979. The FTO board voted to advance me to Step V. They almost had to pass me. Mark Godowsky was on light duty after I flattened his foot on a precision driving course. He'd tried stepping out of a moving patrol car while we were picking up traffic cones. I felt bad. He felt worse. Joanie Ellis was assigned to the surveillance unit as a hooker decoy and drug buyer, and Christiansen suffered a fluke injury to his shoulder lifting his briefcase inside a patrol car.

Chapter Eight
On the Road

It was a surreal feeling, being on my own, working a day shift that consisted of traffic enforcement, policing crashes, or taking reports of crimes that had gone undetected overnight. I remembered what Lieutenant LeGrange had said about backing up other cars on traffic stops. Just the presence of a second car, parked where the motorist could see it, might be a deterrent to someone who would challenge the officer. I backed everybody up on everything—dispatched calls, traffic stops, warrant service attempts—everything. Some veterans became suspicious.

The police productivity system was designed to measure officer performance in a wide range of categories. Every moment of our shifts were captured somewhere in the clocked system. Evaluations, promotions, and even revenue were reliant on those numbers. The lofty goal was to keep the officer active and earning their keep. But the reality was that the standard was arbitrary, and officers used it to position themselves for lateral movement or promotion. Despite its intended purpose, the system created acrimony and wariness among the troops.

One day, AAPOA (Ann Arbor Police Officer Association) vice president and day shift officer Bert Davison took me aside in the report-writing room to ask me why I was following him. He was convinced Command was using me to monitor his activities. When I told him my objective was to ensure his safety, he looked at me oddly. "You're telling me that you're blowing off productivity to back me up?" I nodded my head. His annoyance was tempered by the fact our late moms had been friends through church. He asked me if I wanted to ride with him.

I kept busy. So busy, in fact, that when my first productivity report came out, I finished sixth out of sixty-six officers. That exorbitant number prompted counseling from veteran officers on the importance of reining in the system. One stat in each category would keep you in the mainstream, and supervisors would stay off your back on one end and the veterans out of your face on the other.

And then there were the calls.

Some came close to home. One Saturday morning, riding with Officer Tim Beamon, we were sent to a man-with-a-gun call on Woodlawn, just blocks from my boyhood home on Granger. Beamon was on the Special Tactics Unit (STU or SWAT team), and we were assigned to cover the front of a house. The elderly resident had fired a rifle out the side door, alarming a meter reader. We parked a block away, and climbed fences and crossed backyards near where I played army as a kid. The situation was dreamlike, but my days of make believe were over: we were playing for keeps with live rounds.

Twenty-four years before, and just two blocks away, I was with boyhood friends Will White and Brad Thompson on a half day of school, November 22, 1963. As we played in a backyard across from the Whites' house, a mother emerged from the rear door and told us to "Go home, the President has just been shot." Mrs. White had a television on in her dressing room displaying scattered images from Dallas. When she also suggested it was best to go home, it began to sink in.

We felt a direct link to President John F. Kennedy. Among the notable moms on the block was Mrs. John B. DeVine, the former Marnee Burke. She was the niece of Joseph P. Kennedy as well as President Kennedy's first cousin. The DeVines attended St. Francis Church like the Brady family and ours. We shared brunch every Easter at the Mayflower Hotel in Plymouth. The connection with Mrs. DeVine gave the Kennedy presidency an intimacy not everyone shared. We felt connected to the energy the First Family generated.

The DeVines' oldest daughter asked to watch the funeral at our house so she didn't break down in front of her younger siblings. She remained composed, but my dad wept, the first time I had ever seen him do so. It was my first profound sense of personal loss. American life was never quite the same to me, or as safe, after that moment. Now, a quarter century later, I was trying to keep the peace myself, back in my old neighborhood.

Back at the call on Woodlawn, the gunman surrendered less than an hour later, saying he had only fired at a pesky squirrel pilfering seeds from his bird feeder. Still, the homecoming incident brought my new occupation into clearer focus as the days of being "in the shit" had begun.

Finding a Rhythm on the Beat

I considered myself lucky. I arrived in policing just when old school intuition and modern technology intersected. Working smarter saved valuable time and I was anxious to contribute. I rotated shifts and ran and worked out constantly. When running and lightheaded I worked through scenarios like the ones I'd read in Gene Fear's *Surviving the Unexpected Wilderness Emergency.* His technique of creating situations in your own mind and crunching solutions to resolve them appealed to me, as did my survival. His theory was that even if one didn't have firsthand experience with a particular emergency or threat, having thought through a scenario beforehand would ready you with a reasonable response.

I began keeping a journal. I was so wound up after work I couldn't sleep for hours anyway. I was focused like never before in my life. When I got home, I'd analyze each call, trying to find the flaws in my performance.

And I studied all the calls where officers lost their lives, trying to learn. In the first week of November, 1987, a Detroit officer named Andre Barksdale was killed with his own weapon on a domestic call. Three days later, a hit-and-run driver killed an officer from Roseville, Albert DeSmet, during a vehicle pursuit. That driver was found innocent by reason of insanity—an apt description of what went on out there every night. I paid close attention to the nature of the calls and the part tactics played in such fatalities. I didn't want to become a case study for another officer but with the risks that come with the job there were times I came pretty close.

Tuned Up By a Flautist

Greg Hanson was the department's Walter Mitty, without the Danny Kaye or Ben Stiller likability. He shared amazing stories of his Vietnam exploits but was prone to embellishment. Wired by a hefty thermos of coffee, he never stopped moving, talking or operating lights and sirens in an annoying sequence on emergency runs. Each shift with him was an experiment in sensory overload. As irritating as he could be, there was one time I was particularly glad to see him. James Lee Bynes was originally from Flint, Michigan, but mental health issues had brought him to Ann Arbor. He kept a pair of spring-based hand strengtheners clipped to his waist and he used them to maintain his iron grip strength. Big, bulky and unreasonable, he would often intimidate the other patrons of the free homeless breakfast at St. Andrew's Church. One morning he got into a dispute with another man at breakfast and Bynes throttled the hapless victim in the head with the flute he always carried.

A BOL (Be On the Lookout) was broadcast, and I located him in the temporary bus shelter on South Fourth Avenue. I notified the dispatcher I was checking on Bynes and went inside to speak to him. I was brand new and only knew him by sight. My attempt to elicit even basic information was met with a series of angry grunts. I told him I was investigating what had been classified as a felonious assault, and his failure to cooperate would result in my arresting him. He gave me a distant look and called my bluff.

I got behind him and applied a handcuff to his right wrist. His muscular arm sprang to life as I struggled to maintain my position. I tried to summon help on the radio, but the dispatcher was in the process of exchanging a recipe with another officer and I couldn't get a clear channel. James went berserk, and tossed me like a rag doll around the confines of the bus shelter while I clung to his arm. He backed me into steel-framed windows and body-slammed me onto the concrete floor as I desperately held on.

I knew if I let go, the single cuff on his right wrist would become a lethal weapon in the possession of a deranged man. I could hear the dispatcher blathering on the radio and wondered if it would be the last voice I ever heard. Her singsong tone actually gave me an incentive to hang on. Just as I was thinking about what I would say to her if I survived, I looked outside and saw Greg Hanson strolling up to the bus shelter entrance.

He registered that look of shock, like Lee Harvey Oswald's escort in the Dallas police station when his prisoner was shot. He quickly recovered though, and brandished his nightstick, jabbing James in the small of the back until he brought his left arm back and allowed the second cuff to be applied. I felt like I had been run over by a stampede. My arms, legs and back were sore from the battering I took. I was so grateful, I could have listened to Hanson's stories for days.

* * *

"Don't Try To Get Human with Me"

I stopped a car driven by Gary Holman from Ypsilanti for equipment violations one afternoon. I asked if he was related to Rodney Holman, a tight end for the Cincinnati Bengals. Gary had such a pronounced stutter he was a challenge to converse with but after some difficulty, he told me Rodney was his cousin. I was a fan and Holman was cooperative. I let him off with a warning.

Three weeks later, I was assigned to search for the suspect in an armed robbery at the SuperAmerica gas station at West Stadium and South Maple. The suspect was seen fleeing on foot toward the freeway and I remembered Charlie James' advice about not giving up too quickly.

On a hunch, I drove to an intersecting point between the woods where the gunman fled and a low-income housing project that provided refuge for several known criminals. It was dusk and I parked in the shadow of a building under construction and watched the roadway intently. After what seemed like an eternity, a subject finally emerged. So much time had elapsed since the robbery nearly all the assigned cars had called complete and gone on to other duties. I put my spotlight on him and put the patrol car in gear. The suspect fled like a man on fire as I radioed in the sighting.

I closed the distance as quickly as I could but Officers Terry Johnson and Ted Randall had already had the same hunch I did and were waiting for him in the complex. The suspect had no identification and was unable to formulate a single word, let alone give his name, but I immediately recognized him as Gary Holman.

"Hey, Gary," I said.

Losing his stammer he came back with, "Don't try to get human with me."

I'd done my best. That was the first time I'd outguessed a suspect like that and it was just dumb luck I already knew his name.

NBD — *Red Roof Inn Robbery*

I rotated back to day shift and was sent to back up new recruit Doug Rouse and his FTO Ron Russell on a bank robbery at the National Bank of Detroit on Plymouth Road. With US-23 a step away, several patrol cars sped over to check the highway while I headed across the street to the Red Roof Inn. An officer called for assistance on the freeway, and I hustled down there for backup. It wasn't the right car, and the dispatcher ordered all units not actively involved to return to the station for shift change.

I had an impulse to check the hotel before going home and drove to the rear of the Red Roof Inn, finding the suspects' car parked near a dumpster. Red ink from the explosive dye pack was everywhere, and dye-stained clothes and money had been thrown in with the trash. The plates on the car were stolen, and the actual Missouri plates stashed in the trunk. The suspects had switched cars and, after ordering a takeout from the attached Big Boy, drove away slowly on their getaway.

Handguns were found stashed in the men's room trash. The suspects were still armed with a shotgun and a submachine gun. Maybe it was a good thing I hadn't confronted them with my .38 revolver when they were changing cars after all. Another hunch had paid off though, and I was gaining more confidence. The next day in the squad room, veteran Vic Mitchell congratulated me on recovering the car and a small portion of the money. It meant more to be recognized by old-school officers than anyone else. I was on a mini roll.

Later that afternoon, on a South First Street traffic stop, I heard radio traffic of a fleeing shoplifter from Kline's Department Store on Main Street. Vic Mitchell was in foot pursuit as several units converged on the area. The suspect was described as a black male, short, with a hooded jacket tied to cover his face. I looked in the rearview mirror to see the suspect cross the street behind my patrol car and run up a driveway and into the next block.

I cleared the stop and drove around the block, where I saw him cross the street and into a backyard. I was pumped and roared up the block and got out right on his heels. He jumped a fence and landed in another yard just as I tackled him. I handcuffed him, sat him up and pulled down the hood to reveal that "he" was a girl. "Beverly Webber," Mitchell said as he reached my side. "Officer Stipe has the suspect in custody," he advised dispatch. A great feeling to have your arrest broadcast to all other units. Right place, right time, for two days in a row! Beverly Webber came from a long line of thieves and ripoff artists, all with distinctive looks to go along with their notorious last name. I was to get to know each of them soon enough.

Cruising Speed... 115 MPH

Kenny Marr Jones had experience fleeing from the police by the time he was just seventeen. With a suspended driver's license and riding a stolen motorcycle, he sped through a flashing red light at Stadium Boulevard and Liberty Street at 3:50 a.m. on April 5, 1988. His fifteen-year-old female passenger clung to his waist and gave a passing glance to Officers Clint Seaver and Christopher Sager, stopped at the corner. Jones continued north as Stadium turned into North Maple and increased his speed as he closed on the M-14 interchange. Seaver and Sager, in the department's first new Caprice Classic, initiated a pursuit.

Clint Seaver was a twenty-five-year police veteran known as "Mr. Felony" to his disciples. He'd trained my FTO, Charlie James, sixteen years before. Sager was a rookie like me but a fine driver and cool-headed U.S. Army veteran. In pursuits, the primary unit is given the main radio channel to ensure they can report progress without interruption.

Joanie Ellis and I were on Green Road near Greenbrier on the northeast side of Ann Arbor. We were about as far away as possible while still being in the city. I was driving a 1984 Dodge

Diplomat equipped with the same 318 V8 my Belvedere had. We raced over to US-23 and headed north to intercept them where the M-14 crossed over. At least that was our plan.

We monitored the pursuit channel and radioed our assist on the backup frequency. Clint was composed and sounded more like a golf commentator than a man traveling one hundred five mph. The dispatcher, evidently with a command officer breathing over her shoulder, asked about traffic conditions. Clint reported it was clear and open ahead (it was just after 4:00 a.m.).

We roared up US-23, well past the interchange with M-14, and could see the chase ahead. It was like being in a video game long before I'd ever played one. They were moving in tandem, with the patrol car directly behind the fleeing bike, their headlights painting beams on the road and the light bar on the Caprice bouncing red, blue and white light off landmarks along the side of the road.

Clint responded to a speed check from the dispatcher by advising they were still at one hundred five mph. I looked down at the Diplomat's speedometer, and we were doing one hundred fifteen. The tunnel vision one acquires in a pursuit was evidenced by the fact Clint and Sager had no idea we were closing in on them. We were entering Livingston County and the thirty miles we'd just gone had passed in a blur.

Jones abruptly exited at Clyde Road, and we were right behind them. He turned left off the ramp, and we could hear Clint telling the dispatcher they were going to give way as we must be a local unit knowing the back roads. What a priceless look on their faces as we passed on the bridge over the freeway. We assumed the primary radio traffic and the operator, Cheryl Berry, informed us that Clyde Road came to a T intersection shortly and to use caution.

Jones went left, and we were now on a gravel road where traction was tentative. A sweeping right-hand curve lay ahead of us, and out of it came a Livingston County sheriff's cruiser, sliding sideways from the opposite direction. Jones took one look, leaned left, and plunging straight off the road, crashed into a cornfield. Both he and his passenger went airborne but landed uninjured.

Two more Ann Arbor cars joined us shortly and transported Jones and his stunned passenger separately. We had been running on fumes, and the Livingston County sergeant offered to top off our tanks at their station.

I had driven my GTOs and Grand National at some hair-raising speeds, well over one hundred mph, but I had never driven forty miles with the pedal to the floor the whole way. Despite my sense of composure during the pursuit, one of many intense adrenaline dumps followed, making just filling up the car a difficult chore. The pursuit was described in *The Ann Arbor News* that afternoon, and I felt genuine pride at being mentioned in my hometown newspaper for the first time as an officer. I wished my mom and dad were alive to see it.

Chapter Nine
"I'll Talk to Him"

Randleman & Zasman

The University of Michigan contracted with the City of Ann Arbor for police protection in the days before they created their own department. Three officers working Shift V (2100-0500 hours) rotated in turn, riding a double car each night. I worked this shift with Joe Randleman and Ryan Zasman.

Ryan had been a security guard at Eastern Michigan University where he was ambushed one night by a shotgun-toting gunman who shot him in the side. Surviving that ordeal transformed Ryan into a serious student of officer safety and survival. He exercised the department's option of buying his own .357 instead of carrying the issued Smith & Wesson .38.

He became a crack shot and was particular about tactics. Watching him clear buildings and responding to potential threats convinced me that the next person to take him on would regret doing so. He loaned me Charles Remsberg's *Street Survival: Tactics for Armed Encounters* and I read it every morning after shift before I went to bed.

Joe Randleman was a veteran of several police departments when he joined the Ann Arbor PD. Joe possessed Sherlock Holmes-like powers of observation when it came to human behavior. He just knew when someone was up to something.

Neatly trimmed hair, wire-rimmed glasses, and a soft-spoken earnestness gave him a professorial air as a road cop, and his sincerity instantly set him apart from the persona so many officers adopted. He was a marvel to watch as he projected a genuine interest in everyone he came in contact with. Randleman's passions were the booked arrest: warrants, crimes in progress, or a conspiracy to commit an act yet to occur. He cracked more cases alone in uniform than a bureau of plainclothes detectives.

We called in service one night to find our patrol car out of gas, a serious lapse by the officer who had just turned it in at shift's end. It was five blocks to the city garage. In three separate attempts to get there we made three arrests of subjects Randleman sniffed out of the woodwork. Randleman preferred running out of gas to missing a possible booked arrest.

He seemingly picked out cars arbitrarily and said, "Stop him" or "Stop them." I'd say, "What for?" and Randleman would respond, "I'll talk to them." He would rarely, if ever, cite a driver for moving or equipment violations, but they gave him a legitimate reason to talk to them. The residents of Ann Arbor had no idea how lucky they were to have him out there. He was a legend when he was still in his prime. I was watching an artist at work.

I began to recognize his cues, and adopted Randleman's soft-spoken style, and it paid immediate dividends. I'd tell Zasman, "Stop that car; I'll talk to them." If a driver didn't possess his license and his behavior ran up a red flag, we made a custody arrest. Cuffing the subject and placing him in our car, we'd explain the mere formality until we verified his identity and driving status. Once we did, we'd release him or take whatever enforcement action we thought he had coming. If he was wanted or if he was lying to us, he was already handcuffed, preventing a struggle. Uniform pants ran ninety-nine dollars a pair, and I preferred mine not getting scuffed or torn rolling around on the ground.

Zasman's vigilance rubbed off on me. My reflexes improved

just riding with him. On a South University traffic stop one night, the driver opened the glove box revealing a pistol. As he reached toward it, I snatched and pulled him out of the driver's window. I needn't have worried; Zasman cleared leather and had the drop on him at the same time. As it turned out, the pistol was a .177 caliber pellet gun. They looked dangerously close to the real thing.

Zasman and Carl Brooks

Taking a break from the rigors of working midnights, Ryan Zasman took a temporary position in Special Services. That unit coordinated all special events: Michigan football games, crossing guards, animal control, traffic escorts, etc., and was also responsible for vehicle maintenance. On a bright spring morning, a week into his new gig, Zasman was driving a patrol car to Perfect Fit Auto to have a windshield replaced. Stopped at a red light on Jackson Road at Maple, he heard the sound of gunshots coming from his right. He looked to see a man emerging from Veterans Memorial Park firing a handgun at his patrol car.

Pandemonium ensued with horrified motorists exiting their cars and taking cover wherever they could find it. Zasman jumped out of the patrol car and took a position behind it with his .357 drawn. Despite his warnings to stop, the gunman continued to fire while converging on his position. With noontime traffic and pedestrians at risk, Zasman returned three rounds from a distance of about one hundred feet, striking the gunman twice. He went down immediately.

Zasman asked for an open channel for priority radio traffic. He calmly advised that he had shots fired, and that he'd downed the suspect in the exchange. Hearing radio traffic from an officer under fire sends a chill through one's spine. A tribute to Zasman's composure that he could transmit in the midst of exchanging gunfire.

The gunman was Carl Brooks, a disgruntled City of Ann Arbor crossing guard who had called in sick to work. Ironically, Zasman was now assigned to the office supervising Brooks' duties. Zasman had transferred to the day shift administrative position to limit the risks he was exposed to but he was still the wrong cop to ambush.

On the midnight shift that night, I was sent to U-M Hospital Intensive Care Unit to guard the wounded Brooks. Nurses coming on duty glared at me when told the police had shot their patient. The implication was that there'd been an overreaction on Zasman's part. The notion that he could have waited until Brooks ran out of rounds and arrested him without shooting him was absurd. Every motorist on that road was grateful for Zasman's decisive action. He was awarded the Medal of Valor, the department's highest honor for officers who survived a potentially fatal ordeal.

Stipe & Stark: Forging Friendship with the Hungarian Fireball

Nick Stark was a new officer assigned to ride with me on afternoons. Nick was a stocky kid of twenty-four who'd played fullback for the College of Wooster in Ohio. He possessed uncanny instincts and a simmering temper he used with calculating effect. We got along well, and on a gray November afternoon we were sent to check the welfare of a U-M graduate student who'd missed class for several days.

The student lived at the Tradewind Apartments, located one block north of Michigan Stadium at South Main and Hoover. We knocked on her door and got no response. The indifferent mailman continued to stuff her mailbox even as it overflowed. Her next-door neighbors hadn't seen or heard from her since hearing her sob through their common wall a week before. We looked up at her windows from the ground outside and could see a living room light on.

The building maintenance man was summoned and we un-locked the apartment door with his passkey. We knew where she was the moment the door was cracked. Death has an unmistak-able odor. Nick confirmed it just two steps into the apartment. Peeking around the corner, he recoiled from the sight and stench and said, "Oh my God, it's a ninety-forty," the code for sudden death.

We grimly checked the apartment. The heat was up to eighty degrees and the foul smell so overpowering we were nauseated. We turned the heat down and called for a command officer, required protocol on death incidents. Lieutenant LeGrange referred the scene to a detective, fortunately one who smoked cigars.

The student had shot herself in the head with a seven-round German revolver. Her contorted and bloated body lay on purple, bloodstained sheets with her blackened, wide-eyed face aimed at the ceiling. We found a suicide note saying she was failing a statistics class required for her graduate degree. She also wrote she was infatuated with her therapist, who had apparently not responded in kind. We found the ad she cut out to purchase the revolver.

It is a solemn duty to stand by with a body wherever it's found, but the mood is always more somber when one is posted amid the personal possessions of the deceased. I looked around her cluttered apartment, taking in what life must have been like for this girl—a recluse in the midst of a buzzing college campus.

I agreed to log the gun into property if Nick removed it from her iron grip. Initially, it seemed like a bargain as he snapped each of her fingers to remove it. But the deal disintegrated quickly as I struggled to read the tiny serial number on the frame. The gun itself stunk up the station lobby, and I was woozy with my nose inches away from the splattered barrel.

When we cleared, we were sent to eat. As we sat across from each other at a Big Boy, the scent from the apartment remained seared into our nostrils and we were unable to order. The call had struck both of us the same way, and we were bonded by it from that day on. I became very dependent on partners like that.

I doubled up with Nick on a regular basis for the summer of 1988. We were a contrasting pair: the stocky, Hungarian fireball with an innate sense of human nature, and the skinny, nearsighted townie who knew every street in the city. I was still trying to integrate Joe Randleman's cerebral techniques into my program, but Nick preferred to meet people head on.

Nick Stark grew up in Taylor, Michigan, the son of a magistrate. He was tough and extremely bright. He could articulate his point of view clearly and could often repeat verbatim the entire text of a conversation. He contrasted a rough exterior with an extremely sensitive side and like a crusader, he aspired to elevate the lot of the underdog and expose bullies for what they were. Many withered under his glare.

Nick modulated his pitch like a welder controls the flame on his torch. There was always heat, but the degree varied according to the situation. One could tell that some of our adversaries were being called out for the first time in their lives and Nick was fascinating to watch, striking fear in men twice his size. He had an uncanny knack for separating fiction from the truth. He never wasted time asking *what* had happened—he already knew. What he demanded was the motivating factor behind people's actions. When evidence pointed to a specific suspect, he went on full burn. That the suspect had committed an offense was never in question; Nick wanted to know *why*. It was amazing how quickly he could get to the gist of a story.

My humble contribution to these inquisitions was that as an Ann Arbor native and former building department inspector, I knew the city intimately. If you named a business, I could cite the address. Give me an address, and I could almost always name the business. I got us to the right place in a hurry.

One night, while patrolling alone, I pulled into a crowded court, and a guy took off running at the sight of the patrol car. I leaped several fences and sidestepped a couple of dogs before catching him three courts away. I asked him why he was running, and he breathlessly said, "I thought you was Stipe and Stark." I laughed. I wasn't aware our reputation extended beyond the squad room and into neighborhoods. "I *am* Stipe," I said. He looked at me like I must be an imposter.

North Main CCW Stop

On July 6, 1988, Nick and I were assigned to Ann Arbor's west side. We spotted a '62 Rambler on North Main near Ann Street with red tape partially covering a broken rear taillight. Nick was driving and we stopped it in the driveway of the Salvation Army Red Shield store on the 200 block of N. Main. Nick approached the female driver, Jilly Ritterton, whose thick British accent suggested she was not a townie. I covered the passenger side.

The front-seat passenger was Benjamin Cares, arrested by Mark Fleming on another traffic stop a month earlier for carrying a concealed weapon (CCW). The rear-seat passenger, sitting behind Ritterton, gave the name "Charlie Brown." Seeing we weren't convinced, he offered to go to the pay phone across the street and call someone who could verify that name.

Nick and I got back in our patrol car and consulted for a minute. Cares was nervous, and I wanted to pat him down. Something wasn't right with all three of them. Nick and I both went to the passenger side of the car, where I had Cares step out and patted him down. He was clean, but before I allowed him back in the car, I checked the immediate area where he had been seated. I moved an open-top camera case aside to feel under the seat when I realized how heavy the case felt. I looked inside to see an upside-down TEC-9 submachine gun with a fully loaded magazine.

I drew my revolver and ordered them all out with hands up. I handcuffed Cares as Nick walked around to the driver's side of the two-door vehicle. Before he could get there, the rear-seat passenger pushed the seat forward and sprang out of the car, running down Ann Street. Nick took off in pursuit. I called it in while covering Cares and Ritterton. Officers exited City Hall a block away to assist, but Stark ran the suspect down without any help.

The camera case with the TEC-9 also contained a prescription bottle in Cares' name, filled with rocks of crack cocaine. Beneath the seat in front of the rear passenger was a .357 Magnum loaded with hollow-point "cop killer" bullets. Narcotics detectives at the station identified our "Charlie Brown" as Elmo Zombolis, a known drug courier wanted in connection with the killings of two New York State Troopers (no link was ever proven).

Ritterton insisted she was merely giving the two men a ride to the Arrowwood Apartments on the north side to visit a friend. We'll never know what kind of visit it was to be. Cares pled guilty to a violation of the Controlled Substance Act, and Zombolis was convicted at trial of a CCW charge.

That fall, the city council approved the acquisition of semi-automatic handguns for Ann Arbor police officers. In doing so, they cited our traffic stop and the recovery of the submachine gun and the cop-killer rounds as the impetus for the policy change.

Call Jumpers

Because of the interminable wait for the police when my parents were stricken, I understood the anxiety families suffer in a crisis. When people are compelled to call the police, it is often for the most stressful event of their lives. One of our objectives was to minimize the time they had to endure that difficulty alone. I was also personally motivated by a sense of duty and service to hustle to every call, no matter whether I was the primary or backup unit. Stark subscribed to that same philosophy and as a result, we acquired notoriety as compulsive call jumpers.

Initially, the old-school cops on the shift resented our eagerness and brought their grievances directly to us. No one was more peeved than Larry Van Borne, who had found his pace long before, and resented being contrasted against hard-charging rookies. He was convinced we were unscrupulous ass-kissers who only wanted to impress our commanders.

Van Borne held all rookies in abundant contempt. "If you two go-getters want to jump our calls, you're going to have to write the reports," he lectured us one night.

"Larry," I said, "I'm afraid you won't be writing any more reports because we will beat you to every call."

He threw up his hands muttering, "Phew. Rookies."

Chapter Ten
The Officers

Every time an officer deals with somebody while on patrol, he is setting the stage for that citizen's next encounter with the police. It doesn't make much sense to humble a guy in front of his friends unnecessarily or to alienate him for no reason. A citizen shown respect is more likely to extend it in return. It's a constant challenge to gain compliance in a quick, courteous way.

It's up to individual officers to adopt techniques that win people over. Fighting should be a last resort. Some cops never get it, and tend to create more issues than they solve. There is a time for restraint and a time to employ a degree of force. They have to know how to do it in advance; there isn't time to think about it when it's needed. I was in a lot of fights, but I diffused many more.

There is pride and satisfaction when you can be proactive on the job but it isn't always easy to do. Controversy is stressful and avoiding it can be a full-time job but you still have to try and do your best. Some officers had a hard time with this and looked for easier ways to get through their shifts. That's why there were productivity systems, meant to light a fire under those officers who may want to coast through a shift without doing too much work.

There were constant challenges. It was always a long night if a lazy cop with seniority got behind the wheel of a patrol car.

The driver controls the tempo of your shift and democracy can go out the window. All that being said, some cops gave you a quality product every time they worked.

Jay Edwards

There was a time when all a Texas Ranger had to know how to do was ride and shoot. Jay Edwards would have been a good one—he could do both as well as anyone I've ever seen. Jay wasn't a horseman but he was a Harley rider. He could propel a bike places even the manufacturer hadn't counted on. Police motorcycle officers comprise a special breed. Not all who ride fit the mold, but Jay was among those casting it.

Jay also was likely the finest handgun marksman in a department endowed with elite shooters. Immensely calm, he could park his rounds wherever he wanted, usually in the bullseye, but he could also hit objects on the move. He proved as much on a SWAT training day when he fired two Simunition rounds (simulated bullets made from soap) into the side of a darting Officer Tim Laird's head. Jay was visibly pleased with himself.

He'd worked with Joe Randleman at the Tecumseh Police Department and followed him to Ann Arbor. Joe spoke highly of Jay, and once he arrived, it was evident why. He had the likability and reliability that made Thomas Magnum so popular on TV. Jay took the job seriously, but instantly recognized the humor it engendered. Police work is largely assessing a hastily assembled pyramid of bad decisions and it could help if you had the ability to laugh at yourself sometimes. This was a surprisingly rare phenomenon among wired-tight cops but Jay could do it. He brought big arms and an abundance of common sense to the SWAT team—a great combination to have in a fight.

I was in the station one night when I heard a radio report of a patient who'd fled with his brother from the University of Michigan Psychiatric Unit. The escapee was a huge man, and he was literally certifiably crazy. His vehicle had been impounded, so I headed up to the lobby to inform desk Officer Roger Poppek. When I got up there, I noted a hulking figure exiting the double doors. "Who was that?" I asked. He showed me the hold card, and sure enough, Roger had just released a car to an escaped mental patient.

I called for backup to meet me at Glen Ann Towing to recapture him. Jay Edwards was riding with a partner known as "Jane Wayne" Boblitt, known more for her bravado than her brawn. I was unconcerned, at least until I pulled into the Glen Ann Station and got a good look at this guy. The escaped patient was six-foot-four-inches and at least two hundred thirty pounds. He wore a heavy jacket and thick glasses that hinted at mole-like vision. Edwards and Boblitt arrived when I did, and the patient turned to confront us.

The escapee eyed Jay and me, eyes moving back and forth as he backed up against the door. He'd expected to it to be locked and when it fell open, he tumbled back for a moment, and Jay and I sprang on him. He regained his footing and the fight was on. It was close quarters, and he was strong. Jay and I had trouble getting any kind of grip on him as display racks tumbled all around us. One rack fell against the entry door, wedging it closed and locking Boblitt outside. There wasn't room for her anyway.

Jay finally got behind him and wrapped him up in a bear hug. Jay was powerful enough to lift him off the ground, but the patient probed Jay's side, trying to locate his holster. Jay was left-handed, confusing the escapee momentarily. I grabbed the guy's left arm so he couldn't reach the gun. Jay was trying to body slam him, which created a crack-the-whip movement with me at the tip. My head came within inches of a heavy metal gate. Some men can summon up inhuman strength and resistance to standard methods of control. This guy was definitely one of them. I'm not suggesting we were overmatched, but a draw was possible—until something strange happened.

Jay lifted the fellow up and tried to slam him again, but the guy planted his feet while his head snapped forward. When it did, his thick-framed glasses skittered onto the concrete floor. I cried out, "Your glasses!" He immediately stopped struggling, squinting to see where they had fallen. While I gently picked them up and slipped them back over his ears, Jay easily cuffed both wrists. The guy transformed into a completely different person. Quiet and subdued, he repeatedly whispered how grateful he was his glasses hadn't been stepped on. We cleared the debris from in front of the door and stepped outside.

Jane Wayne and the subject's brother just stared at us as we walked to Jay's car and closed the guy up in the back seat. Jay asked me how I'd thought to mention the glasses. I explained that anyone who has ever worn them panics when it appears they're going to break or be stomped on. In an entire career of police work, it was the only time I used that gambit. Once was enough.

Benny Joe Dyer

Officer Benny Dyer was an unsung hero. He never sought credit for anything he did, but he once confided to me that he felt unappreciated by many of his coworkers. If Benny Dyer was working and someone needed help, he would be there the way he was for me countless times. I don't remember the first time I met him, but he treated me decently from the start. He also had no pretensions, just a wide grin with a gap in the middle. A notoriously hostile cabbie once referred to Joe as "that porky pig motherfucker." He didn't strike me that way, but you could kind of see how Joe could get under someone's skin. He saw the humor in everything. He giggled a lot, especially when filling out a Mace requisition form after bathing officers and suspects with his last canister.

Nick Stark and I were dispatched to 1900 Geddes, a four-story apartment house, on a fireworks complaint. We climbed to the third floor and found the hallway choked with acrid smoke.

We made our way down the hall and found the carpet on fire in front of an apartment door. Nick hit the alarm while I called for dispatch to send the fire department. "They have canceled; they advise it's a false alarm," the operator replied.

"Well," I told her, "I'm here to tell you we have a fire. Have 'em step it up!"

Nick and I unreeled an emergency hose and started working the fire as Benny Dyer, Ryan Jazzman and Mark Fleming arrived. They reactivated the fire alarm and worked on evacuating the building while Nick and I assessed our situation. Fleming joined us for a moment to make sure we were okay. We were tempted to leave with him. Despite our efforts, the flames were spreading and the carpet fabric emitted toxic black smoke. We crouched as low as possible and agreed we would hang there a bit longer. We'd knocked on every door to clear the building and we thought we were the only ones remaining on that floor.

Then we heard the sound of a baby crying. We couldn't pinpoint it until we heard voices in the apartment directly across the hall from the fire. The door opened, and a sleepy couple emerged holding an infant. Nick and I exchanged wide-eyed glances, realizing they would have been trapped had we bailed out just moments before. We got them out and were relieved by firefighters, thankful to be outside in the fresh air.

Benny Dyer was with the residents of the apartment where the fire originated. One girl suffered serious burns to her foot when she stepped through the flames outside their unit. The three girls had been feuding with some boys on the second floor and the injured girl had rejected one of them, a Michigan student. He'd been harassing her for weeks. Arson investigators found a flammable liquid had been poured on the carpet outside the girls' door and ignited. The student was arrested and the fluid seized from his apartment. Had it not been for the fireworks complaint, the result may have been tragic.

Benny had a way of showing up when others wouldn't. I was once asked to drive three female recruits around the city and show them the landmarks. None of them brought lunch, so we stopped at a restaurant on North Maple Road. Before we went in, I explained my reluctance to eat out in uniform, due to untimely interruptions and the cop-bashing stories you'd often overhear.

My food had just been set before me when a woman came up and tapped me on the shoulder. "Officer, I hate to disturb you, but there is a man with a gun at the tire store down the street." I stood up, giving the recruits a knowing look. The witness gave me a description, and, leaving the recruits behind, I headed for the tire store. I radioed the nature of the call and requested an assist unit.

A patrol car was just pulling out of Veterans Memorial Park across from me, but inexplicably, the officer turned the other way. I parked in a concealed location and watched as another patrol car, this one driven by an administrative lieutenant, exited the restaurant across the street from the store and also left the area. I couldn't believe it.

I awaited real backup, and it arrived in the formidable figure of Benny Dyer, racking a round into his shotgun. Also hustling to help was Amy Atchinson, who pulled up a moment later. It's good to know how fast an officer will respond when you need them.

The suspect sat in a chair with his back to the front window, a revolver clearly visible in his back waistband. He wore a blue windbreaker with an emblem on one side. I knocked on the window and motioned for him to step outside and as he did, Joe pointed the shotgun directly at him. He raised his hands and I recognized the logo on his jacket as being from the International Association of Chiefs of Police.

The man was Bert Loney, Police Chief of Milan, Michigan. He sheepishly apologized for his carelessness. I drove back to the diner to eat my lunch, disgusted at the officers who bailed out on the call for backup. I'd never witnessed such police timidity firsthand. In all fairness to the lieutenant, she may have been in "administrative tune-out" and not had her radio on anyway. I would never look at them the same way again.

Not long before Benny retired, a lone robber who claimed he was armed robbed a downtown bank. Several of us checked the area when I found a backpack containing some miscellaneous papers at Ann and Ashley streets. I called Benny over to look at the bag, and he was convinced the suspect had dropped it. That seemed a little farfetched to me, especially because the bag appeared to belong to a street person. I gave Dyer some papers with a name on them anyway, and he broadcast the guy as a suspect.

Larry Stevens, a beat cop watching the bank's videotape, heard the name and recognized the man on the screen. A transit officer knew the man's daily routine and directed detectives to where they could find him. Thanks to Benny's instincts he was arrested and the money recovered.

Benny Dyer had a blowout retirement party. He bought a mobile home and went camping with a handful of officers. He joined us for shift parties after work sometimes, and was proud when his son joined the department. We stopped seeing him after a while. He retreated into his home and rarely left his easy chair or his computer. His health, mental and physical, betrayed him and he died in December of 2003. Benny Joe took part of me with him.

Joe Calumet

Officer Bert Davison and I doubled up frequently on afternoon shifts one fall. Normally reporting at 1500 hours, Michigan football Saturdays dictated a much earlier time of 0900 hours. This freed the day shift for stadium assignments. Inexplicably, we also signed up to work a Party Patrol one Saturday that ran to 0300 hours, past our normal 2300-hour quitting time.

Football Saturdays are bad enough without stretching them to eighteen hours, but we'd endured a steady stream of calls amidst a driving rain and had just fifteen minutes left when we heard the call. Officer Joe Calumet was call sign Frank 61.

Dispatcher: "Frank 61, copy a man with a gun."

Calumet: "Go ahead."

Dispatcher: "Frank 61, 3300 Creek, three-three-zero-zero Creek, a man with a gun, we'll get you more."

Marilyn Kelly was sent as the backup, but Davison and I were much closer and volunteered to assist. We were buzzing south on Huron Parkway in the pouring rain when an update advised: "Units heading to 3300 Creek, caller advises there are shots fired, subject is armed with a shotgun." I was driving as fast as the Dodge Diplomat would allow on wet pavement, and as was becoming customary, we arrived first.

It had rained the entire shift, so Davison and I both wore our raincoats and waterproof covers on our garrison hats. I got to the kitchen door with my gun drawn when a man, showing me his empty hands, beckoned me in.

"It's my brother, he's down there, in the bedroom," he said as he pointed down the hall. The living room was full of hushed, sobbing women, and before I moved another step I asked the man, "Where's the gun?"

"It's in there, with him; the shooting is all over," he said, gesturing again to the door with his hands.

The bedroom door was closed, but music blared from within. I recognized the Jackson 5's "The Love You Save." I stood around the corner and slowly pushed the door open. A man lay back on the bed with his feet on the floor, a shotgun by his side. He was clearly no longer a threat—his head was blown to pieces. A crimson mist spattered the walls and ceiling, and I heard the crunching of skull and bone fragments as I walked into the room. I glanced at the snowy, flickering picture on the black and white television, equipped with foil-covered antennae. You could barely make out the grainy images, but the volume was cranked to the maximum.

I could also hear a strange, rhythmic sound but I was so taken aback by the grotesque form before me that I couldn't place it; I just stood there, listening. Then I realized it was the sound of brain matter dripping onto my hat cover and the shoulders of my raincoat. I stood, transfixed, until Davison asked me if I was secure. There were firefighters and Huron Valley paramedics standing by to check the victim, Moses T. Clinton.

I walked out into the hallway where Joe Calumet now stood and as I slumped against the wall I took off my hat, and said, "God, Joe, that is grim. I've never seen anything like it."

Calumet just shrugged. "Oh, I've seen a lot worse," he said. I strained to imagine what he could possibly have seen that was worse than that spectacle in that bedroom. Later I realized it was just Joe and his calculated attempt to divert my thoughts from the blood-spattered scene. It kind of worked.

Clinton's network of family and friends had turned out faster than the rescue personnel, a not unusual occurrence. When this happened it could present both emotional and logistical complications as the victim's loved ones responded not only to their tragedy but also to the presence of the authorities. The medical examiner on the scene, the ancient and hard-drinking Dr. Meeker, had apparently left his bedside manner with his last live patient because he chuckled to himself as he came out of the bedroom, saying, "Hell of a way to stop drinking." The buzz of the packed kitchen and living room fell silent and the entire entourage directed their collective glare at me.

I asked the bereaved brother if he wanted to take a walk, and we went outside into the driving rain. We sat in the patrol car for some privacy. He told me his brother had suffered substance abuse problems and the family had scheduled a stint in a treatment facility for him. The resulting argument sent Moses into a rage, and before anyone could stop him he grabbed the shotgun and slammed the bedroom door. Moments later, a terrible blast signaled the end of his torment. Our talk was interrupted by a frantic knocking on his window. A firefighter opened Mr. Clinton's door and asked, "What was his name?"

I thought that Dr. Meeker must have trained the fire department in sensitivity. I leaped from the car, walked around the passenger side, and pulled the fireman away while closing the door. "Look, I'll give you the victim's name when we're done. This man hasn't even come to grips with his loss, and you're referring to his brother in the past tense. Do you *mind*?" Firefighters, of course, leave a warm bed at three in the morning when they respond to such calls. They don't have the time for pleasantries when they have to compose their one-line report.

Davison and I had worked twenty hours by the time we logged the shotgun and wrote the report. Because of how he'd tried to help me, the incident went some way in softening my view of Joe Calumet. He'd offered me a distraction in exchange for us handling the gruesome call. I was even more surprised weeks later when he radioed me he wanted to meet, car to car.

Joe coached a men's softball team comprised of veteran officers and he invited me to join his team. To be included was a defining moment in my career. I don't know that I can convey the utter awe in which I held these old-school officers. They were legends still in their prime. They were the quiet minority representing the silent majority. Like Vietnam-era veterans, there was no glory, or groundswell of public support for their cause. They had only each other to rely on.

Despite their similarity in age to college activists and campus protesters, they were considered by many as blue-collar bullies, bent on suppressing an enlightened generation of free thinkers. The Ann Arbor police were a formidable force, but relatively restrained for the times. Their uncomplicated motive was to keep the peace when allowed to, or restore order when forced to. Joe Calumet was on the line for every event.

When the dust and smoke of the protest movement settled, the cops held the streets where the battle for America's future had been fought. Many of the movement leaders defected to corporate boardrooms to exploit the capitalism they so loudly rejected. The legends of your profession are the benchmarks to which you aspire. Whether a sign of desperation on his part, or a nod of acceptance for me, I got a kick out of being asked to play for his team. His quiet voice forced me to hang on every word he said, and I strained to listen. He was worth hearing; his one-line wisecracks alone were gems of wisdom.

The Boss of Bosses

When Charles Glazier was the lieutenant in charge of the Special Investigations Unit, he was known as the Boss of Bosses, for good reason. Glazier was among the finest people I'd ever met or worked for, anywhere. Lieutenant "LT" Glazier was there for me a number of times. One night when recruit Steve Scott and I arrested a drunk driver near the VA Hospital, the man offered us a bribe to let him go. While we processed him in security, he made the offer once more. I warned him not to mention it again, especially to my boss. When the lieutenant came into the room to view the man, the suspect told him we'd solicited money. The LT blew his stack. He embarked on a blistering, five-minute rebuke about the cowardly nature of spurious claims. It worked. His anger prompted the suspect to confess his offer as well as my warning about baiting the lieutenant.

As my shift lieutenant he knew of my documented injuries. As durable as I thought I was, the job inflicted its share of hits. My ailments included a shoulder injury I'd suffered while tackling a drunk driver, smoke inhalation at a number of fires, a concussion suffered subduing an arsonist in his parent's home, and a back strain that happened while carrying an accident victim to safety. Each incident required an injured officer report be filed or else no subsequent claim could ever be made. I loved my job, but I wasn't indifferent to the toll it was taking. I hadn't missed a single day. Still, human resources considered me a "chronic injury problem."

I was summoned to an injury conference with an HR representative and Lt. Glazier. The rep itemized my injuries and described the pattern he saw developing in a careless officer who didn't exercise safety precautions in the course of his duties. The lieutenant politely listened, but I recognized that familiar simmer. He was more restrained than he'd been with the drunk driver, but when it was his turn he let the HR man have it.

Like a tenured professor lecturing a first day student, he pointed out that I was tied for the department lead in incidents handled and that dispatch cards showed me to be the first to arrive on nearly every call I was assigned, either as the primary or backup. He suggested these injury reports could be avoided if I stopped taking a proactive approach to the job and let nature take its course. He also asked the HR assistant if he wished to join me for a ride-along. He declined, saying his assessment may have been hasty.

I felt very well supervised.

One night we sat in Shift V briefing and heard a call for help from the radio in the command office. We could hear screaming in the background and that heightened the urgency. Nick Stark and I ran out to our car and headed to the west side. George Westwood had responded to a disturbance at 800 South Maple Road, a troublesome housing complex. "LT" Glazier was backing him up. The whole neighborhood turned out to watch as two plus-plus-sized women, Betty Ann Soames and Barbara Jo Cartwright, duked it out in the courtyard.

We were running a full signal west on Huron Street as intermittent radio traffic updated us on their situation. I was driving fifty mph in light traffic as we approached a green light at Seventh Street. A car coming south on Seventh ran the red light and crossed directly in front of us. The evasive maneuver I used had us up on two wheels as I swung right and then left to avoid hitting them.

When we arrived at South Maple and sprinted to the courtyard, we could see LT, standing like a pillar between the two struggling women, his hat cocked to one side and his clip-on tie dangling by the clasp. He looked like he had survived a stampede. Westwood kept the crowd at bay as Nick and I handcuffed the two women so we could transport one while LT took the other. When we got to security and removed the handcuffs, the two women immediately charged at each other with LT caught between them again. They were all breasts and hair, with the lieutenant grasping whatever he could to keep them apart. I was struck by the irony of such a decent man, wedged between two of the world's meanest and angriest women.

LT's secret weapon was his temper, and he very rarely broke the glass. At this point you could tell an alarm was about to go off. His animated face turned crimson and veins popped out of his neck. Those two women were loud and obnoxious and were used to bullying others to get their way. Not so this time. When LT bellowed "SHUT UP!" they did, freezing in place. We were able to lead them to separate rooms and they were booked for disorderly fighting and assaulting a police officer.

LT waved me into the command office to thank us for our rapid response. He looked like a rock star that had been mobbed by obsessed fans. His normally crisp, clean uniform was in a shambles. He was chuckling to himself, and I asked what was so funny. All he said was, "Imagine being married to one of them."

Retired Ann Arbor Police Chief Jack Lee was a rookie in his first phase of training one December when he and I were dispatched to a fight at the South Quad cafeteria on U-M's campus. A dance hosted by a sorority had morphed into a brawl. Officer Flynn Jeffries and LT Glazier also responded. It was the largest indoor melee I'd ever seen. Furniture, potted plants, bottles, shoes and anything not nailed down was being thrown around the room.

Young men were entangled in rugby-sized bunches punching, kicking and wrestling on the tile floor. We waded into the crowd but were outnumbered fifty to one. LT and Flynn released Mace from their gun belt canisters into the tightest formation of combatants. Just a couple of strategic sprays broke the group up in a hurry. Several more scattered fights broke out before we got the building cleared. We didn't make any arrests because we didn't have enough officers.

Afterward, East Madison filled with dance guests and curious onlookers. Assistant City Attorney Annie Littleton, whose daughter had been one of the party hosts, confronted me on the sidewalk, angry about the use of Mace. She demanded to know who ordered it, and why we singled out African-American students even though everyone fighting was black.

"I did," a familiar voice called from behind me. "I'm responsible for the conduct of the officers," LT Glazier told her. He was always one to take immediate action and responsibility. Ms. Littleton could not be pacified, and a personnel complaint was filed though all of the injuries incurred stemmed from the fighting itself. No one involved sought treatment for Mace exposure. Lt. Charles Glazier was an honorable man of unquestioned integrity but maybe the complaint made him think he'd overstayed his welcome. He had also been passed over for captain in favor of Larry Fiske and that had to be as inexplicable to him as it was to us. Whatever the reason, he submitted his retirement papers the following month.

The days of leaders rolling up their sleeves and wading into the fray with their men were nearly over. Supervisors were to become police officers in name only. Charles Glazier retired in January and when he left he took with him a good deal of the initiative that had made me a successful officer. Lt. Glazier's genuine enthusiasm over a job well done was infectious and I was never more pleased with myself than when I made him happy about an arrest or a lifesaving effort.

Shortly before he left, I bought two cups of coffee and asked to meet him at Yost Ice Arena on State Street where I told him what a privilege it was to serve under his command. I asked him if he had any personal highlights in his career he was most proud of. Despite an impressive record of accomplishments and high-profile arrests, he said his most memorable moment belonged to someone else. As then Officer Glazier, he had stopped a subject wanted for rape at State Street and Packard Road. The suspect resisted arrest and they struggled on the ground.

While Glazier fought to get him under control, he saw bodies flying through the air, one landing on the sidewalk and two others in the street. A large chunk of concrete rolled harmlessly away. He turned around to see the towering figure of Officer Max Burleson, who'd singlehandedly dispatched three of the suspect's friends as they converged on the unsuspecting Glazier. "My career highlight," LT Glazier explained with some emotion, "was having my life handed to me by Max Burleson." His was a life worth preserving. Lieutenant Charles Glazier breathed life into the police profession for many of us and enhanced my own career considerably.

Larry Fiske

In direct contrast to LT Glazier's inspiring leadership style was Lieutenant Larry Fiske. A member of the special tactics unit, Fiske was a fast, fluid runner and a capable marksman who routinely aced the obstacle course portion of the team recertification. It was baffling how he ascended the ranks as quickly, however. He lacked both tact and discretion. It was said that he once issued a restraint citation to a grieving widow consoling her child en route home from her husband's funeral. His philosophy was to hammer the public and hammer them hard, a policy he impressed on those under his command.

Once, I arrested a man named Jack Reznor and his sister Julie Ann on a traffic stop at LaSalle Street and Packard Road, just a block away from their house. Julie Ann gave me her sister's name, Sue Ann, though both girls had outstanding fugitive warrants for prostitution out of Ypsilanti. Jack Reznor also had a warrant, and being barely a week after being talked out of a parking structure suicide, he complied readily. Julie Ann was going either way, but she did not want to go quietly. She was dressed for the evening in a shimmering top, miniskirt and stiletto heels.

One of the easiest ways for officers to get injured is to be too delicate with a woman who is actively resisting arrest. The area outside the car was littered with large rocks the size of softballs and though Julie Ann was fighting I was reluctant to take her to the ground with force. Fortunately, Matthew Caswell arrived to assist and we were forced to pin her down in order to get her handcuffed. As I feared, Julie Ann's long legs were a little scuffed up.

Lieutenant Fiske was the station supervisor and came back to security to view the arrests. He was displeased when I told him that the female prisoner's legs incurred some scratches. He proceeded to scold me on my excessive use of force and entered her interview room to solicit a complaint. He was met with the four legs of a chair she clobbered him with as he walked in. The door partially closed and was blocked by the chair as it fell to the floor. Fiske responded by body slamming the short-skirted Julie Ann onto the table, exposing "too much" information to detail here. "Book her!" he said as he stomped out of security, without his complaint.

Once, at the scene of a burglary at Lamp Post Plaza, Fiske announced through the broken entry window: "Ann Arbor Police, were coming in!" He then racked a shotgun at the opening for emphasis and ordered two of us to go in and clear the building while he covered from the outside. I preferred my entries a bit quieter and unannounced. The lietuenant was much better at second-guessing others than thinking ahead.

He was also constantly uptight. He didn't seem motivated by any personal dislike or grudge; he just didn't think anyone deserved a break. He'd been the product of an old-school system where merit was based on generating numbers. He certainly did that. It was hard to believe that he bested Charles Glazier in any leadership category, and his promotion to captain and later to deputy chief left many heads shaking. Discretion is the understanding that one can't effectively enforce all the laws all the time. Fiske did his best to do it anyway.

"Wingnut" Roger

Roger "Wingnut" Poppek was brought on in the recruit class ahead of mine, which included Ted Randall and Terry Johnson. Roger finished last in his in-house academy, putting him just ahead of me on the seniority list. That fact grated on me my entire career because Roger exemplified bad form. The "Wingnut" nickname was in reference to his outsized ears, but he was always spinning something, usually a story. Roger claimed to have worked at the Detroit Police Department, but had actually only served a brief stint with the Wayne State University Public Safety Department. He was notoriously unreliable.

The productivity system gave officers credit for self-generated activity. After a women's advocate spray-painted the word "Rape" on dozens of stop signs in the Burns Park area, Roger initiated a separate malicious destruction of property (MDOP) report for each sign in order to pad his numbers. He also did things like take credit for discovering an "open door," or an unsecured business after hours. Roger would check one off every night Arbor Dodge took a scheduled midnight delivery.

One night I was working a U-M hockey game when a stabbing occurred in the parking lot of Yost Ice Arena. I disarmed and handcuffed the suspect then attended to the victim. Roger showed up too late to be of any help but removed the suspect from my car, transported him to the station and booked him, taking credit for the arrest. Roger was usually tied up on something else when we needed him.

I think I was angriest with Roger on a shift change, when I'd worked the Saturday night before and had to transition to day shift and work a double into Sunday morning. It was spring, and warm weather brought people downtown early in the day. Sometime around noon, I was dispatched to Liberty Plaza to look for a man having a heart attack. I had just gotten him stabilized when a bystander informed me that two women were having a knife fight in the library lot next door. I called for a backup, and they sent the sluggish Roger. I disarmed the two women and had to handcuff them together because Roger hadn't shown up yet.

I held the link in the cuffs while the heart attack victim was loaded into an ambulance, tying up traffic for a moment. An elderly man in a Cadillac tried going around stopped cars by cutting through some parking spaces. He ran over two Harley-Davidson motorcycles, and they wedged under his car. Somehow he thought he could dislodge them by backing up rapidly, grinding the shiny bikes into the pavement and sending up showers of sparks.

Roger pulled up as I removed the keys from the man's ignition, still holding onto my two knife fighters. Roger offered to help with the crash while I locked the two women in my patrol car. After I did, he handed me a slip of paper, hopped in his car, and was gone. The paper had the two vehicle identification numbers for the motorcycles scribbled on it. The wife of the heart attack victim was asking me for a ride to the hospital. The Harley owners had to be restrained from attacking the man who trashed their bikes, and my prisoners had resumed their battle in the back seat of my car. Meanwhile, Roger called out for lunch.

Chapter Eleven
Rapid Response and a Courageous Kid

The police department set minimum staffing levels throughout the day, projecting how many officers and cars were needed at specific times based on carefully compiled data. Cars could get tied up on calls coming in at all hours and sometimes several cars were needed on a single incident, leaving the road short. At those times non-priority calls were just held. On one such predawn shift I found myself as the only available unit left in the entire city. The other cars were either all in the station on arrests or on follow-up. Having twenty-eight miles to cover is a daunting task and though one method is to try to "stay central" and equidistant from every perimeter point, I usually tried to rely on my instincts.

At 4:00 a.m., I found myself off North Maple Road on the city's far northwest side. I had just turned down Sequoia Parkway when my unit was called. It was an ambulance request for a heart attack and of all the places I might have been, I happened to be just a half block away. I always wondered what the dispatcher thought when I told her I was already there. I arrived while the caller still held the receiver to her ear and she gave me an astonished look as she pointed to her stricken husband on the hallway floor.

I tilted his head and adjusted his airway to assist his breathing. I borrowed a blanket to keep him warm and assured him he would be okay. The look of grateful relief on his wife's face was precisely what motivated me to hustle to every such call. The fire department and Huron Valley Ambulance (HVA) arrived shortly, and her husband survived his ordeal. There is a reason that the Supreme Court recognizes an officer's intuition.

Jim France, Theo France and Tony Webber

In 1988, downtown Ann Arbor was plagued by a series of violent street robberies targeting young white students. They were typically struck from behind, knocked to the ground and kicked until they gave up their wallets and money. One hundred eighteen such assaults occurred between May and October. These "white boy bashings" were committed by roving gangs of young black males who disappeared down darkened alleys or into nearby apartments. The epidemic prompted police command to assign Christopher Sager, Doug Rouse, Nick Stark and me to pounce on any assault reports in the Liberty-Maynard area.

The extra patrol paid off on its first night, December 10, when three robberies were committed in just eight minutes. One victim was crossing the U-M Diag when he was knocked down from behind and robbed of his wallet with his ID and credit cards. The second victim was standing in front of Dooley's Bar on Maynard when he was knocked to the ground and kicked repeatedly until he gave up his wallet. Five minutes later, a student withdrawing cash from an ATM was grabbed from behind and punched in the face while his wallet and money were taken from his pocket. This assault prompted a bystander to report a "fight" which Sager and Rouse rolled on instantly.

Stark and I drove west on Washington while Sager called out the description and direction of travel. Two suspects emerged from an alley just ahead of us and crossed Washington into The Prescription Shop parking lot. Nick was driving and closed the distance until bumper blocks prevented further vehicle pursuit. One suspect broke right, behind the pharmacy building, and I jumped out of the car behind him. He leaped a series of chain link fences dividing businesses, some apartments, and a church. All those hours of running the par course and the track were paying off as I easily closed the distance on him. At one point, I called ahead for him to "look back here." When he did, I drew my gun and told him to stop and put his hands up. He continued to run around the First Methodist Church rectory building toward East Huron Street.

As I bore down on him, I holstered my gun and prepared to tackle him. He turned around just as I hit him hard and he slammed onto the frozen ground. He was gassed, so I was able to grab his arm and flip him over with a simple twist and cuff him. Benny Dyer pulled up right then and I lifted the suspect to his feet while Benny searched him. He pulled a U-M identification card in the name of Henri Boyce from the guy's back pocket. I asked him his name, and he said "Jim France," a notorious downtown predator. "Where'd you get this ID?" I inquired. "I borrowed it" was all he would say. Boyce had been the first victim.

Sager and Strauss captured France's cousin, Theo France. The third suspect was caught by Nick on Division Street. Not many bad guys were getting away. All of us on duty then comprised a very effective midnight platoon. This "team policing" was fast, efficient and effective, and became the prototype for the department's Special Problems Unit, formed to combat gang activity and serial crimes. Our goal was to solve crimes before the victim knew they'd happened.

On Christmas Eve 1988, Nick and I were parked on Maynard Street, talking to some bar patrons, when we heard the squeal of tires and the grinding of a transmission unable to find a gear. We looked east on William Street and saw a Honda with the windshield frosted over, lurching forward like the first day of driver's ed class. A bare hand reached out the driver's window and attempted to clear the windshield with a snow scraper. We pulled behind the car, activated our top lights, and suddenly the chase was on.

A novice at driving a stick, the driver squealed his tires each time he let out the clutch. He scooted down William to Fourth Avenue, and turned onto Madison heading west to Third Street. He beached the car in a driveway and it began rolling backwards. I pressed our front bumper against it to secure it in place. The suspect hadn't run a dozen steps before Nick slammed him onto a tangle of frozen roots.

The driver turned out to be Tony Webber, a member of a dubious family of criminals that had plagued the city for years. His father Richard was in the Washtenaw County jail for domestic assault; his brother Bo was in Jackson prison for a Christmas Eve bank robbery the year before; sister Beverly was still working off the shoplifting conviction at Kline's Department Store after being the subject of my first foot chase. We notified the Honda owner that he'd been the victim of an auto theft and that his car had been recovered in the same visit.

The Wrong Rear Window

One night Nick and I were sent to a breaking and entering in progress on Red Oak Drive off Miller. The suspect fled before we arrived but the facts of the incident were as amazing as they were disturbing. A grandmother was watching her daughter's children while the mom worked a midnight shift at a west side laboratory. The eight-year-old granddaughter and four-year old grandson were sharing a bed because the boy didn't like to sleep alone. The girl woke up in the dark to feel hands pulling at her nightgown and she shrieked.

Someone continued to tug at her clothing, and she screamed at whomever it was to stop. She heard a man yell, and a commotion arose in her room as he slammed into walls and furniture, cursing. She turned on her lamp and recognized her mother's boyfriend. He made eye contact with her and scrambled out the window. Her brother was out of bed and standing by her book-shelf. The grandmother heard the noise and called police.

When we arrived, the children sat composed and quiet on the couch, the brother holding his sister's hand. Nick interviewed them while I inspected the bedroom. The aftermath of a fight was evident: pictures were knocked off the wall or hung crooked, books were scattered on the floor, and everything atop a desk had been swept off. It seemed improbable that one subject could wreak such havoc while stumbling about in the dark. I rejoined Nick in time to hear the girl's account. She was bright enough to give us the suspect's name, his address and vehicle description. Dispatch sent Sutter and Sager to find him.

The girl was unhurt but the boy had marks on his back where he'd fallen. I called the mother at work, but she was in complete denial. She was so adamant about her boyfriend's innocence, she hung up on me so she could call him. Sager and Sutter were just staging at his house when the suspect burst out of his front door, ran to his car, and tore off with them in pursuit.

They caught up to him just as he arrived at the lab, and the mom ran out to meet him. They took him into custody and impounded his car. The suspect looked as though he'd been mauled by a small animal. Once they relayed this information, the girl's story and condition of the room began to make sense.

The four-year old boy had been awakened out of a sound sleep by his sister's screams. He instinctively leaped on the suspect's head to defend her, and began clawing him. The suspect backed into several things, trying to scrape the boy off, but he clung like a rodeo rider, inflicting as much damage as he could. The intruder finally freed himself from the boy's grasp and threw the boy against the bookcase. The brother's heroic actions likely saved his sister from a horrific assault.

The mother returned home but continued to insist that there had to be a mistake, even suggesting her daughter might have enticed the boyfriend. We felt for those kids with a mother like that but to their credit they were smart enough to look out for each other. Nick and I went to Hobby Center in the mall and bought them a couple of sacks worth of gifts. We left them on the porch with a note of commendation for their bravery.

Hardy Cooper and One Tough Victim

An Ann Arbor native, Hardy Cooper was fast, instinctive and seemingly indestructible. He had a knack for being in the right place at the right time. On the night of March 1, 1989, Cooper and Mickey Witmer were sent to the Westgate Kroger Store at 2500 Jackson on an assault call with the suspect still in the area. The call had an authentic ring to it because so many reports were coming in simultaneously. We heard phones ringing in the background as the dispatcher keyed her mic.

Nick Stark and I zipped out Jackson Rd. and were there in a minute. Cooper sorted through a gauntlet of curious onlookers to get a statement from the victim. She was beaten brutally, bleeding from lacerations to her forehead, the bridge of her nose, both nostrils and the inside and outside of her mouth.

The victim described the assailant as a white male, five-foot-eleven-inches, slim build, gray knit ski mask and a waist-length blue nylon jacket. As Cooper broadcast the description, Stark and I were on Jackson approaching I-94. He no sooner got the information out than Nick said, "Turn around, I think I see him." I flipped the patrol car around and we were out of the car and on the man as he crossed the road behind us, trying to duck behind a bus shelter on the northern edge of the shopping center. He matched the suspect description perfectly.

His name was Mitchell Lee Adderley of Jackson, Michigan. A Law Enforcement Information Network (LEIN) check and complete criminal history (CCH) showed Adderley had twice served time for kidnapping and sexual assault. He pointed out his pickup truck and consented to a search of the vehicle. The unlocked truck had attached, tradesman-type utility boxes containing a variety of tools. Inside the cab were several empty Budweiser cans and a No-Nonsense panty hose wrapper. Adderley didn't have the keys on him and said he didn't know where they were.

Cooper filled us in on the victim's account. The twenty-five-year-old woman was shopping in Kroger when she noticed the suspect following her around the store. At one point, she felt something brush against her leg and turned around to see the man bent down directly behind her, as if he had dropped something. It struck her as strange that he was wandering around the entire store yet had no groceries. When she went to the deli counter, she noticed he was still watching her, but he now held a six-pack of beer. The subject waited until she was ready to check out, and stood a few registers away instead of using the express lane for his one item.

Returning to her car, she placed her grocery bags in the trunk. She got into the driver's seat holding a package of cookies and placed her clutch bag in her lap. Her car door was suddenly pulled open and a man wearing a ski mask told her to "get over" while he pushed her toward the passenger seat. The victim screamed "*No, no!*" and kicked at the suspect. He punched her several times in the face as he continued to push her over. She realized she was being abducted.

This victim was predisposed to never allow herself to be kidnapped, preferring to fight in public than be taken to some remote location. Kicking as hard as she could, she inched herself back into the driver's seat until she slid out of the car and onto the ground. The suspect pummeled her again, using his right fist to punch her face repeatedly. Enraged, the victim struggled to her feet and started toward the suspect while still screaming to attract attention. As she closed in on him, he turned and fled in the direction of Westgate Standard.

Once Huron Valley Ambulance arrived, they took the victim to U-M Hospital while we surveyed the scene. Witmer, Nick and Hardy spotted a set of GM keys and a small cutting tool on the ground below the driver's door of the victim's car. The keys fit Adderley's truck. Mickey used a tape measure from Adderley's toolbox to note the exact distance from Adderley's truck to the victim's car. He drew a sketch to scale using a narrative continuation report form. It was included in the report.

Adderley told Nick he'd driven to Ann Arbor to buy a video game at Perry Drugs. When he couldn't find it, he went to Kroger to buy a six-pack of beer. Putting the beer in his truck, he decided to walk across Jackson Road to check Kmart for the game. Still unable to find it, he was returning to his truck when he encountered us. When Nick asked him why he had hidden behind the bus shelter, Adderley didn't answer.

We impounded Adderley's truck and headed to the station to work on the report. When the victim arrived at the department, I was struck by the extent of her injuries. Although she'd suffered no concussion, her entire face was puffy and swollen. She looked like a bare-knuckles fighter. She held an ice pack to the most painful side of her face, but was stoic considering what she had just been through. The blows to her mouth impaired her speech.

We told her that her resilience had undoubtedly saved her from more serious injury. She switched hands to secure the ice pack and placed the chilled hand into the pocket of the smock-type coat she wore. She got a puzzled look on her face and removed a watch from her pocket. "Is that yours?" I asked.

"No, I've never seen it before," she said.

I took the watch back to police security and showed it to Detective Jim Wysocki. I stood by as he opened the door to the first interview room where Adderley sat at the table, facing the door. Wysocki walked in with the watch in his open palm.

"My watch!" Adderley blurted out. Something seemed to dawn on him, and he asked, "Is that my watch?" He suddenly became disgusted. "That's not my watch; I've never seen that watch."

Nick and I knew we had somebody here. This victim was beaten to a pulp, and the suspect had two prior kidnapping/sexual assault convictions on his record. He'd struck her so hard his watchband snapped and the watch fell into her pocket. The woman was so defiant that in his haste to escape, he dropped the keys to his truck under her car. We were on a supreme roll of arrests, but nothing matched how this man was caught so quickly. Hardy Cooper's ability to isolate the victim and broadcast a timely description resulted in this rapid arrest. I consider it the best of my career.

The media had just won the right to use cameras in Washtenaw County courtrooms. Mitchell Adderley was the first defendant to be photographed at an arraignment. When his picture appeared in *The Ann Arbor News*, Ann Arbor police detectives received calls from several women who told them that Adderley had also followed them around local stores.

Because Adderley was unable to successfully force the victim from the scene, and because he was unable to initiate a sexual assault, a district court judge dismissed the kidnapping/criminal sexual conduct charges, and Adderley was charged only with attempt to do great bodily harm less than murder. At his trial, the jury was visibly puzzled by the sidestepping testimony of detectives. They not only couldn't allude to Adderley's criminal history, they had to carefully tiptoe around the premise of the interrogation. Their measured responses were an attempt to avoid a mistrial. The irony is that only the victim's active resistance precluded the intended crime.

One could see that the jury knew they were getting only part of the story. You knew they were asking themselves "Why would he just randomly beat this woman up?" Dodging Adderley's motive was tricky. The victim's testimony was compelling, however, and the photographs taken of her facial injuries at the station shocked the jurors. Mickey's location sketch, enlarged to fit a courtroom easel, occupied the jury for some time during deliberations. Witmer wasn't the hardest charger on the road, but he knew that tangible exhibits helped put facts into perspective. Mitchell Adderley was convicted and sentenced to a minimum of fifteen years in prison.

The victim recovered and is an internationally renowned pianist. She married one of Ann Arbor's most prominent citizens, who gave an emotional speech thanking me at my retirement.

Chapter Twelve
Action Oriented: A Gun, a Fire and a Shootout

"Cart"

Dave "Cart" Carter had ridden road patrol in the late sixties. He'd dodged land mines as an infantryman in Vietnam and returned to encounter members of the Weathermen, the radical student group committed to political violence. Some of their members had been linked to bombs planted at the ROTC building and the Ann Arbor CIA office. One premature blast killed Ann Arbor radical Diana Oughton and two other extremists in a Greenwich Village bomb factory. It was serious business long before "domestic terrorism" had become part of the American lexicon.

Cart and Joe Calumet were regular partners working Shift VI, from 2300-0700. As a rookie on my first midnight shift, there was a seventeen-year gap between myself and the officer next in seniority. It was a lesson in humility. Calumet took off the entire month of August each summer, leaving Carter to rotate with a number of partners. He and I were assigned as single units on the south side one Sunday night.

Sent in response to a prowler on Dewey Street, I was just a minute away. I parked at the top of the block and made my way through the shadows until I reached the address. I saw the prowler standing in a driveway, peering into a house. I drew my gun and moved to within a few feet of him. Identifying myself, I ordered his hands up. He turned to face me, and I ordered him to turn back around. When he did so, he put his hands in his coat pockets. I told him to pull them out again. He no sooner complied than he returned them to his pockets once more. I radioed Cart that I had him.

"GET your hands up," I said, and he raised them slowly.

"I have a gun on me," he replied before sliding his hands back into his pockets.

"Down on the ground," I ordered, pushing him forward. As Cart pulled up, the suspect was lying prone, with his arms extended from his sides. "He's got a gun," I said. I motioned toward him with the barrel of my own, pretty torqued up at this point.

"Go get it," Cart said, as if talking to a dog waiting to fetch a Frisbee.

I disarmed and handcuffed the guy before putting him in the back seat of Carter's patrol car. Due to double with Cart later at 0200 hours, I asked the duty sergeant if we could do so before booking the prisoner, allowing Carter to share in the arrest credit. Cart processed the guy, while I completed the paperwork; an adrenaline dump distorted my penmanship

We dropped the suspect off at the jail on our way to lunch. After eating, Carter asked if I'd like to ride with him while Calumet was on vacation. Such an invitation was an honor, and I immediately accepted. The next night, Mr. Felony himself, Clint Seaver, congratulated me on the arrest. "I heard you did a good job last night," he said. It was a defining moment in my career.

Cart turned me on to advanced patrol techniques that I hadn't seen before. He would cant the patrol car spotlight to illuminate buildings we had already passed to avoid telegraphing our presence on our approach. He reinforced light discipline, the advantage of being acclimated to the dark, and not lighting up our position. To this day, I still scold my kids on excessive flashlight use when camping.

Delaney Craig

A stocky, curly-haired, baby-faced rookie, Delaney Craig got off on the wrong foot when he joined the department. He shared a condo with one of the department's most notorious womanizers, who warped his outlook with frequent bellyaching. Craig's first evaluation reflected that attitude but he soon got a lesson in discretion.

One Saturday morning, Craig impounded a car belonging to North Central Property President Bettye Radcliffe. A respected voice in the Michigan Republican Party, she parked in Wheeler Park while she unloaded supplies for a benefit picnic near the park pavilion. The duty command lecture Craig received did little to improve his outlook.

He redeemed himself quickly and thoroughly, however. On August 18, 1988, Craig and I were assigned as single cars downtown during an intense lightning storm. A staffing shortage left us as two of the only cars in the city. Concentrated lightning sparked a flurry of false burglar alarms all over the north side, and we alternated following each other from one to another. After the last of several alarms, we parked car to car, awaiting the next run. When it looked as if the alarms were over we started downtown, or "moving central," as the dispatchers called it.

We were halfway back when the dispatcher sent us Code One to a structure fire at 1070 Greenhills Drive. When I pulled up, Craig was already speaking to a neighbor who told him that lightning had struck the condo next door, an end unit attached to several others. The cedar shake shingles were ablaze and the resident was still inside. The condominium was fully involved, and flames could be seen ripping through the roof. Dense smoke rolled through the complex. Craig stepped back and launched a series of kicks to one of the two double front doors. On the third or fourth kick, the heavy door gave way and we rushed inside. I had tried kicking in much less formidable doors without success.

The place was beautifully furnished. The resident was Margaret McGibbon, an affluent patron of the University Music Society who traveled extensively. We announced our presence several times, but received no answer. Ascending stairs to the landing between the first and second floors, we saw the figure of a woman in a nightgown at the top on the second floor. We beckoned her down to us, but she raised her hands and retreated into her bedroom. Whether it was a moment of modesty or the uncertainty of who we were, it cost us time we didn't have.

Sprinting to the top of the stairs, we were enveloped in the searing heat and roar of an inferno. Craig acted instantly, and leaped to snag the woman, but she struggled, reaching for a housecoat or a robe. I stood at the top of the stairs, wondering how a guy who could bust through a reinforced door could have so much trouble overpowering a senior citizen.

I kept an anxious eye on our diminishing avenue of escape and warned Delaney that time was up. Indeed it was. My skin and throat were scorched. Fire was consuming everything around us. Flames dripped from the ceiling. He urgently coaxed Mrs. McGibbon ahead of us down the stairs, as fire screamed at our retreat. I looked at the elegant collection of art and artifacts she had displayed and realized they would be fuel for the swift-moving blaze behind us. I wondered if the passengers abandoning the Titanic had had similar thoughts as they passed the trappings of the doomed liner.

We barely made it. We made our way to the front door and stepped outside into fresher air. I was grateful I hadn't been alone. I had never cut anything so close in my life. The neighbor who reported the fire offered our victim a place to stay just as the fire department arrived. The Ann Arbor Fire Department had staffing level issues themselves and just two firefighters manned their North Campus Station after midnight. The driver set the gauges as the lieutenant started to deploy the hoses. There was little time to lose, so I assisted him while Delaney Craig evacuated neighbors and interviewed the victim and the neighbor for the report.

Fire Lieutenant Kerr asked me to help him place a ladder in front of the garage, and he climbed up with the hose over his shoulder. I followed him up and spotted him to make sure the pressure of the hose didn't topple him backwards. The smoke was worse once water was poured on; it rolled over us in a thick wave of black, choking fog. The lieutenant was equipped with an air pack and a mask. I tried holding my breath. I thought how little sense it made to have just two firefighters on a pumper truck when it took two to deploy the hoses.

Lieutenant Kerr's efforts checked the spread of the fire to adjoining units, but Mrs. McGibbon's residence was still a cauldron of melting antiquities. After what seemed like an hour, other engine companies arrived and they worked the flames until her beautiful home was just a smoking, wet ruin. My throat and my lungs felt charred. The sergeant sent me to St. Joe's Hospital for an exam. I suffered some smoke inhalation, but was due for my two days off anyway.

Although fire departments are staffed twenty-four hours a day, it takes time to wake up, get dressed, and be on the way in the middle of the night. Patrol officers in their cars can respond much quicker. I'd attended several structure fires by now, and was getting wary about my frequent exposure to smoke. I had a conscious respect for the danger of fire but I knew I couldn't stand by and wait for the fire department when someone was trapped.

The Influence of Colors

In April 1988, the movie *Colors*, starring Robert Duval and Sean Penn, opened at the Fox Village Theatre in Ann Arbor. Nick, Patrick Christian and I went to see it shortly after the opening, and just a handful of viewers were in the audience. The indifference to human life by the L.A. gangs made me sick.

They were dependent entirely on violence. Few escaped those neighborhoods. I was glad I wasn't working in Los Angeles. The movie continued its run and crowds began to swell. The film became a catalyst for gang wannabes to assert their own affiliation, and drive-by shootings at crowds lined up at theaters became common.

One such incident at the Fox Village Theatre involved a car that was spotted at another shooting in the Pinelake Village Cooperative off South Maple Road. Riding alone and anxious to find the suspect's car, I was relegated to running an errand for Shift Lieutenant Bob LeGrange. As I waited for his submarine sandwich at the Cottage Inn Restaurant at Winewood and Maple, I heard frantic but muffled radio traffic.

Gale Johnson, a tough, unflappable Vietnam veteran, sounded agitated. He'd been in more documented shootings than any other Ann Arbor officer, all were found justified and within policy. He was conducting surveillance on active crime targets for the Special Investigations Unit. SIU had a radio channel of its own, but when it needed a marked unit or assistance, officers identified themselves on the patrol frequency by their badge number. You could instantly sense the urgency of his situation on his first transmission.

Gale Johnson: "506"

Dispatcher: "506, go ahead."

Johnson: "506, *10-12*." (Officer needs a clear channel for priority traffic.)

Dispatcher: "All units 10-12."

Johnson: "506, *shots fired*, 2700 block of Pennsylvania, suspects heading west toward South Maple."

Gale had found the car from the two shootings and was following when it suddenly stopped on Pennsylvania. The front passenger hopped out. Gale stepped from his car, identified himself as a police officer, and ordered the man to put up his hands. The subject whirled around, fired at him, and took off running. Johnson returned fire, striking the subject in the buttocks. The vehicle sped off toward South Maple, and Gale broadcast his radio traffic.

I jumped into my patrol car and was there in an instant. I cut my headlights, using streetlights for visibility. The suspects' older sedan pulled onto South Maple right in front of me. Using the open channel, I radioed the dispatcher that I was behind the car and Wanda Caswell dispatched units to assist me. We were both running without lights, and I wasn't sure whether they had seen me behind them or not. They turned east on Pauline, and I gave an update on our direction.

They turned sharply into the Walden Hills apartment complex, coming to a stop. I opened my driver's door, covered the car and occupants with my handgun, and lit it up with the driver's side spotlight. This group had been involved in three shootings in one night—I wasn't going to fool around with them. I announced that if any one of them moved I would shoot them all.

It was late. The windswept parking lot was unseasonably cold and desolate. Despite my adrenaline, I felt isolated and extremely exposed. I realized that the entire police department still thought I was eastbound on Pauline. The suspects stopped so quickly that I hadn't had a chance to call it in. I also hadn't had time to turn on the headlights or activate the top lights. I noted that the suspects were remarkably still.

Other responding units jammed the radio channel, preventing me from transmitting my location. Finally, using my portable radio, I was able to call the stop in. Just moments later, the suspect vehicle was flooded with the lights from several patrol units led by the department's best marksman, Jay Edwards. We conducted a felony stop, an arrest procedure used when the suspects were involved with serious crimes and could be flight risks. Weapons drawn, we ordered the occupants out one at a time, backed them up toward the police cruisers, and put them face down on the cold ground.

As the last suspect was ordered down, I was thinking that justice was truly being served at that moment. Lit up by a dozen spotlights, shivering on the frigid pavement and held at gunpoint by several veteran officers, there was an element of uncertainty in the suspects' minds. No gang signs, no dirty looks, no defiant double-talk, just strict compliance with the arrest. It was a rare moment of vulnerability and clarity for some otherwise tough hooligans.

Once the men were secured, I examined their car. The trunk lid was riddled with bullet holes. It dawned on me why they had been so compliant—someone had already lit them up. Gale Johnson later confided that he may have expended a few rounds their way after the gunman had fired at him and they fled in the opposite direction. The wounded gunman was found hiding in a freezer at a nearby Farmer Jack's supermarket, with the detective's round right in his ass.

Gale was grateful the suspects had been captured and that the car, with evidence of the previous shootings, had been recovered. I was thankful for Jay Edwards and the other officers who had hustled to back me up. The gang culture that had seemed so distant a few months before had moved into the neighborhood. Once the suspects were safely in the station, they reverted back to defiant belligerence. But for those few fleeting moments in that parking lot, they experienced the same fear they tried so hard to instill in others.

"Fortune Favors the Prepared Mind"

The Ritual

I'd learned to keep riding boots spit-shined at Culver. I carried that same compulsion through the police academy and back to Ann Arbor PD. I kept my uniform sharp and my leather spotless. Each day before my shift, I followed the same ritual of fitting my uniform with my nametag, badge, whistle and silver pens, in that order. There were other trappings that we were authorized to display (shooting pins, award ribbons) but I preferred a spare look. I polished and buffed my boots until my arms were sore.

I tried to prepare for work the same way every day. Nick and I were performing at an unprecedented level. Our location, availability and timing for emergency calls were flawless. Even Larry Van Borne had stopped griping about our call jumping. To keep us off the radio in the early morning hours, he and Joe Calumet bought us coffee and met us behind Ann Arbor Buick on Washtenaw Avenue.

My fitness routine was grueling, I pushed myself to the limits of physical endurance while running likely work scenarios in my head. I still ran the eighteen-station par course on the U-M North Campus almost every day, usually taking my well-trained dog Augie with me. In the coldest days of winter, the wind across Mitchell Field would create chest-high snowdrifts in the swales. The only footprints were remnants of my previous day's efforts.

I knew if I were to pursue suspects outside, I had to train in the most difficult conditions. Running laps at the U-M track, the spiraling wind whipped an alternating pattern of dry lanes and knee-deep snow. Jesse Owens had set four world records there, and his ever-present plaque kept me company in those frigid, lonesome hours of training.

I saw a news photo of Cincinnati Running Back James Brooks running the Riverfront Stadium stairs the day after losing the 1989 Super Bowl. I was impressed. Living one block away from the largest collegiate stadium in the world, I adopted his routine immediately. Constructed in 1927, Michigan Stadium seated more than one hundred six thousand fans. The entry portals brought you to the top of seventy-six rows of seats that descended down to the field. Running up and down the forty-four sections meant climbing and descending some thirty-three hundred stairs. In good weather it took about twenty minutes.

It was a torturous regimen, but my legs were carrying me to personal record times at the track and on the par course. Despite wearing a gun belt and jump boots, I was routinely running down kids half my age. For maximum mobility and comfort,

Nick and I had pared down our winter garments to long underwear, uniform shirt and pants, and a commando sweater.

Psychology is a key component of success on road patrol. If
we don't appear scared, don't show the cold, and look our adversary right in the eye and invite him to take us on, he'll usually
flinch without fighting. Of course, that doesn't mean that we're
not scared stiff, freezing our ass off and hoping he gives up
without a struggle. But I was ready.

There were many practical applications. On Christmas Eve,
1990, Katie Quine and I were sent to a burglar alarm at the
Columbia Cable offices on South Industrial Highway. A heavy,
drifting snowfall blanketed the area on a holiday night with no
other foot or vehicle traffic. The suspect broke in through a
north window, ransacked the snack cart and coffee money, and
fled out a south window and into the quiet night. Quine secured
the scene and I followed the fresh tracks.

This was why I ran against the clock in the snow, to replicate
these conditions. I was wearing schoolboy rubber boots that
zipped up the front. I pursued the suspect for half a mile at a run
when I spotted him a hundred yards ahead on the Eisenhower
Parkway bridge near Boardwalk. His unbuckled boots had filled
with snow, and he'd stopped to dump them out.

I was joined by former Michigan hurdling champ Patrick
Christian. We closed the distance and arrested the ex-convict
without incident. At his trial, his defense attorney claimed I had
followed the wrong subject. The judge suggested his client get
better boots or a different story. The defendant was convicted.

I was working harder and smarter. For instance, we had long
secured crime scenes where the suspect or suspects fled on foot,
leaving tracks in fallen snow. K9 handlers were adamant that the
scent not be contaminated and the policy was clear on this point:
do not follow the trail. I tired of waiting, knowing that suspects
were making their getaways while we waited for tracking dogs to
arrive.

One night I simply backtracked the prints leading *to* the

crime scene from their origin. There was the suspect's car. He'd taken the most direct route to get there, but took pains to lead us in another direction when he fled. I was waiting for him when he returned to his car. It took the dog nearly a half hour to catch up to us, tracking the route of his getaway.

The NCAA Tournament Incident

Near the end of the NCAA basketball championships final game between Michigan and Seton Hall in early April 1989, I sat behind the wheel of the Ann Arbor Police transport van parked in an alley off Maynard Street. A squad of uniform officers sat in back, waiting to be deployed. I watched several Michigan fans reacting to the game's progress several floors up in the twenty-eight-story Tower Plaza.

Patrol Deputy Chief Ford Walters organized a detail of thirty-eight officers to respond to the revelry of a Michigan win and the potential carnage of a U-M loss. Judging by the fans' exuberant gestures, it was going to be a celebration. Our detail remained staged while the final seconds of the game ticked away. Screams, honking horns, and the sounds of fans streaming into the streets announced Michigan's victory.

South University attracted the largest crowd, so I wheeled the van around the maze of one-way streets to the command post. In what has now become an American sports tradition, dozens of revelers ballooned to crowds of hundreds. Our detail was composed of loosely grouped officers from various agencies watching in amazement as the celebration spiraled out of control.

Little by little, the seeds were planted: trash containers were overturned, bottles smashed, daredevils climbed the light poles to ascend the cables suspending the traffic signals. The more daring the aerialists became, the bolder the crowd got. They rocked vehicles attempting to traverse South University and a misguided Detroit cab driver tried to run the gauntlet by using his horn and bumper to push the crowd out of the way. He was barely able to escape his cab as the frenzied group flipped it over.

Nick Stark, Hardy Cooper, Ron Lindsey and I watched from the corner of Church and South U. Reports were pouring into the command post of escalating violence, but no order was given to take action. A group was working on turning over a second car when dispatch reported a man being attacked by ten subjects in the Forest Street parking structure. The four of us pushed our way through the crowd blocking the intersection and hustled to the scene via an alley.

As I looked over my shoulder, I saw we were pursued by a charged-up group of about fifty people. We reached the structure and checked for the assault but found nothing. As we began to emerge, we could see that the pursuing crowd had grown to about two hundred chanting rowdies. Bottles began to rain down on us as we backed under the overhang of the garage. The four of us spread out side by side, with our nightsticks drawn and cocked, prepared to strike anyone who ventured too close. We needed to protect ourselves. Beer spattered our legs as bottles fell a few feet short of the line we tentatively held.

A pile of concrete rubble, leftover from ongoing construction, offered an attractive arsenal for a mob searching for more projectiles. From nowhere, a Good Samaritan scaled the rubble pile and held a small crowd at bay by threatening to chuck blocks at anybody foolish enough to call his bluff. Strategically, we could have been worse off, but there were no threats from our flanks or behind us. The second floor of the carport offered some protection from lofted rocks and bottles but the disparity of four of us against two hundred had me plenty worried.

A few in the group taunted us and tried to enlist more to pelt us. It was an awkward standoff. We'd done nothing to instigate the crowd, but our jackets were covered with spittle from the rabble we'd passed en route to the bogus call. I'd heard and seen enough. I took a step forward with my nightstick cocked against my shoulder and beckoned the closest heckler toward me.

I made solid eye contact with him and invited him to get close enough for me to whap him one. He shook his head as if to say "no thanks," so I pointed to the man next to him. He, too, declined to come closer as the crowd quieted down to see what we intended to do next.

If I was going to be in a spot like that, I was thankful I had a trio of tough companions like Lindsey, Stark and Cooper who had all surmounted long odds in street fighting. The crowd was dying for something to happen, but no one wanted to be the one it was happening to. Gradually, the back of the crowd started to drift away, quietly. First one by one and then by twos, they dropped their rocks and debris and migrated toward the sounds radiating from South U. Soon we found ourselves alone with the guy who said he had just happened by and took the high ground. If we didn't have a riot to attend, it would have been a great time to debrief over some cold beers. But bedlam reigned up and down South University and the gravity of the standoff didn't sink in until later. We didn't defy those odds every day.

More cars were overturned, storefront windows smashed, and there was still no word from the top to restore order. We acted on our own. Stark, Cooper and I combined to arrest five window-breaking vandals and delivered them to the command post. When it was all over, close to eighty thousand dollars in damage had been done and ours were the only arrests made. Merchants made their feelings known and the department took some heat. A new game plan was drawn up for future Michigan basketball postgame festivities.

Honored Recognition

In May, 1989, I received an invitation from Chief James Colby for the AAPD Annual Awards ceremony on June 2nd. Patrol Deputy Chief Ford Walters had stopped me in the hallway to mention he'd seemingly "been doing nothing lately but signing letters of commendation" for me. It wasn't long before that I'd been baffled as to what one had to do to be recognized. Nick Stark and I had been so busy hustling for the past year that we were oblivious to the scope of our achievement. We agreed to attend and stood together in formation as the alphabet dictated.

Deputy Chief Charles Erskine read off the names and the citations in his uniquely somber way. Nick was called and received four Professional Excellence awards, for the capture of Mitchell Adderley in the Kroger attempted kidnapping incident, suppressing the 1700 Geddes fire, the capture of the trio of downtown robbery suspects including Jim France, and the arrest of a subject who had stabbed two U-M students.

Chief Erskine called me up next for the same four Professional Excellence awards as well as the Medal of Valor for the rescue of the Mrs. McGibbon at the Greenhills fire with Delaney Craig. The Medal of Valor was the department's highest award for those who survive their action. After he read the citations and I returned to my spot in formation, he added: "I believe that is the most awards ever given to one officer."

A rush of blood flooded my ears, and I felt lightheaded for a moment. In my entire life, I had never been honored in such a way. I felt a surge of pride and was thrilled to share the moment with Stark and Craig. It didn't hurt that my sons were watching from the audience. Rhonda, as usual, skipped the ceremony.

Delaney Craig and I were called back up to receive *The Ann Arbor News* Award, presented to recipients of the Distinguished Service Award or Medal of Valor. Veteran police beat reporter Thomas "Flash" Walcott interviewed me for a story in *The Ann Arbor News*. It was a very flattering piece, written by an outspoken police supporter at the paper. A picture showed me saluting Chief Colby, who recruited me in the first place. He'd whispered, "I knew I was right about you," as he handed me the Medal of Valor.

I wasn't particularly heroic or courageous. I was empowered

by the fact the welfare of people was dependent on my taking action. Barney Fife explained it best when he said that his badge represented a "lot of people." They didn't all have to be there for me to make a stand on their behalf but their presence was real. Without them, I'd have just been another skinny guy standing alone. It made all the difference in the world. I finally felt I had accomplished something significant in a very challenging profession.

After the article was published, I received cards and letters from friends of my parents, commending me and telling me how proud my mom and dad would have been. One woman had worked with my mom at a Kaiser-Frazer plant after the war; she enclosed several photos of my mom I had never seen. She invited me to visit while she was in town watching her daughter's home nearby. It was great hearing old stories for the first time.

Chapter Thirteen
The Special Tactics Unit

The day that I received commendations at the AAPD awards ceremony, a notice was posted for three vacancies on the special tactics unit (STU). Candidates, once selected, had to attend three weeks of "intensive training" at a SWAT School hosted by the Western Wayne Special Operations Team. To qualify for consideration, a candidate had to maintain a "high degree of physical fitness" and be otherwise eligible according to department policy.

The department policy on special threat situations (e.g. hostage taking, barricaded gunman, suicidal subject) specified that patrol officers would be the initial response to all such situations. However it went on to say that patrol officers were not trained or equipped to handle such incidents. I wanted to resolve that contradiction.

Once a year, the Incentive Selection Test was held to test officers on various aspects of criminal law and department policy. A passing score allowed one to bid on in-service positions like temporary detective, or long-term posts like field training officer or special tactics unit member. To ensure impartiality, an outside vendor designed and administered the test.

Studying for the test was largely a matter of reading a stack of policy and procedure orders from front to back, and lifting every rule that could be put in the form of a question. The rest was a mix of common sense and a grasp of Michigan state laws.

Reading those P&Ps was a sure way to induce sleep after a stressful midnight shift. No matter how much or how little I studied, I finished fourth out of seventy odd test takers for several years in a row.

Still, I had some mojo going for me. I had a great test score, I was in an elite state of fitness, and I was having a career-making year on the road. I did have some strikes against me, as well. The most daunting hurdle was the commander himself: Robert LeGrange didn't like me. I'd been called in on my day off the year before to be a uniformed presence on a drug raid. The captain completed the briefing instructions and because I'd not assisted on a raid before, I raised my hand and asked, "If someone runs out the back door where I'm posted, what do you want me to do?"

"You weren't my first choice for this operation," he said. "If you keep your mouth shut, you just might learn something." I was missing Frank Sinatra on *Magnum P.I.* for this? Nice to be humiliated in front of the entire tactical team.

Two other worthy candidates, Ted Randall and Seth Connery, had distinguished records on the road and were readying themselves for advancement. Every time I passed the command office when Capt. LeGrange was working, Ted and Seth were seated behind the closed door, soliciting whatever advice he would share with them. I had tremendous respect for those guys, but I thought schmoozing with Bob was beneath them. The other viable candidate was Mack Livingston, who had been kind enough to offer me a place to sit when I had otherwise been rousted at my first solo shift briefing.

I had another reason to believe I wasn't on Bob LeGrange's short list. As shift commander, he had once tried to call me at home to summon me into work early. I was in the shower and three-year-old Jacob answered the phone. When Bob said: "This is Captain LeGrange, may I speak to your father?" Jacob replied, "Shut up, butt face," and hung up. He'd called a second time with the same result.

Four officers, three openings, and I knew I was going to be the odd man out. A thorough (intrusive) medical examination was required as well as a psychological exam from the department psychologist. The physical agility test consisted of a one and a half mile run in twelve minutes or less; a one-hundred-yard dash in less than sixteen seconds; a one-hundred-yard, one-hundred-eighty-pound man carry in less than forty-five seconds; five pull-ups; thirty push-ups; and as many sit-ups as possible in one minute or less. I saw no problem with any of these except the man carry. I only weighed one-sixty myself. The other candidates weighed significantly more and I had never tried running while carrying someone on my shoulders. The agility test was held at the U-M track, where I often ran.

None of us had difficulty with the pull-up, push-up and sit-up portions, and we all ran the sprint easily. The man carry was something else. I hoisted Livingston onto my shoulders using a fireman's carry. I thought my spindly legs would snap as I weaved back and forth down the track. It was scarcely a walk/run that I was doing, as each agonizing step found my legs wobblier. Livingston kept slipping off to one side as I struggled to stay in a straight line to minimize the distance and reduce time. I reached the finish line and crossed with barely a moment to spare. My legs were screaming, and we had yet to run the mile-and-a-half leg of the test.

Several current members of the SWAT team attended the agility test. As they gave us a few minutes to rest up for the run, they stood together and talked about us in inaudible mutterings. A couple of them shook their heads in what I was sure was a condemnation of my carrying skills. Finally, we lined up for the mile and a half run. I had been running it in just over ten minutes, so I was feeling confident. Ted and Seth took off fast and I was tempted to push by them and show what I could do without baggage, but Livingston was just jogging from the get-go. He just couldn't run any faster, so I fell in beside him and tried to coax him into a realistic time.

He obviously hadn't been running enough and with his labored breathing, he told me to go on without him. Ted and Seth were close to lapping us anyway, so I figured we would just move as quickly as we could and work it together. It was damn close. As we neared the finish line, some members of the team flanked us and rooted Livingston on. We crossed in 11:58, and I breathed a sigh of relief. We had all passed the physical fitness portion of the process.

That night, Sgt. Mark Zawicki met me on the road.

"You looked good out there today," he said. "I was very proud of you. Did you know that part of the SWAT code is that you never leave a team member behind?"

"No. No I didn't," I said.

"Helping Livingston says a lot more about you than your time." He was nodding his head like I might have a shot after all.

I called Livingston and invited him to join me at the Huron High track in the afternoons to tune up his time. Livingston soon became a running fanatic, and for years after logged several miles each day. We waited for word of who would be invited to the SWAT School.

The Summer of 1989: Murder on Whitewood

On a sweltering June 18th, Nick and I were sent to a burglary in progress on Whitewood Street. We were four miles away when we got the call, while another unit handled a noise complaint a block away from the address. We were sure they would clear their call and beat us over there—they didn't. On crimes in progress, the dispatcher keeps an open mike to update information as it is passed on to him or her. One can hear the operator relaying what the caller is actually saying. The frenzied tone of the operator's voice telegraphed the urgency of the call, and we were running Code One down Packard Road.

The initial dispatch was of a burglary in progress. The second report indicated that subjects were forcing their way through the front door. An update said they had entered and were attacking the occupants with a knife. The 2634 Whitewood address was part of the Pittsfield Village Apartments, a post-war housing complex offering the tiniest two-story units one could imagine. The 2634 residence was set two hundred feet back from the street, making the address numbers difficult to find.

As we approached, the front door was open and we could hear a woman was screaming from within. A much quieter one met us at the door and told us the suspects had already fled. The doorframe was split in half, and the window pane shattered. The apartment was in shambles with the dining table overturned and dirt from potted plants spread across the floor. We moved into the living room where one apparent victim lay face down at the foot of the stairs. I did a double take as I recognized a second victim.

Donna Reading was a longtime employee in the city clerk's office. She was present the day I was sworn in as an officer and was well respected. Donna was a stout woman, with a roly-poly neck that was gaping wide open with a deep slice from front to back. I directed the other woman to find a towel and apply pressure to Reading's wound while we attended to the man on the floor. A wallet lay next to him and a Michigan license identified him as Walter Carlson.

Carlson lay in a large pool of blood, so we rolled him over to find his wound. Rolling up his shirt I could see a sucking chest wound in his right upper quadrant. I asked the two women to find a plastic bag or some cellophane while Nick tried to locate a pulse. Carlson was unresponsive to any verbal communication and had stopped breathing. Reading gave me a plastic bread bag, and I inserted my hand inside and placed it over the wound, a technique I'd once heard mentioned in a first aid class.

Walter began gasping for breath and appeared to be reviving for a minute. He lapsed back into unconsciousness shortly afterward, never uttering a word. But with his airway sealed, he was now breathing. Huron Valley Ambulance (HVA) paramedics relieved us to turn to the investigation.

The woman at the front door was Walter's sister. She explained that they had been watching a boxing match on HBO when Walter's wife Hester, her brother Mitchell Walker, and a third woman had come to the door and tried to push it open. The door was deadbolted, so Mitchell kicked it in. Walter picked up an umbrella and tried to fend them off, but became pinned in a corner. Hester ran to the kitchen, where she rifled through drawers until she found a steak knife. Mitchell held Walter with his arms at his sides while Hester stabbed him. Carlson collapsed near the stairs where we found him.

Mitchell and Hester then converged on Donna Reading, who was backing toward the door while calling the police. Hester slashed Donna several times with the knife. It was small wonder the operator sounded so agitated. The third intruder remained by the front door the entire time. After Donna was wounded, all three fled back out the front with Hester retaining the knife used in the attacks. A description of the three suspects, along with a vehicle and plate, was relayed to communications.

I headed up to St. Joe's Hospital to check Walter Carlson's status and was told he was in very critical condition. After an hour and fiteen minutes, the attending nurse returned to tell me he had died. Fifteen minutes later the nurse returned to tell me Walter had again been revived and was tentatively holding his own. He was a very tough man. Walter Carlson was stabbed at 2300 hours (11:00 p.m.) with the knife puncturing his aorta. He died at 0415 hours.

Hester's Mercury Zephyr was abandoned a few blocks away at Pinecrest Avenue and Oakwood, where a witness saw Walker exit the car and run over to a sewer grate, dropping something inside. The three suspects were on foot, heading toward Washtenaw Avenue. Newly promoted sergeant Diane Seagram recovered the murder weapon from the sewer and impounded the car.

When planning the perfect murder, one wouldn't leave living witnesses who know you. One wouldn't drive a battered Mercury Zephyr that frequently stalled, and wouldn't commit such a crime when Hardy Cooper was working. It all caught up with Hester Carlson, Mitchell Walker and accomplice Ginny Raines in the parking lot of the Holiday Inn East at Washtenaw Avenue and US-23.

Cooper and partner John Stevens spotted Raines crossing the lot toward the Amoco station next door. She was making a not-so-subtle attempt to avoid the officers, and they stopped to identify her. Hardy saw a Yellow Cab at the entrance to the motel and went over to check on it.

The taxi was exiting the lot with Carlson and Walker inside when Officer Cooper, in true McCloud-like fashion (another of my favorite police characters on TV), thrust himself in front of the moving cab and drew down on the occupants. Outgunned and overmatched, Hester and Mitchell surrendered. They claimed the victims had injured themselves in an attempt to attack *them*. The episode would just get stranger as it proceeded to trial.

The officer assigned to the noise complaint a block away from the Whitewood homicide showed up when it was too late to offer assistance. How he could have failed to hear the stabbing call was beyond me. I expected everyone to be as aggressive as Nick and I were but that was naive. If they had come immediately it might have made all the difference for Walter Carlson and Donna Reading. To be fair, there was a rookie in that unit but he wasn't driving. It is a hard thing to commandeer a patrol car from a senior officer. But there would come a time when that particular rookie was among the fellow officers I most relied on.

Greg Heschendorf — A Victim of Circumstance

Just two Sundays after Walter Carlson was killed, Nick and I were handling a burglary at the Dom Bakery at Main and Liberty.

While wrapping up the report, we overheard Zasman and Bruno Stevenson dispatched to a shooting at 715 Plum Street. Sergeant Diane Seagram was sent to assist. Like always, we were determined to get involved.

I was familiar with Greg Heschendorf, who had been confined to a wheelchair after a motorcycle crash. He lived in the childhood home he'd inherited from his mother and made a meager living selling drugs. A year or so before I'd arrested two men who'd robbed Heschendorf at gunpoint in a drug deal gone awry. But now, tonight, he'd called 911 and told the operator he'd "shot his friend."

Zasman and Stevenson were responding from the south side, and we easily beat them to the north side address. The dwelling was just off Pontiac Trail, so we cut the lights and rolled to a stop a house away.

Nick and I flanked the front porch. Having the better view, I assessed what was going on inside. I could see Heschendorf's overturned wheelchair on the living room floor as he lay side by side with the apparent victim, crying and wailing incoherently. A woman appeared and came running toward the front. She pushed the screen door open and beckoned Nick and me inside.

Nick grabbed her and dragged her off the porch, handing her off to another officer; he wanted to make sure she was safe. Satisfied that backup had arrived, Nick and I simultaneously leaped up the steps and entered the living room with guns drawn. As we closed on the two men, Heschendorf screamed, "I've shot my friend, I've shot my friend."

He had indeed. His companion lay motionless on the floor with bullet wounds to his stomach, forearm and head. I tried to rouse the victim, Manny Michaels, to no avail. I dragged the paralyzed Heschendorf into the dining room by a wrist and handcuffed him with his arms over his head. Nick cleared the dwelling and rescue personnel swarmed in, kicking expended shell casings around and destroying our crime scene while attending to Michaels.

Nick read Heschendorf his Miranda rights and interviewed him in his sparsely furnished dining room. He told us that Michaels was his best friend and that he and his girlfriend were staying with him. Heschendorf and Michaels were in the midst of a drinking binge and the girl began arguing with him when Michaels stepped outside. Heschendorf grabbed her arm and she screamed. At that moment Michaels reentered the house and they exchanged heated words. Heschendorf retreated into his bedroom but left the door unlocked.

Soon thereafter Michaels charged into the bedroom and Heschendorf shot him with a pistol he kept for protection. He continued to converge on him, so Heschendorf shot him again. Michaels staggered out of the bedroom and collapsed in the living room. Heschendorf called police and attempted to render aid to his "friend." Heschendorf said he was unsure how many times he fired.

His statement conflicted with the wounds. Michaels had been shot in the stomach and it looked like after turning away to retreat, he'd been shot again, both in the forearm and in the side of the head.

The victim was transported to the hospital and Nick and I helped Heschendorf into his wheelchair so we could take him to the station. We secured the handgun, a .380 Walther, in our patrol car, but firefighters and paramedics had kicked around the rest of the evidence. Medical wrappers and waste materials were intermingled with the shell casings we left for investigative personnel. Michaels died at 0730, about four hours after the shooting. Heschendorf was booked for murder and taken to Washtenaw County Jail.

Ann Arbor averaged one homicide a year and Nick and I had been called to two within the span of three Sundays. I'd smelled the stench of death, felt brain matter drip on my head, and saw the life seep out of two separate homicide victims in a very short time. If I had been naïve and sheltered before, I wasn't the same guy anymore. I was very fortunate that Nick was a terrific partner, and we could handle just about anything.

The summer madness continued. A few days after Michaels' killing, Stark and I were driving up Liberty Street and saw a woman running across Thompson with an axe handle held over her head. She came up behind another woman and brought the stick down, striking her hard on the back and shoulder. Nick grabbed the mic and called it in, then hopped out and ordered the woman to drop the axe handle. Instead, she turned and faced him, again raising it above her head with both hands. When Nick drew his sidearm and ordered her to drop it, the stick clattered to the pavement.

She had a male companion who appeared out of nowhere. He jumped at Nick, grasping his gun arm. I handcuffed the woman and pinned her against a storefront window while Nick shook the man off. Then he leaped at me while Nick holstered his pistol and attempted to wrestle his companion free. Nick tackled him on the sidewalk and cuffed him.

The victim explained that she and two friends had been dancing and singing down the block. The suspect told one of her companions that the victim looked like she had gonorrhea and when the victim uttered a response, the suspect rushed across the street and attacked her with the axe handle. The suspect claimed the response had been a racial insult; the victim was white, the suspect black.

For his part, the suspect's boyfriend had a much nobler motive for hindering the police: His girlfriend was two months pregnant with his child. He was compelled to intervene when Nick pointed his gun at her abdomen. "I wouldn't have done anything if you were pointing it at her head," he said.

We returned to the station and went down to the communications desk to draw arrest numbers for the two. They played back Nick's transmission that gave our location. I couldn't make out a word, but two cars had responded to assist us while a crowd was developing. The LEIN operator had been busy running a check when Nick called out. While no one else present could figure out what Nick had said, the operator calmly swiveled in her chair and said, "Thompson and Liberty." When lives depended on a single transmission, it was incredibly helpful to have people that could pull the information out of garbled, crackling radio traffic. There was mayhem every night and on every shift and Nick and I—all of us—were dependent on the talents of our dispatchers and operators.

Chapter Fourteen
One Tough Cop

I served the Ann Arbor Police Officers Association Executive Board as an officer or board member for fifteen years. At times I had my hands full just representing my partner. Nick Stark was intelligent and perceptive but he and I were polar opposites in personality. I would have objected to his style and intervened on behalf of beleaguered suspects if he wasn't so right most of the time.

Bullies lumber through life, bowling over every passive person they encounter, but Nick was one to call them out. Officer Tim Hammer coined him "Pitbull" and maybe that's how Nick was. But I wasn't about to call my dog off anyone that would seize the opportunity to attack me or someone else. Nick's brutal, in-your-face honesty prompted several complaints from a newly empowered public, informed to demand a business card from every officer they had contact with. One could divert attention from his crime by questioning the officer's method of investigating it. I was usually his union rep *as well as* a witness to the alleged misconduct.

We weren't beating anyone. As a matter of fact, our use of force was restrained compared to other departments. I had yet to see or hear of any Ann Arbor officers removing their nametags and thumping people. There were a few, isolated instances where Ann Arbor officers engaged in extra-curricular punches at the end of a pursuit or at the conclusion of a prolonged fight to subdue a suspect, but Nick took no part in them. It was only his tone that got people in a twist. That same tenor of treatment netted countless felony arrests and elicited unchallenged confessions. He would be elite in any agency.

Nick once loaned me a book called *One Tough Cop* by veteran New York Police Detective Bo Dietl. A courageous undercover detective, Dietl had busted dozens of serious felons numbering more than fourteen hundred arrests over a fifteen-year career, for an average of ninety-four per year. While reading the book, I checked our current productivity report to see how we measured up. Working 1,572 hours, we each averaged a booked felony arrest every 20.822 hours. That was seventy-five arrests *each* for the productivity period, or about two hundred fifty per year apiece. We kept the back door swinging.

One thing Nick and I weren't doing well was writing hazardous (moving violation) tickets. I ranked seventy-seven out of seventy-nine officers during that same period. The bottom four officers were typically Stipe, Stark, Edwards and Randleman, in random order. We were routinely counseled on the value of hazardous tickets to city revenue, accident prevention and police visibility.

But we far exceeded the department average for traffic stops, and none of us could justify taking money out of the pockets of taxpayers while burglars took money out of their homes. It made little sense to work dedicated traffic enforcement when there was little or no traffic to watch. Our stops for moving violations often resulted in a custody arrest, and it was bad form to "double-dip" by piling paper on a booked arrestee.

I had one sustained citizen complaint in my career. We'd stopped a U-M student for a moving violation on South State Street. A resident of Detroit, he failed to pay a fine for a misdemeanor drinking violation, and a warrant was outstanding. He was cooperative and friendly. We wanted to avoid vehicle impoundment because he had just enough money to post his bond and be released at the station. I asked his girlfriend if she could drive his car and follow us in. She was not so friendly, and insisted our stop was prompted by the fact they were African-American. Despite our assurances, she was resolute in her vocal disapproval of her boyfriend's arrest. We allowed them to talk privately for a moment, and she agreed to drive the car.

While following us to the station, she inexplicably made a prohibited left turn onto a one-way street, nearly striking another car. We stopped, and Nick ran back to drive the vehicle to City Hall himself. While we bonded her boyfriend out, she was registering a complaint about our "profile" stop. She told Captain Red Burton that I had deliberately forced her to drive in an effort to humiliate her. As it turned out, she was unlicensed. Once released, her boyfriend was visibly dismayed by the commotion in the lobby and asked to speak to the captain alone. When they emerged from Burton's office, he went directly to his girlfriend, whispered something to her, and they left the building together.

Burton summoned me into his office and told me what was said. The boyfriend had told him he had never received more professional treatment by the police and that we had gone out of our way to help him resolve a ticket he had ignored. He told the captain that his girlfriend was a campus activist, and he didn't want her antagonism to overshadow the courtesy we had extended to him. Captain Burton sustained the citizen complaint but resolved it with verbal counseling.

"Stipe, you did the wrong thing, but for all the right reasons." I was as thrilled with the driver's intervention on my behalf as I was steamed at the girlfriend's dishonesty. It gave me a brief glimpse into the minds of cops who hammer everyone without exception. After all, if you could be disciplined for giving someone a break, why do it? Obviously, you did it for people like the boyfriend.

Nick's citizen complaints were few compared to his commendations, and he showed tremendous sensitivity to emotional victims, but the department's new, enlightened approach to policing was destined to emphasize engagement over enforcement. By June of 1989, Nick and I were long off probation and able to successfully bid for the midnight shift. The quandary our shift commanders faced was how to reign in Nick's blistering tongue without slowing one of their most productive employees. His deductive reasoning skills continued to flourish.

The Pitbull Finds a Bone

The University of Michigan C. S. Mott Children's Hospital is world-renowned for its treatment of critically ill kids. Parents of stricken children were allowed to park mobile homes in the hospital's lower lot near the Huron River to be close by, rather than commute or stay in a hotel. One such mother of a terminally ill daughter returned to the lot and found her mobile home missing and called 911 to report it. Her husband came to drive her back to Canton, Michigan.

Passing the Huron Towers, she immediately did a double take. Tucked in a back corner of the apartment lot was their mobile home. Nick and I were dispatched to recover it. Although the camper was only missing a few short hours, it had already been ransacked, adding insult to injury.

A bag of personal hygiene items typically carried by homeless men was left inside the camper, an indicator the suspect intended to return. The Huron Towers were a pair of high-rise apartment buildings built in the early sixties. The view of the Huron River was spectacular and the complex boasted a pool, a small convenience store and a bar. It seemed unlikely the suspect would be in an apartment, so we headed for the bar.

The Apartment Lounge was a throwback to places I avoided in the seventies, but of course, had I lived there, I'd have probably been a regular. The dimly lit lounge emitted a combined scent of Old Spice and cigarette smoke as Nick and I walked in. I surveyed the tables along the windows to the right while Nick scoped out the patrons seated at the bar.

Almost as soon as we entered, a longhaired white fellow with a shabby overcoat left a stool and headed for the exit. Nick was right behind him. I caught up as they got outside, but for some reason, I was sure this wasn't our guy, though Nick was just as adamant he was. For one thing, it had been too easy to find him. The man carried no identification and sent me on several wild goose chases checking an array of bogus names. Nick was hammering him with questions about where he was from, where he had been, what he was doing there, all creatively answered with some variance of the same lie.

While Nick was consulting with me, the guy tried to ditch something he pulled out of an inner pocket. Nick retrieved it and finally gave me a name with authenticity. A lengthy criminal history showed several felony convictions in Detroit for various offenses. Nick told the suspect that he knew he had taken the mobile home, but Nick was wondering what the guy was afraid to tell him.

Nick reasoned with the guy. "If it's something else you did, tell me now so I can say you volunteered the information. Believe me, if you have a deal coming, it'll be easier to make happen."

"It's not something I did. It's something I saw," the man explained.

Nick just continued to look at him, waiting for the other shoe to drop.

"It was a shooting," the man continued. "I saw someone shoot a guy."

"Dead?"

"Yes."

"Okay, good job, now tell us about the mobile home," Nick said. Stark was something.

The man confessed to hotwiring the mobile home and, seeing a big parking space as he drove by, choosing the Huron Towers lot to hide it. He found some money in a cabinet and was drinking that up when we walked into the bar. The homicide story checked out, too. Nick had solved it in a handful of questions within five minutes of arriving on a completely unrelated call. The suspect testified for the Wayne County prosecutor in exchange for dismissing the unlawfully driving away an automobile (UDAA) charges. As usual, Nick was right again.

"I've Got Just One Question..."

A short time later, Nick and I were sent on a road trip to pick up a prisoner. A lot of cops loved road trips. They could take their time, go out to eat, and kill a significant portion of their shift. Nick and I much preferred to handle the dispatch calls and leave the highway driving to someone else.

While we were on the transport, we heard cars being sent to a robbery at the Crowne Plaza Hotel on Hilton Boulevard. The incident continued as a Michigan state trooper found a 5.0 Mustang matching the suspect vehicle behind a store on Jackson Road near I-94. Officer Byron Maxwell was sent to bring in the suspects and tow the car to police security.

When Nick and I got back to the station to process our prisoner, Nick asked Maxwell about the robbery. The two male suspects matched, as did the car, but Maxwell could find no money or weapon, and a handgun had been seen by the victim. Captain LeGrange was the duty commander and ordered Maxwell to release the suspects unless he could find something to link them directly to the robbery.

One of the suspects was already sitting in the lobby, awaiting the arrival of a cab. Nick gave me one of his incredulous looks, like what is wrong with this picture? Nick knew the hotel had been robbed just a few weeks before because he had worked the call. He asked LeGrange if he could speak to the suspect who remained in security. LeGrange gave his consent and while I booked our prisoner, Nick stepped into the interview room.

"I've got just one question to ask you," he said to the

Mustang's driver. "Why did you hit the same hotel twice?"

The suspect looked at Nick wide-eyed and shrugged his shoulders before replying, "We already knew the layout, and where to park and how to hop on 94. It just seemed to make sense."

That response drew a follow-up question: "Where is the gun and the money?"

"Under the spare tire, bolted down, in the trunk. It's all back there," he replied.

Nick excused himself and with Maxwell in tow, he recovered the gun and the money, stashed in the trunk of the Mustang right where the suspect said it would be. I was standing in the squad room when the door to security flew open, and Maxwell sprinted to the lobby to grab the second suspect just as his cab arrived. Relieved, Captain LeGrange wrote a glowing letter of commendation for both Stark and Maxwell, omitting the part about nearly releasing the suspects prematurely. A typical day for Officer Nick Stark.

Chapter Fifteen
Western Wayne SWAT School

The department elected to send all four candidates to the Canton SWAT School in September, 1989. I wondered if they weren't hedging their bets should one of us wash out or be injured. I wasn't sure if Bob LeGrange was giving Ted Randall and Seth Connery inside tips on SWAT School survival, but all he gave me were grave warnings of how grueling the course would be.

On the day before SWAT School began, I watched a Detroit Lions game and tried on all my equipment to make sure I had it down. I'd been to Culver Military Academy and the Detroit Police Academy, so I felt I was ready for the rigors of SWAT School. After all, I was now a four-year veteran and in great physical condition. How hard could it be?

The Canton Police Department on Sheldon Road was a state-of-the-art facility and the site of our school. An auditorium, lecture halls and plenty of parking made it an inviting place to conduct police business as well as training sessions. The first day I drove myself, arrived early, and stood in the lobby with thirty-two other wired candidates in various tactical uniforms.

The school commander was none other than Captain Bob LeGrange. The Ann Arbor Special Tactics Unit was formed in 1980, with LeGrange a charter member and its lone commander. His hand-picked coordinator for the school was Jack Mauser, a sergeant from Northville Township and the leader of Western

Wayne County's SWAT team.

SWAT was not just an acronym or a specialty to Jack Mauser: it was a way of life. He looked and stood like a soldier with close-cropped hair, trimmed mustache and a ramrod straight posture. He was so much more ready for us than we were for him. Trim and lean, he was in outstanding condition and exuded an intensity bordering on madness.

The first day was intentionally benign to lull us into a false sense of comfort. We met in a large conference room with plenty of coffee and a large platter of doughnuts. I didn't eat doughnuts as a rule, and the large, pink-frosted one looked like an obvious trap, so I remained seated. Several other students scarfed a few under the watchful gaze of LeGrange and Mauser. It was clear that this captain was not the same man constrained by collective bargaining agreements or the measured restraint he commonly displayed at the Ann Arbor Police Department. He had his own island of command and a hardened first mate to help him mold his own brand of cutthroats.

"Although this is a democratic society, this school is not, and there is no time permitted for group discussion and voting." Thus, the training manual set the tone for fifteen days of breathless physicality and mind-numbing head games.

After the first day, Ted Randall, Seth Connery and I elected to carpool together. They took turns driving to my house in Ann Arbor and we would rotate driving to the school. The carpool rides became our sanctuary before and after the daily grind of class and we took turns talking one another into enduring just one more painful day.

In addition to LeGrange and Mauser, the cadre included Sergeant Aaron Heath of AAPD. He was a strange combination of tedious bookishness and stunning athleticism rolled into one body. Heath specialized in narrating sleep-inducing training videos shown with alarming frequency at the department. He was also known for making precision, high-powered rifle shots in pressure situations that earned him the nickname "Iceman." Heath's focus on instruction rather than conditioning made him a breath of fresh air among some of the self-important cadre of teachers.

Perhaps the best was Corporal Joe Warnacki of the Dearborn Police Department. He was a six-foot-five-inch timber tree of remarkable strength with a voice that sounded like a bellow from the bottom of a cavern. Gifted at every aspect of tactical performance, he was an impressive physical specimen. I was lucky to be assigned to his team due to his clear, patient instruction.

Each day began with physical training (PT) formation at 0800 sharp. As we lined up facing the parking lot, we could hear the cadre emerge from the Canton PD building, uttering a simultaneous "Oorah" as they jogged, shuffle step, to our formation. They broke ranks and descended upon our respective teams, ripping apart our uniforms, equipment and posture. Failure to address our cadre by the appropriate rank resulted in an alertness drill (twenty push-ups). No one, aside from lieutenants and above, was to be addressed as "sir."

After the initial inspection, Mauser or Warnacki would lead us in marathon PT sessions. Many of the exercises had unique SWAT titles, like side straddle hop (jumping jacks) that we committed to memory. Once the name of the exercise was announced, we had to assume the "position of exercise," or the starting position. Failure to snap into this resulted in an immediate alertness drill. Most of the exercises were designed to work the various muscles we would need for rappelling.

Before I'd begun, I'd gotten an inside scoop from an unexpected source, Larry Fiske. The former FTO program coordinator may have been a petty micromanager, but he was also fast, conditioned and had a firm grasp of the physical demands of SWAT. At lunch one night in July, I'd asked him if there was anything I should know about the PT portion of the daily regimen. He suggested I start doing multiple repetitions of leg lifts.

He told me the cadre used marathon sets of these painful reps to punish the group for the mistakes of individuals. No one else mentioned them, but I added the exercises he described to my workout right away. It was a key piece of advice and I was so grateful. During these punishments, students around me were in genuine agony, straining to keep their necks and legs aloft in an endless series of Hello Dollies (side to side leg lifts) and flutter kicks (up and down).

Following PT, the daily ranger run was led by John Mauser. He was in superb condition and intent on proving it, leading us around a giant par course adjacent to the Canton PD site. The first run was pretty tame after our physical pre-test that first Tuesday. We'd been given five minutes to get inside and change into our gym clothes and there were thirty-three nervous, breathless men jammed into a locker room designed for a dozen. We struggled to make the transition in time but we did it... barely.

My head was spinning from the overload of directions, instructions and screaming but my body was in good shape and I managed to buzz through the first stages of the pre-test handily. I was nervous about the man carry that I had practiced but not yet perfected. We paired up in two ranks with the front man picking up his partner and racing the corresponding man in the other rank for one hundred yards. I was alarmed when I turned around to see six-foot-three-inch Martin Curtis from Washtenaw County behind me. Although lean and muscular, he weighed one hundred ninety-five pounds while I was just one hundred sixty.

The fireman's carry begins with one man flat on his back, face up, extending a hand to allow you to pull him up and launch him over your shoulders. Balancing his weight evenly on both sides is ideal, but it takes both practice and leg strength. Curtis tried to assist me by leaping up, but the butt of his holstered, semi-automatic pistol struck me square in the face, cutting my forehead and knocking off my glasses. The impact threw me back five steps before I could regain any balance at all.

I wobbled down the runway, woefully behind my counterpart. Curtis was so tall that his legs continued to slip off my shoulders as I ran. By the time I reached the finish line, I was carrying him nearly upright, with his tiptoes making intermittent contact with the driveway. I was one second under the requisite time. It was only our second day.

We were divided into five teams, or squads, with two cadres in charge of each. Six of us comprised Team 1, including Ned Roth, Washtenaw County; Ron McIvor, Dearborn PD; and Randy Matthews, Canton Township.

Everywhere we went and everything we did was done "on the hop." That meant we ran—and I mean everywhere—for everything. A drink of water (when we were allowed), a box of ammo, taking a piss—every aspect of the training was done at a run. The only time we weren't running was during instruction or if we were conducting some aspect of training or doing alertness drills. I thought I worked out a lot but if I combined the daily time spent running the Michigan Stadium stairs, the par course and the track, it would amount to only an hour and a half or so. It hardly prepared me for spending eight to twelve hour training days sprinting everywhere.

Like competitive sports teams, the initial phase of tactical team training consisted of weeding out those who couldn't hack it either physically or psychologically. The cadre was relentless in the criticism of everything everyone did. If we slowed to assist someone on a run, we were screamed at. If someone fell behind and no one slowed down to help, we were all chastised. Each successive day saw our numbers dwindle. Our initial team of six was down to four by the fourth day.

The rigorous punishment did include some training. On Thursday morning, I stood on the third floor of the five-story rappelling tower. Corporal Warnacki showed me how to hook my carabineer to a rappelling rope dangling outside the window. He instructed me to run out the rope slack, which I thought I had, before climbing out the window and beginning my descent. I placed my right (brake) hand in the small of my back and slid off the windowsill.

I'd left too much slack and unexpectedly dropped a couple feet as I exited the window. I tried to stop myself with my left arm clinging to the rope, but the sudden jerk snapped my left shoulder, and stinging pain ran up my arm. When I reached the ground, I could barely lift it and cursed myself for getting injured on only the fourth day of training. It only took the one jump to learn to run the slack out of the rappelling rope, however.

My lifeless left arm was useless for the remainder of the school, making push-ups and weapons handling an exercise in agony. All of us on Team 1—Roth, McIvor, Matthews and I—suffered an injury that first week, but we pledged to ride it out together.

The ranger runs got longer and longer with the added component of donning gas masks for wind sprints sprinkled in to break up the monotony. Students were dropping like flies due to injury or exhaustion. We knew that no one from Ann Arbor PD had ever dropped out of a SWAT School and Ted, Seth and I were committed to not being the first.

The beginning of the second week brought Black Tuesday. It began with a forty-five-minute ranger run through swamps and over obstacles, punctuated by low crawls through sharp field grass. At the completion of the ranger run, a delirious recruit uttered, loud enough for Mauser to hear: "We got 'em on the run now." Mauser, looking like John Wayne's angry Ethan Edwards in *The Searchers*, turned and glowered at us like we had just spat on his baby. Mauser's next exercises punished the memory of that next hour right out of my mind.

At the firing range that afternoon not one of us could do anything right. We did so many push-ups that my ragged left arm lost all feeling for a day. Our initial class of thirty-three was now down to seventeen. In the midst of cleaning weapons, Ronnie McIvor commented that he could disassemble and assemble an

MP5 with his eyes closed. One cadre overheard him. As we stood in formation waiting to be dismissed, Mauser invited us into the conference room to watch the demonstration.

The stakes were high for Ron. If he broke the weapon down and put it back together, we could go home. If he failed to do it, we were going to run till we died. McIvor was blindfolded and placed at a clean conference table. We were either too tired or too timid to speak while he took the gun apart. But aside from a couple of brief hitches, he was as good as his word. He ran the gun through a function check, and to my great relief, it worked perfectly. It was all I could do to get home, polish my boots, clean my gun, iron my fatigues and study weapons nomenclature until I collapsed with exhaustion.

I was proficient with my Smith & Wesson .38 caliber revolver. For the SWAT School we were issued Steyr 9mm semi-automatic handguns. They were called "boat anchors" for a reason. Cumbersome and heavy, they cycled, not revolved, and I couldn't get the feel I had with the revolver. The H&K MP5 submachine gun, the Ruger Mini-14 .223 caliber assault rifle and the Styer .308 caliber sniper rifles were all new to me, and it took all the focus I could muster to qualify on the various targets.

Aaron Heath taught the MP5 block, and his "isometric tension" technique helped me keep the weapon under control and clean my targets. I slowly got the hang of the .308 long rifle, and the combination of breathing, trigger control and scope relief got me qualified.

The Ruger Mini-14 was kicking my ass, however. The .223 course of fire required a two-hundred-yard run to the target and back, plus placing ten shots inside the body of the target. The Ruger's bladed gun sight was incompatible with my cumbersome glasses. That, combined with my weary left arm struggling to hold the barrel steady, resulted in scores of nine out of ten shots again and again.

My nemesis was Corporal Rod Michaels, said to have once been a Special Forces operator. He was a special kind of an ass to me. He lay next to me on the firing line, grilling me on the weapon's nomenclature and critiquing every aspect of my technique. A wrong answer or ocular orbit resulted in more alertness drills and additional running up and down the range. I was beginning to crack and was convinced I would not make it to graduation.

To add more stress to my fragile existence, the trials for both of our earlier summer homicide suspects had been scheduled during the school. The cadres were dubious about my absence. I attended PT, the ranger run and gas mask drills before running to my car and changing into my suit for court. Despite my military haircut and no matter what I did, my hair stood on end from the effects of perspiration and the gas mask straps.

Testimony for the Hester Carlson trial was seemingly uncomplicated and straightforward: a crack-addled wife broke into an apartment and stabbed two people. The Greg Heschendorf trial was more convoluted for a number of reasons. First, responding rescue workers had contaminated the scene by kicking evidence around and leaving several medical packets and wrappers on the floor. This raised questions about the recovered shell casings and where they had been when Stark and I had entered. I hadn't paid close attention to those items while covering the suspect and securing his weapon.

Second was the issue of the wheelchair location. There was a grease pencil board exhibit in the courtroom detailing Heschendorf's living room, and I could see where Nick Stark, testifying the day before, had drawn in the wheelchair. Defense Attorney Robert Rigan asked me to draw the wheelchair where I remembered it being, using a different colored marker.

When I did, he made an issue of the distance my figure was from Nick's. I reminded him that he asked me where I remembered it, and not where Nick had. He told me that I was bordering on being a hostile witness. He went on and on about the discrepancy, and that it tainted our entire testimony. I wasn't sure how telling the truth compromised our integrity, but then I hadn't gone to law school.

Rigan was most tenacious attacking the circumstances of Heschendorf's confession. Before his demise, the victim Michaels had trashed several items of furniture, including the dining room table, and pieces of it lay around the perimeter of the dining room. Rigan asked me where I took Heschendorf when I removed him from the living room. When I testified that I dragged him into the center of the dining room, he asked if there had been a light fixture directly above as Nick questioned him. I replied that there was.

Rigan continued: "Officer Stipe, you've stated that you dragged a distraught, crippled Mr. Heschendorf into the dining room, under the direct glare of a ceiling light fixture, and allowed your partner to Mirandize and question him under these adverse conditions? Didn't you think of a more appropriate place to take my client's statement?"

My reply was, "If Mr. Heschendorf was uncomfortable in the house he grew up in, in the home that he helped furnish, under the dining room light that he had eaten his meals under for years and years, I would be hard pressed to think of a place that would have put him more at ease." I could tell by the jury's reaction that I had scored on the prickly lawyer.

Despite my clever comeback, both murder cases, Hester Carlson's and Greg Heschendorf's, unraveled with the testimony of two "expert" defense witnesses.

Hester Carlson's attorney engaged the Safe House coordinator, who testified that her attack on her husband was a culmination of years of spousal abuse. The fact that entry was forced, the victim was held, and a premeditated knife attack was launched didn't seem to carry much weight. Hester Carlson was herself a victim of "battered wife syndrome." She was acquitted of murder.

Robert Rigan called a psychologist who testified that Heschendorf's confinement to a wheelchair had rendered him incapable of rational decision-making. His confrontation with Michaels fueled a survival instinct that made the shooting inevitable. Was he just as justified shooting Michaels in the side and back as he fled as he was firing on him as he converged? Rigan said he was.

Heschendorf himself made for a pathetic figure. The jury acquitted him, too. Unfortunately, sometimes one *can* get away with murder.

Back at school, at the end of the second week, I'd mastered the PT portion of the daily grind. I could keep up with both Mauser and Warnacki on the leg lifts. My proficiency did not go unnoticed by Commander LeGrange, who chose that morning to walk up next to me in the midst of the exercise and step up on my abdomen with his entire weight. To his surprise, I continued to count the reps aloud until they were completed. Again, I silently blessed Larry Fiske for giving me the heads-up on the one exercise that was killing everyone else.

I reluctantly called Joe Calumet to tell him I was going to miss the fall softball games during the school. I'd fully intended to play, but I had so much equipment to clean and so much studying to do, I just couldn't manage both. Unfortunately, I was committed to work the Michigan football games the first and second Saturdays of the school. My whole body ached, but there was no getting out of the detail, so I toughed it out.

During the second football game, I walked through the tunnel entrance of Michigan Stadium and onto the field to assume my place in the north end zone. I was lost in thought, with my back toward the stands, when I heard someone yelling, "Hey, hey you, Barney Fife, get the hell out of the way." I turned around to see who was getting yelled at when a guy pointed directly at me. "Yeah, you, fucking sit down or get out of the way."

I didn't like my glasses; they made me look like a nerd. So much so that Larry Van Borne referred to me as "Boz," the geeky computer hacker on the TV show *Riptide*. I started the SWAT School at one hundred sixty pounds two weeks before, but lost weight due to the constant running and sweating. I suppose I looked like a skinny little wimp to this drunken loudmouth, who was stuffing his face and barking at me to move. But I had endured two weeks of the most grueling punishment a thirty-four-year-old man could expose himself to. I knew I was going to make it to the end.

I walked over to where the man sat, pointed at a little boy seated nearby, and said: "We don't permit profanity in the presence of women and small children. If you don't want the entire stadium to see Barney Fife drag you up those seventy stairs and out of the stadium, you will kindly keep your cussing to yourself." The guy sank back in his seat, contemplating that image.

"Thank you, Officer," a lady one row back said, "he has been cursing the entire season." I never heard another peep out of him.

The last week of school was devoted to a practical exercise, helicopter rappelling and testing on every facet of the course. Detroit Police sent out a helicopter for us to launch jumps from the landing skids from an altitude of seventy feet. Two students would exit the chopper on opposite sides and, at the direction of the jumpmaster, drop off the skid and rappel to the ground. Seeing my fleeting glances at a razor-sharp axe on the floor of the helicopter, the jumpmaster told me if the pilot encountered any trouble, he would cut the ropes.

"Regardless of height?" I asked.

"Yup," he replied.

My counterpart on the other side had some trouble clearing the skid. I was halfway back, when the jumpmaster gave me the closed fist signal to hold. With my brake hand pressed into the small of my back, I waited for what seemed forever for him to get underway. Once he did, I tried to release, but could not get the rope to slide through my glove to get going. In an ill-advised maneuver, I extended my brake hand far from my right hip until the rope began to slide through my glove. Once it did, I could not get it back in position. I sizzled the seventy feet down the rope with my right-hand smoking from the friction. My left arm and shoulder were already toast, and now my right hand was a seared piece of meat. It was only Wednesday.

On Thursday we demonstrated the tactical rappel, a timed climb up and rappel down from the rappelling tower. Teammate Ronnie McIvor broke out 800mg tablets of Motrin for Roth, Matthews and me. It was like a miracle drug as the aching in my left arm disappeared. I completed the rappel flawlessly.

I dreaded the firearms qualification, especially the .223 shoot. It was left for last, and I sprinted the two hundred yards down to the target and back and pressed ten rounds down-range. As usual, nine of them hit home and the tenth was just outside the scoring ring. Two more attempts left me spent and frustrated as I still failed to quality. I stood off the line, waiting for another turn, when someone tapped me on the shoulder.

I turned to see Range Master C. J. Jameson. "Give me that magazine," he said, nodding at the fifteen-round mag I held in my hand. "Give me that weapon," he demanded. "This is how you cheat with the Ruger Mini-14." With that, he tossed my magazine aside and produced a thirty-round magazine from his pocket.

He slapped his magazine in the receiver, laid on the firing line, cradled the gun in his right arm and planted the magazine on the ground. Without even steadying the rifle with his left hand, he fired ten one-handed rounds downrange.

"Go get it." He nodded toward the target. I returned with it, all ten of his rounds in the center scoring ring.

I loaded his magazine into the Mini-14, waited for the word, and sprinted downrange. Warnacki stood near my target, Jolly Green Giant-style, as if he intended to remain there while I fired. He nodded silently as I turned around to return to the line. I was the last one needing to qualify. All eyes were on me as I flipped at the firing line, lay down, planted the magazine, and shouldered the weapon. With more hope than focus, I looked down the bladed sight and gently squeezed off ten rounds.

Jameson announced that the line was safe, and I ran down-range. I wasn't close enough to see where my rounds had hit but Warnacki waved me away, signaling that I had qualified. As I bounded back to the firing line, I wondered if there was a possibility he'd given me a pass. *Naw, he wouldn't do that*, I thought. And even if he had, there wasn't a man on Earth that could get him to admit it if he didn't want to. He was as tough as they come.

The next day, Friday, was the final physical test followed by the written exam. This time I humped a lightweight on the man carry and finished in plenty of time. The four of us comprising Team 1 ran the one-and-a-half-mile distance together. With about a quarter mile to go, I prepared to sprint to the finish when Ronnie McIvor grabbed my arm. "Take it easy," he said. The four of us that had started this ordeal together and endured so much as a team, finished together. Two of McIvor's coworkers from Dearborn finished the mile and a half in 8:53 and 8:51. We clocked in at 9:40.

SWAT School Postscript

I came out of that three-week school in the best condition of my life. I shaved my one and a half mile time from 10:00 down to 9:20. I learned tactics I'd never seen before, like closing on adversaries in armed encounters and taking definitive action as soon as I assessed a threat. Thanks to Aaron Heath, I had also become handy with the MP5 submachine gun. It became my preferred weapon to dominate armed encounters. Other things I learned included a lesson from guest instructor John George, who taught me how to enter a door and clear a room at minimum risk. I passed that knowledge on to my partners, and ultimately the entire patrol division. I felt in control of every armed encounter I was in for the rest of my career. I also started to win over Capt. Bob LeGrange—first choice or not, I was now part of his team.

One student, Ferndale Police Officer Lawrence "Lean Beef" Warden lost thirty pounds in the three-week school, going from two-hundred-sixty to two-hundred-thirty pounds. Unable to complete the long run in the required time, he returned a month later and passed. Then, a few months after that, he stopped a car carrying two men who leaped out and opened fire, wounding him several times. His return fire killed both men and Warden credited the rigors of SWAT School for his survival.

Jack Mauser remained a cadre at the school and the commander of Western Wayne's team for some time to come. A year after I knew him at school, his team responded to a prison escapee who'd sought refuge in a remote house, taking a lone woman hostage. Attempting to leave the scene in the woman's car, the suspect engaged my former teammate Randy Matthews, who killed him with an MP5.

While SWAT School provided enhanced training and made us better at our jobs, it could hardly guarantee success. The challenges ahead loomed larger and larger.

Chapter Sixteen
Man With a Gun and the Drowning Pool

The McDonald's Incident

Now that I'd completed SWAT School I was ready for my first special tactics assignment. I didn't have to wait long. Within a week we were being briefed. Detroit drug dealer DeAndre Parks had taken up residence in a west side Ann Arbor apartment complex, menacing neighbors and laying the groundwork for what would become a violent turf war. An undercover Ann Arbor officer, working with the Michigan State Police, was able to wrangle his way onto Parks's client list.

Buy/busts don't always go down like you see in the movies. There are no wharfs, deserted piers or abandoned warehouse districts in Ann Arbor. The undercover officer was trying to negotiate a favorable location for us but Parks was wary of being ripped off or busted. He selected a very public place for the ultimate deal with the officer, the McDonald's at 2310 West Stadium.

Team leaders weighed the urgency of getting Parks off the street against the logistical challenge of protecting the patrons of a very busy restaurant. A relatively simple plan was devised using several members of the special tactics unit (STU) and veteran uniformed officers. The deal was scheduled to go down at the height of the dinner hour, around twilight one night in October, inside a vehicle in the parking lot.

Tim Beamon and Bob LeGrange were posted as marksmen on a rooftop across the street. Two marked patrol cars, driven by veteran Officers Vic Mitchell and Rod Spangler, stood by as a uniformed presence. STU Operator Mack Livingston, also on his first SWAT assignment after the school, was armed with a submachine gun and rode with Mitchell. Their job would be to converge on the object vehicle and make the arrest.

But then there were complications.

Parks employed two armed henchmen to cover his movements and engage anyone who might try to rip him off. The two were staged in a booth on the north side of the restaurant, overlooking the lot where the exchange would take place. For the AAPD, the operation required an innocuous-looking fellow to cover them from inside the restaurant. He would be in plainclothes and armed with a submachine gun. He was charged with protecting the customers should the gunmen open fire. This task was assigned to the most humdrum looking guy they had: me.

I wore a full-length cashmere coat that belonged to my dad and slung an MP5 under my arm. I sat on a stool just outside their booth, nibbling on dinner and reading the paper while they engaged in animated conversation. Outside, it was taking a while for the deal to unfold. The place was packed at 6:00 p.m. with someone seated at nearly every table. As with all plans, the unscripted occurred when uniformed Washtenaw County deputy Dave Keel walked in. He placed his order at the counter as Parks's gunmen eyed him warily. I spun my stool to ensure he didn't recognize me, gripped the MP5, and anxiously waited for him to leave.

Just as Keel got his food and turned to leave, sirens began screaming and the arrest was initiated. Keel dropped his order, drew his gun and ran out the north entrance, followed closely by Parks's men.

I was on my feet immediately. Looking outside, I could see Livingston pointing his weapon at the exiting suspects while motioning to me with an open palm to get down. I whipped open my overcoat, displayed the machine gun and announced, "Police officer, everybody down!" The response was immediate—without exception, everyone dove for the floor. Drinks, fries and burger wrappers rained down among them.

My intention had been to get the crowd down only if rounds were fired but it was evident that initially I was seen as the threat; just five years before, a shooting in a San Ysidro McDonald's left twenty-one people dead. I announced several times that I was a police officer and would advise when it was safe to stand. A subject I didn't recognize burst through the south doors and I ordered him to the floor while he yelled that he worked there. This was confirmed with a nod from behind the counter. Then Rod Spangler entered and said the scene outside was secure.

Parks had been taken in custody along with his men. There were no injuries and no complaints, and McDonald's reimbursed their customers for their spilled drinks and food. There had been thirty to forty customers in the restaurant and in the weeks to come, I heard many stories about how everybody knew somebody that had been there, and of the carnage that resulted. The witness pool swelled and expanded.

The event illustrates how you can't plan for everything but that you can train for it. I never liked plainclothes duty, especially with a displayed firearm; I preferred it when the public could easily recognize me as a police officer. But I was supremely confident in our team and leadership and the results bore that out. Compared to SWAT School, this event had been like just another exercise.

Weber's Inn Fight

Not a week later I was back on the road. Nick was taking some well-deserved time off. At our Shift V briefing on October 29, 1989, we were given the description of two runaway girls who were thought to have fled to Ann Arbor. A tip suggested they might be staying at Weber's Inn on Jackson Road, on the city's west side. Since Weber's was in my area, I went there to check.

When I stopped in at the desk, the staff told me they didn't recognize their descriptions. As I was pulling out, I saw a guy exit the hotel and start walking to a car. I pulled up to him and noted his car had Kentucky plates. He was short but stocky, with a thick Southern accent. He looked a little wired, so I asked him if he intended to drive. He said no, he was just getting something out of his car and going back to his room. Satisfied that he wasn't driving, I left.

Detroit Academy classmate Ryan Jazzman and Tim Hammer were riding together and I met them for coffee at Main and Madison, where my dad's tire store had once been. I told them about the Kentuckian I'd spoken to at Weber's. Hammer said an updated broadcast mentioned the suspect matched his description.

They followed me back to the hotel, and we told dispatchers we would be out checking for the missing girls. As I pulled up, the guy looked out of a second-floor window and closed the curtain quickly. Hammer agreed to cover the back stairway while Jazzman and I headed upstairs to check it out.

Jazzman and I took the elevator to the second floor, stepped off, and turned right to see the suspect marching toward us. "Hold up," I said, signaling him to stop. He lowered his head and tried to bulldoze his way between us.

Jazzman weighed less than one hundred seventy pounds, and I was still a rail from SWAT School. This two-hundred-twenty-five-pound bulldog was possessed, trying to bowl us over. We each crooked an arm under one of his and tried to stop his momentum but there was no pushing him back. The best we could do was to let him fall forward and ride him to the floor.

As we landed, the contents of a package he carried with both hands spilled onto the carpet. Syringes and a number of boxes of Buprenex Injectable (a morphine derivative) covered the floor in front of the elevator. The combination of his strength and some extra chemical help made him nearly impossible to control. Jazzman and I each held an arm, but were unable to get either of them pinned behind his back.

Jazzman was an unassuming figure, but he was extremely tough. A native Detroiter of Polish descent, he'd been groomed on Motor City streets. I had yet to tap into my SWAT School reservoir as the suspect continued to surge forward, doing little except for grinding his face into the carpeted floor.

The police department had recently transitioned to an 800-megahertz radio system that was supposed to be the last word in urban police communications. Among the features was an orange emergency button which sent an audible tone to the dispatcher. They in turn would give a predetermined code asking if the officer was all right. Failure to respond with the prescribed code would prompt the dispatcher to send assistance. It was designed for incidents where officers may have been taken hostage.

We were at a stalemate. Jazzman finally released his grip with one hand and pushed his emergency button. The dispatcher responded by calling Hammer's badge number, asking him if he was okay. Hammer, posted at the foot of the back stairs and oblivious to our situation, responded that he was fine. Jazzman and I looked at each other with "What the hell?" expressions. Once again, Jazzman hit his button and, once again, the dispatcher asked Hammer if he was secure.

When Jazzman and Hammer called into service, the operator switched their radio and badge numbers. Hammer remained puzzled, but Buck Revere and several other units around the city sensed trouble and began heading to the hotel. We couldn't wait. Our man was possessed with some unearthly power and we had to get him secured before we burned out.

Finally, I wrapped both arms around his left arm and thrust my entire body across his back, over to Jazzman's side. The sickening snap was unmistakable. The suspect screamed an agonizing cry of pain and for a moment went limp. Jazzman handcuffed his now cooperative right arm to the broken left one. We kept him pinned, face down on the floor, until Buck arrived with an apologetic Hammer behind him.

The man from Kentucky's name was Harley Stanford but what he had ingested remained a mystery for a time. He quietly rode the elevator to the lobby, wincing in pain from his broken humerus. But once we approached a patrol car, he got jumpy as a horse, struggling against being placed in the back seat. We got his head and shoulders clear of the roof and tried pushing him in, but he began kicking wildly, and we had to back off to protect our legs. I took the toe of my boot and pressed it against his anus. Stanford shot across the backseat as if propelled by a rocket, bouncing his head against the opposite door.

While he headed up to U-M Hospital, we went back to check his room. Both of the missing girls were there. While they collected their things, I walked out to where we had struggled. Jazzman collected the syringes and Buprenex boxes for evidence but I wondered where Stanford had been going with them. I looked in the trash can below an ashtray outside the elevator and found a baggie with fifty-six grams of powdered cocaine inside. Assorted drug paraphernalia had also been disposed of and it too was retained.

The girls told us they had met Stanford through a mutual acquaintance. He'd driven to Ann Arbor two days earlier, where he met them before embarking on a binge of cocaine and synthetic morphine use to enhance his sexual prowess. Already paranoid from his first encounter with me, he stalked back and forth across the room all evening, checking the windows until I returned. Then he made several trips to the trash can until he literally ran into us.

After logging the evidence at the station, I headed to the hospital to check on his injury. The doctor told me his arm had suffered a clean break and it would be okay. His concern was that a broken pen had somehow punctured his sphincter. I asked how a pen could have become lodged in his anus and the doctor relayed Stanford's account of inserting it in his rectum as a means for intensifying his sexual pleasure. In the midst of the struggle with officers, the pen was broken, causing extreme discomfort. I didn't have the nerve to tell him of my one-time technique of nudging his sphincter with my boot.

On the following Wednesday morning at court, I stood bleary-eyed, having slept for just two hours, looking at the court docket for preliminary examinations. I felt someone come up behind me, breathing down my neck. I turned to see the rug-burned, scabbed face of Harley Stanford, sling on his left arm, smiling at me and asking me when we were up, as if we were boarding a train together. His detoxified state impressed the judge enough that he ordered him back to Kentucky and to never return to his jurisdiction.

A Turning Point — Argonne

On the Saturday after the Weber's Inn incident, three Huron High School sophomores, Melanie Adams, Heather James and Dawn Gibson, toilet-papered a house hosting a party on Waldenwood, ironically, our old address. As they left the girls thought they were being followed and panicked. Adams, a novice sixteen-year-old driver, sped through several neighborhoods trying to elude their pursuers.

Leslie Richards was a clerical typist working in data processing at AAPD. A redheaded knockout, she also had a lot on the ball, and had shown an interest in becoming a police officer. Clearly overqualified in her current post, Chief Colby suggested she ride along with me because, the way things were going, she was bound to see something.

Joining the Special Tactics Team added more responsibilities to my daily routine. Among them was having to carry a cumbersome tactical bag. It held cold-weather gear, rappelling harnesses, extra ammunition, gas mask; the works. Each shift I removed the ball-busting bag from my car and tossed it into the trunk of the patrol car I'd been assigned.

We hadn't been on the road long when dispatcher Estelle Franklin told us to respond to a report of a car plunging into a pond at Argonne and Nixon Roads. We were just a half mile away, and arrived in a minute. Three frantic teenagers, one of them soaking wet, waved us down.

"Our friends are in there, you have to get them out," the shivering girl screamed, pointing at a nearby retention pond. I looked at the pond and saw a cauldron of bubbles rising to the surface.

"Our car, our car went in there. Do something, get them out, *please!*"

I ran to the edge of the pond and could see tire tracks running up to a short fence that had been bowled over as the car plowed through it and into the water. The pond was about fifty feet in diameter, and the bubbles were rising right in the center. An Ann Arbor Fire Department engine arrived, followed by Nick Stark and Tim Hammer. A firefighter took one step into the frigid water and high-stepped back up the bank.

It was November 3, and the mild, Indian summer days of the SWAT School a month before were long gone. It was a cold and clear night, but the pond was stirred an inky black. I stripped off my gun belt and handed it to Leslie Richards. I borrowed a rope from the firefighters and tied a bowline knot around my waist. I gave the other end to Nick, asking him to pull me back when I told him to.

I nearly went into shock when I leaped into that pond, feet first. The ice-cold water acted like a paralyzing serum in my legs. It was like treading water in a pond of slush and I became oblivious to the steady arrival of rescue personnel and patrol cars. It was eerily quiet below the surface of the murky water. I knew the girls must be down there. But despite several dives, I could not find the car. Visibility was zero in the churned-up pond. Nick called to me and motioned to a firefighter holding a long pole.

I swam back to retrieve the pole, and returned to the center of the pond where I probed the depths. How deep was this water? The pole was eight feet long but casting it as far as I could reach revealed nothing. I'd been in the water for just a few minutes, but was already stiffening up and having trouble kicking with my trouser-covered legs. I may have been in superb shape but I was already exhausted. Whatever I was doing wasn't working and I called for Nick to pull me back.

I went over to Leslie, got my portable radio and called dispatch, asking them to send the county dive team to the scene. The firefighters produced an inflatable raft that Nick, Flynn Jeffries, Tim Hammer and Sergeant Jack Kirby took turns pairing up in while probing the pond with the same pole. By now, an enormous crowd had gathered, including the parents of the trapped girls. They lived just a block away.

I was so cold I could barely speak. It dawned on me I had dry clothes and long underwear in the bag I'd stowed in the trunk of my car. A U-M Survival Flight helicopter whirred overhead, illuminating the area, but it was blowing a numbing blast of chilled air down on us. I grabbed the long underwear and fatigues and climbed in the back seat to change. The helicopter was producing so much noise that would-be rescuers had to scream to one another to be heard. I left the back door open so I wouldn't be locked in my own patrol car. Seeing Leslie approach, I called to her to ensure she didn't close it on me.

Unable to hear what I said, she poked her head in the back door at the very moment my chilled body was fully exposed. The combined look of shock, bemusement and pity said more than any comment she could have made. She turned her back to guard the door for me.

Yellow police tape tied tree to tree cordoned off an area for the families to stand and console one another while they watched the rescue attempts. Officer Marilyn Kelly acted as a buffer, ensuring the media didn't intrude on their emotional ordeal.

The attempts to locate the sunken car using the raft were unsuccessful too, but the rapid arrival of the county divers gave me a glimmer of hope. For over an hour they blindly dove, using extended hands to scour the bottom for the elusive car. Finally, diver Ron Fleming located the Mercury Sable station wagon, nose down in about twenty feet of water. The car had settled in loose silt that had covered the rocker panels and prevented Fleming from opening the doors.

The retention pond was essentially an inverted cone, like a funnel, the sides sloping into the center. It was here the car had come to rest. Divers hooked the car to a wrecker cable that winched it up from the water at an agonizingly slow pace. Neither prayers, cold water, nor resuscitation could save them. Heather James was found in the back storage area where the last bubbles of air would have clustered. Melanie Adams was still in the front seat, where a broken-heeled shoe and a smashed windshield testified to her last, desperate attempt to escape her watery tomb.

I'd always harbored a phobia of dark, deep, cold water, getting chills whenever I saw a movie that included a car submerged in that way. To be confronted with such a situation and utterly fail to rescue the occupants left me dazed.

Backseat passenger Dawn Gibson said they had mistaken two friends following them for someone chasing them from the house they toilet-papered. Adams had been driving too fast on the winding Argonne Road and missed the last curve, sending them right toward the pond. Gibson already had her door open when they hit the water and was able to slip out while the station wagon bobbed momentarily. Gibson and the girls in the second car, Ellen Brandt and Anne Matthews, made rescue efforts, but the Sable sank too rapidly for them to get to their friends.

Attempts to revive them at the hospital failed as well, and they were declared dead early Sunday morning. Their bodies looked like the lifeless, Resuscitator Annie dolls we used for CPR training. I was numb. We drove back to the station and I dictated the report while Leslie massaged my shoulders without saying a single word.

After that experience stopped keeping me awake at night, it gave me nightmares. It was the first time I'd attended an emergency and failed to rescue the victims of anything but a homicide. The girls were just sixteen years old. Their deaths took the glow off every success I'd had. The follow-up stories in the paper did little to temper my mood.

Captain LeGrange had been the duty commander when the call came in, but he elected to go home when the oncoming shift relieved him. In an interview, the scuba diving SWAT commander questioned the sluggish emergency response and wondered why divers had taken so long to find the car in that tiny pond. Towing company owner, Benny Lewis, was also critical of the emergency responders and said that had he been in charge, the girls would likely have been saved.

Heather James' father, Carl James, was more forgiving, praising the length of time the divers remained submerged. "They gave it their best shot," he graciously said. The tragic loss of those young lives haunts me to this day.

For her part, aspiring police applicant Leslie Richards abandoned any thought of becoming a cop, resigned from data processing, and transferred to the city administrator's office. She found work more befitting her intelligence and became administrative assistant to administrator Hal Jorgenson. She remained there until they moved to Charlotte, North Carolina, where they became Mr. and Mrs. Hal Jorgenson.

The year 1989 was a pivotal one for me. It accounted for both my greatest achievement, the Medal of Valor, and my greatest failure, the loss of those two teenage girls. If I'd peaked out, I sure didn't recognize it.

Chapter Seventeen
A Gunman, a Fire and a Telescopic Sight

In February of 1991, just seventeen miles down the road, Officer Steven Reuther arrived for work at the Milan Police Department. A deranged man was lying in wait and shot him in the head as he entered the building. He was my first Honor Guard assignment. I stood by his casket for several shifts and thought of the vulnerability of turning one's back in uniform. I wore mine to and from work too. Hypervigilance kept me tuned into threats, but not much else.

Less than a month later, Nick and I stood in the command office talking to Bob LeGrange and Sergeant Jack Kirby. A car was dispatched to a "shots fired" call just two blocks north of City Hall. We were out the door and down the block just in time to see a battered van driving West on Kingsley. Calls began pouring in of multiple shots fired in the immediate block.

The van refused to stop at first but suddenly slammed on its brakes at Kingsley and Fifth. The driver hopped out while Nick closed on him. As he spun him around, I could see the guy was armed with at least two handguns, a 9mm in his waistband and a chrome-plated revolver in a shoulder holster. I closed the distance ready to light him up if he tried to draw on Nick.

He was overmatched. Nick had him cuffed and disarmed in a blink. I secured the handguns in our trunk while Nick asked him what he'd been doing. Mickey Callan said he'd fired a dozen rounds into his cousin's car over an unpaid debt argument. He was hoping he'd come out of his house so he could shoot him. Inside his van we found an arsenal.

Sgt. Jack Kirby was a veteran officer and a nice guy but he had an annoying habit of inserting himself into calls in order to bank court overtime. When I went to retrieve the .357 and 9mm out of our trunk to log with the other evidence, Kirby had already removed them and logged them himself to join the chain of evidence. He needn't have bothered as the defendant copped a plea without trial. Callan was one of many men I came very close to shooting.

The tragedy at the pond off Argonne Road may have dissolved the invincible feeling I'd once had, but it didn't slow down our response time. Larry Van Borne shrugged his shoulders in silent resignation and accepted the fact that Nick and I would beat him to each and every call.

On the early morning of July 27, 1991, Larry and John Stevens were sent to a structure fire at the Greenbrier Apartments on the city's north side. We were downtown, but Nick easily beat the big guys to their own call with some nifty driving, as did Sergeant Mark Zawicki. The fire originated in a rear basement apartment and was fully involved. The north campus fire station still had just two firefighters assigned on night shift, barely enough to get water on the flames, which were now lapping up the outside wall of the building.

The Ann Arbor Fire Department's policy was that no one else was to enter a fire once they arrived on the scene. Mark Zawicki was among the supervisors that understood lives trumped policy. We were not going to remain outside an active fire while residents slept inside unaware. Mark, Nick and I each took a floor of the three-story structure to evacuate the building. When I arrived on the third floor, choking smoke filled the stairway and hallway. I pounded on door after door announcing

"Ann Arbor Police" and shouting that the building was on fire.

As I rapped on each door, I checked the door handle to see if any were unlocked so I could sound the alarm more clearly. I found one door unlocked and opened it while yelling "Fire!" A little boy, wearing pajamas, popped up on the couch. He was about five or six years old. A woman came running out of the bedroom, stark naked, and froze for a moment staring at me. "Ma'am, your building's on fire, please grab something, we have to go," I said. I beckoned the little boy to come with me and he ran and jumped up into my arms. I grabbed his blanket and wrapped it around his back, holding the hallway door open and yelling to the woman to hurry.

Other residents of the floor emerged from their apartments and descended the front stairway, where there was less smoke. The woman and a man finally emerged from the bedroom and joined the boy and me as we fled down the stairs and out the front door. I tried to put the boy down so I could reenter the building, but he clung to me like I was a stuffed animal.

It was chilly that summer dawn, and the blanket seemed inadequate to keep the boy warm. I had Nick start the patrol car and turn the heater on, and placed the boy on the front seat. The woman turned out to be an overnight guest of the father and they stood outside the building with the other tenants, all of them watching smoke seep out some open windows.

Nick and I double-checked each apartment to make sure no one had been left behind. We worked on arranging temporary shelter for the displaced residents and I let the boy play with several emergency light functions while we waited. Van Borne and Stevens helped coordinate housing and kept early risers from driving over the fire hoses.

Even after housing was arranged, my little companion did not want to let me go. He refused to leave the scene unless I carried or drove him, so I did. Residents called the department later to thank us for their rescue. We were cited in a letter of commendation and nominated for the Distinguished Service Award. By now

I was on the awards board myself and abstained from voting. The nomination passed anyway and we were recognized in October, along with an *Ann Arbor News* Award, my third in four years.

"American Sniper"

The popularity of *American Sniper*, a 2014 Clint Eastwood film based on former Navy Seal Chris Kyle's bestselling book, illustrates our fascination with true life characters that surmount incredible odds. A public that suppresses the detailed toll of war doesn't readily recognize snipers, bombardiers and torpedo men for their heroism, or the sophisticated mathematical skills required to carry out their assignments. Skilled riflemen save lives. They cover ground movement and the treatment of wounded. They are also an integral part of police SWAT teams.

I served on the Ann Arbor Police Special Tactics Unit from 1989 to 2004. I was primarily assigned as point man on entry teams and carried an MP5. One day, a subject took two hostages in a home at White and Henry Streets a block away from my house and I became the first responder. I found myself behind a scoped .308 rifle covering the entry elevation from a dining room across the street. We trained at one-hundred-yard distances, but my target paced back and forth, menacing two women with a handgun, a mere one hundred feet away.

The balance of our unit took up other positions and Ted Randall assembled a ready response team to disarm and capture the subject at the prescribed time. The owner of the house I occupied made coffee, offered me the use of her dining room table and evacuated to a neighbor's home a safe distance away. The gunman controlled his environment in every way but one: his hostage sister told him to go outside to smoke. He sat on the stoop facing Henry Street at dusk, the glow of his cigarette filling the telescopic sight as I watched. Scene commanders considered taking a shot at that moment to prevent his return indoors. I had trouble controlling my breathing and my thoughts.

I anxiously awaited word. In my peripheral vision, I detected movement on the left. I was advised to maintain cover of the suspect while the response team moved into position. Now cloaked in darkness, they closed on the gunman, threw him to the ground and secured and disarmed him. I breathed a sigh of relief; my hands were clammy and I had a parched tongue. I realized how much I preferred leading a component on a dynamic entry as opposed to the anguishing assignment of a posting behind a rifle. There are lots of unpleasant realities in the process of preserving life. One of those is the necessity of the sniper, who understands that saving lives sometimes means taking one.

Chapter Eighteen
Partnership and Marriage On the Rocks

Success at work often comes with a price at home, taking a toll on your family life. Rhonda and I hadn't been in tune with each other for a long time, and the quality time I spent with our sons William and Jacob took a definite hit with my schedule. I'd play guitar and sing to them, I coached some of their ball teams and watched cartoons and went to movies with them, but it was hardly enough, even when I took them with me to run the Michigan Stadium stairs. I was just too immersed in work and training.

One advantage of living in the city you police is the convenience of being able to stop at home and change a dirtied uniform, use the bathroom or just say hi to the kids. One drawback is finding your wife having dinner with another man. The guy seated in my dining room chair was making himself right at home; I'd never seen or heard of him before. Rhonda had met him at her health club and from later accounts it appeared they'd been working out closely together. I wasn't really surprised. I'd suspected a number of men had been with Rhonda before and after she'd become my wife, but seeing one sitting in my own chair was something else. It had long been paid for at considerable risk to my life.

Whatever spark it was that lit our partnership had been doused. Rhonda tried to be gone for daylong workouts when I was home, which made for a peaceful setting but a fractured parental experience for Jacob and William. I just don't think Rhonda ever really knew what to do with herself while I was at work. She was pretty and fit and good at attracting attention so inevitably she did what she did best.

Marilyn Kelly joined city employment full-time the same day I did. She'd earned a music degree from Western Michigan University and she worked across the hall from me before moving to the police department herself, where she ultimately became a sworn officer. We'd had a vague awareness of one other around City Hall, but in 1991 we were assigned to ride together for the first time.

We were born a month apart and both raised in Ann Arbor. We knew lots of the same people and shared some common interests in music and film. A COP (Community Oriented Policing) assignment put Nick and I on different shifts, and I began riding with Marilyn a lot. It was a change of pace from what I was used to, but we became close confidants.

As much as we may have had in common, we were opposites in our approach to police work. I was fired up, gung-ho, eager for action and recognition. Marilyn was low key, quiet and tended to shun attention. Her work was fundamentally sound; she conducted thorough investigations and wrote concise reports. She was especially adept at interviewing sexual assault victims and handling sensitive details with discretion.

Marilyn was also an equestrian who stabled her own horses. Her compact upper body (she stood five-foot-two-inches tall) was strengthened by years of riding and pitching bales of hay. She was also a crack pistol marksman whose scores surpassed all but a handful of male officers. Her parents were divorced so she endured some of the same disruption I'd experienced with a succession of new mothers. She possessed humor, intelligence and a stunning figure, but like many attractive women, she suffered a bit from low self-esteem. It didn't seem as though she'd ever received due credit for her many accomplishments. We grew closer and I became attached right away.

Marilyn and I made for an effective patrol tandem. Police partners rely on an intimate trust in one another. They endure the same stressful situations at work, and sometimes the same friction at home. I looked forward to every shift with her, and she did an excellent job of looking out for me.

Sent to a breaking and entering in progress at Lee's Market on Dexter Road, we arrived to see the suspect behind the counter, smashing the cash register with a baseball bat. I entered the business to confront him when he turned in my direction with the bat held over his head with both hands. I heard Marilyn yell, "Drop it!" and he immediately complied. I looked back to see her in a classic combat stance, with her chrome-plated .357 gleaming in the moonlight. She was about as capable at covering suspects as they came. I'd seen her range targets, and they were impressive.

On another night, Marilyn and I stopped a drunk driver at Madison and Packard. Driving a flatbed cable lineman's truck, he was visibly fit and bulked up. We called in the stop, and the dispatcher acknowledged our location. He failed all sobriety tests and when I told him he was under arrest, the fight was on.

I was in superb shape but he was too big and beyond my ability to get under control alone. Marilyn jumped in, but he was wired and hard to handcuff. I radioed for assistance but the dispatcher (yes, the same one who jammed the radio when I tried calling for help with James Lee Bynes) asked us where we were. She was a nice person, but very distracted.

Marilyn and I exchanged exasperated looks. We were one of only two cars on the road and the dispatcher couldn't keep track of where we were? Wrestling with this suspect was going nowhere. Marilyn decided she'd had enough. She grabbed a hunk of his hair and slammed his head against the curb, telling him to get both arms behind his back, now.

When he hesitated she slammed him again, repeating her order. As drunk as he was, he knew better than to delay any longer. I cuffed him up and we led the woozy fellow to the patrol car. When we arrived at the station, the shift lieutenant told us he had overheard the puzzling radio exchange. He'd already called down there and counseled the dispatch officer on paying more attention to what we were doing and where we were doing it.

I loved police work and sharing it with someone I had intense feelings for enhanced each shift. Nick and I had always maintained an unspoken code of behavior regarding women: we admired and revered them, but focused exclusively on the job at hand. The two of us worked at a relentless pace and even the toxic and heady mixture of summer nights, alcohol-fueled parties and the attention of amorous police groupies failed to derail us. As unhappy as I was with Rhonda, I had remained entirely faithful. That was about to change.

"In Valor There Is Hope"—Recognition

When I started with the police department, I'd wondered what one had to do to earn the numerous award ribbons and commendation letters bestowed on veteran officers. I'd evidently figured it out. I was awarded the Medal of Valor and two Distinguished Service Awards in just four years. I also received the *Ann Arbor News* Award in 1989, 1990 and 1992. It made me the most highly decorated officer in department history and of course I shared those medals with Delaney Craig, Nick Stark, Mark Zawicki, Tom Hammer, Flynn Jeffries and Jack Kirby. But it felt good to be the common link.

Craig and I were featured on the "America's Finest" segment of the syndicated series *Crimewatch Tonight* with veteran CBS correspondent Ike Pappas. Pappas was the reporter asking Lee Harvey Oswald, "Do you have anything to say in your defense?" when Jack Ruby brushed by him and fatally shot Oswald

November 24, 1963. Pappas later offered key testimony to the Warren Commission.

Delaney Craig and I were filmed putting our hats on, walking out of the police locker room and jetting off in a patrol car while Pappas described the Greenhills fire rescue. It took me three takes to simply walk out of the locker room and past the camera. Despite my affinity for movies, it suggested I wasn't cut out for Hollywood.

Before that first awards ceremony, I'd never been recognized for anything before in my life. My great regret was that my parents didn't live to see any mark of achievement on my part. Many officers outwardly dismissed awards as meaningless while others humbly ignored them, but they meant something to me. They said someone in the department appreciated my efforts, and I was gratified. As a member of the awards board, I reviewed all nominations with Deputy Chiefs Ford Wallace, Greg McDonald and Miller Davis, an exclusive group.

The success gave me some clout with administrators and allowed me to be candid in my role as union representative. I used diplomacy, humor and candor in my efforts to diffuse the many citizen complaints generated by the department's new open-door policy. Community policing empowered a vocal public and expanded the volume of complaints by the hundreds. Sometimes my tactics worked and I was able to work toward a sensible conclusion. Other times the disposition of a complaint was a foregone conclusion.

Rhonda was not impressed with my heroism or my union responsibility. She skipped the award ceremonies, as she had my Detroit Police Academy graduation. She liked the money my overtime produced and spent it accordingly.

Playing with Fire

As is common with patrol partners, Marilyn became my best

friend. A group of us went bowling Monday nights at Colonial Lanes in Ann Arbor and outside of work, it was the only time Marilyn and I socialized together in public. We met for private walks in Saginaw Woods or sometimes a brief, after-shift rendezvous.

As an escape, Marilyn reserved a room at the Marriott Hotel in Ypsilanti. We sipped champagne, nibbled on shrimp and fittingly watched *Women From Headquarters*, a 1950 movie about female LAPD officers. Then we watched *Later with Bob Costas* featuring Bill Murray's account of attending Elvis's funeral. I left about 4:00 a.m., convinced I'd never loved anyone more.

Our private partnership was not the secret we thought it was. I was smitten and distracted. Despite our pretended nonchalance, it was well known that something was up between us. Units working the late midnight shift had seen our cars leaving a couple of our meeting spots in tandem, despite our efforts to be sly.

Rhonda was getting phone calls from a "well meaning" mystery woman who cautioned her that I was involved with the department's "black widow." I was getting reports from friends who also frequented Rhonda's health club that her physicality with her workout partner was not confined to the workout equipment.

Despite my love for William and Jacob, I was ready to leave Rhonda for Marilyn. Time and time again, whenever the topic came up, Marilyn would assert that she was not going to be the cause of my marriage breaking up. She assured me that she knew what she was talking about, and that it just wouldn't work. She was right, of course, but she underestimated the depth of my commitment. Marilyn and I cultivated our friendship through hours of road patrol and the sharing of personal experiences and to me, our intimacy was a consummation of a close, personal bond. I had never admired anyone so much.

In between training new recruits we continued our partnership and our clandestine meetings. And she covered me closely.

One night she came up behind a suspect I was talking to and dis-armed him of an eight-inch knife. The times we were not riding together, she backed me up on every call. Even her recruits knew something was going on. On the calls where we tracked down suspects or uncovered critical evidence together, we shared a bond of achievement I'd not felt with any other partner.

Thinking neither clearly nor logically, I lost all perception of my personal reality. I clung to the hope that Marilyn would relent and become my full-time partner off duty, too. Rhonda and I shared little but the house and our mutual contempt for one another. One night on midnight shift, I stopped home to use the bathroom. Rhonda and the boys had just ridden home with a friend from an outdoor party. I got to the front step just in time to see Rhonda and him disrobe and get to work on the living room floor. It didn't inspire more rational thought. Still Marilyn continued to avoid the topic of going public and our talks became tense while the intimacy remained extreme. But unbeknownst to me, she was lining up my replacement.

The Downward Spiral

Patrick Christian was among the department's most likable guys. He had a wide-eyed eagerness to get involved and do the right thing. He had a considerable number of friends and the guest list for his summer wedding in 1992 was long. Marilyn asked me if it would be okay for her to accompany another officer to the wedding and reception as she would otherwise be alone while I took Rhonda.

It was hard to argue her point, so I told her to go ahead. Several guests were staying at the reception hotel; Rhonda and I hadn't planned to stay as the boys' babysitter needed to get home at a certain time. Near the end of the reception, Marilyn's tipsy companion offered his room key to Rhonda and I, saying he "wouldn't be needing it." Marilyn was avoiding my attempts to catch her eye and my stomach felt as if a cannonball had slammed directly into it.

I felt sick the entire ride home. Over the next week or so accounts of their giddy flirtation at the hotel bar after we left sizzled through the department. Marilyn seemed to have changed overnight. Even as we rode together, my once warm companion turned frosty and downright defensive when I asked what was going on. She asked to be assigned to someone else. My situation was obvious to everyone but me.

I felt abandoned and betrayed. I'd shared every single thing that was of importance to me, everything that mattered. Places, movies, music, even food—every refuge I would normally retreat to in times of stress became an instant reminder of Marilyn. She had come to watch me play softball and run the Michigan Stadium stairs. She convinced me to listen to "The Dance" by Garth Brooks and watch *Against All Odds* with Jeff Bridges and Rachel Ward. She especially liked the movie's title song by Phil Collins. I'd failed to see how prophetic those songs and the film's scenario had been. For a long time I was crushed anytime either song or video played, which was very often at the time.

Of course it was worse at work with the three of us on the same shift. My body was having a chemical reaction to the anxiety. In addition to the constant pit in my stomach, I began perspiring more and my body odor became toxic. I was beset by all the stages of grief at once: shock, pain, anger and depression descended on me as a group, and I became a colossal bore. I just couldn't stop yakking about it. What I had thought was a well-kept secret turned out to have been widely known around the department. What may have made for titillating gossip among co-workers while it was going on turned into an insipid rant as I vented about it. The poor officers who endured a full shift worth of my bellyaching must have wished I worked elsewhere.

I was moody at home, too. Rhonda had no idea why I was suddenly so morose. I was lost, and I tinkered with the draft of a letter to Marilyn to express my feelings. Rhonda found it one night while I was at work and called dispatch to summon me home. The call sounded so grave that half the shift responded, Marilyn included, to find a distraught Rhonda having a meltdown.

I took Rhonda in the house and told her that the relationship had been entirely one-sided and that I was upset Marilyn had found someone else. I thought it necessary to exonerate Marilyn because there was no telling what a manic Rhonda might do to a perceived rival. We'd later find out.

I took the rest of the night off and locked myself in our room with my pistol. Rhonda's alarm overrode her anger for a minute, and she called Nick Stark to the house. My emotional bottom fell out, and Nick calmly listened while I had a breakdown in front of my old partner. I hit my absolute lowest point and remained there for some time. I just didn't know how I could go on after having lost Marilyn's friendship.

Midnight Rides with Buck Revere

At that time, riding with me must have been the worst assignment on the road. Thank goodness Buck Revere volunteered for it. Buck was a hard charger, fast and thorough with an unmatched work ethic. He was also adept at changing the subject whenever I went on about carrying a torch. He didn't employ Nick's calculated anger but he was impatient with drivel and got right to the point. Buck and I were as effective as Nick and I, but we just didn't enjoy the same extraordinary streak of luck. But at six-foot-one-inch and two hundred twenty-five pounds, no one broke away from Buck's grasp and I ran down everybody else. Revere got me focused on work while at work, which was an enormous challenge with Marilyn on the same shift.

I read a book called *Excess Baggage* by Judith Sills. She explained that most of the time, women like Marilyn have moved on and rarely give former companions a second thought.

All the energy I was expending thinking about her was just being wasted. I had become a captive to my imagination, thinking she was wondering about me at any given moment, the way I was about her. She was busy doing the things new couples do: hosting parties, traveling: all the things it had been impossible to do with me. Recognizing my issues only went so far in solving them, however. There was still a lot of healing to do and a great deal of accounting that demanded a reckoning.

The Detective

Inevitably it was a long, painful summer. After a softball game one night, new detective Terry Johnson suggested I apply to the detective division for in-service training. He thought it might offer a change of pace and distance me from the fallout of my relationship with Marilyn. Besides, he said, if I ever became unable to work the road for any reason, an alternative spot in the department would be possible.

I applied for the position and got the nod. I spent sixteen hundred dollars on new suits, sport jackets and the requisite London Fog overcoat. In September, I descended into the bowels of the building to the Detective Bureau. I was assigned a desk in an office with Joe Hazard. I'd ridden with him on my very first day at the police department. He could scarcely understand how I'd leave the relative safety and comfort of the building depart-ment for police work. He had been an artillery officer in Vietnam and every morning he'd play a tape of reveille on his office cas-sette player at high volume—he was a wee bit deaf.

Sergeant Shel Phillips tried to keep me occupied by assigning me every retail fraud, gas station drive-off and vandalism report that came into the bureau. As the trainee, I became the dispose-all for cases real detectives didn't want to deal with. It was nothing like solving homicides but I cleared one hundred shoplifting cases in six months.

We were confined to the City Hall basement with no natural light or ventilation, doing most of our follow-up interviews over the phone. I answered calls as "Officer Stipe." I didn't want to imply that I had any intention of staying; I failed to see the prestige in being a detective.

I was assigned the imagined assault case of a mentally disturbed graduate student, who insisted "iridium triggers" emanating from the North Campus cell towers were molesting her in her sleep. The attacks persisted, despite wrapping herself in aluminum foil. Instead of dismissing her claims I submitted the report to the prosecutor, who denied authorization. The student filed a personal protection order against me, the prosecutor and the local FBI Special Agent.

A retail fraud suspect I was booking confided that two West Side thugs had moved into his disabled father's apartment, establishing a headquarters they used to commit several armed robberies. He was concerned for his dad's safety. I passed the information on to the Special Investigations Unit who actually caught them in the midst of robbing a Jackson bank. I was a bit dismayed that the unit received all the credit for solving the string of crimes when part of it rightfully belonged to a beleaguered shoplifter and his part-time detective.

The highlight of my stint was two weeks of working surveillance with super veteran Max Burleson. He was an imposing presence, resembling Sean Connery's Jimmy Malone character from Brian De Palma's film, *The Untouchables*. Max began his police career the same week Johnny Carson debuted on *The Tonight Show* in 1962, and retired the same week Johnny did in 1992. Max had been deferential to me from the start and I never could tell why. He was known as the toughest man in the department and didn't get on with just anyone.

I trusted him with my profound sense of loss and grief over Marilyn's abrupt dismissal. When I told him that I'd shared everything of meaning to me—movies, music, places—and that they now served as painful reminders, he said simply, "Find new things," as if he too had undergone some emotional baggage handling at one time. One would never guess it, he looked so unflappable.

Undercover officers all had nicknames, like Rebel, Rodeo, Disco, Buster, etc. If Max (known as "Pache," short for Apache) didn't like your suggestion he'd assigned you one of his own. I picked "Stryker," John Wayne's sergeant in *Sands of Iwo Jima*. Max seemed to think it went well with Stipe.

I was schooled in crime scene processing, warrant applications and fingerprinting, all tools I could use on road patrol. But when my six months of in-service training was up, I just wanted out. Detectives with tenacious follow-up skills are critical components of the legal process and the interview techniques of the best of them were a marvel to watch. The problem was I longed to be out of the building and on the road. It was a different kind of energy and I missed it. Joe Hazard had done his best to make me comfortable but when it was over, I left him and his reveille tape behind.

Chapter Nineteen
Kelly and Lauren and Gladys

Kelly Shayne

Buck Revere was not easily impressed. But he saw a lot to like in the April, 1992, class of police recruits. The future foundation of the department was built, in large part, on this stellar group. He drew former Eastern Michigan University basketball player Kelly Shayne to train, and the combination of what she brought and what he imparted to her resulted in a very effective officer. Tall, muscular and quiet, she combined a passive demeanor with an imposing presence. Right away she was able to inject herself into action without getting in the way.

As officers arrested a disorderly subject on Maynard Street near Nickels Arcade, a couple of drunken companions attempted to interfere. Shayne moved to intercept the two, grasped both ends of her nightstick, placed it against the chest of the bigger of the two men, and drove him backward the length of the sidewalk.

In stark contrast to rookies who recite their resumé and try to dazzle with their knowledge, Kelly rarely spoke unless she was asked a question. She blended inconspicuously, but invariably was there when needed. I took a liking to her right away.

Officers from several departments gathered at the Holiday Inn West for a "Battle of the Badges" weightlifting competition. Kelly was one of the Ann Arbor Police entrants. AAPD competitors and supporters were huddled in the corner of the large banquet room and Shayne slid a seat up next to mine and put her feet on the bars below my chair. She was releasing extra energy by fidgeting her feet. I started laughing at my vibrating perch and asked her if she was nervous. She nodded her head yes. I asked, "Didn't you play college basketball in an arena full of people?"

"Well, yeah, I did."

"Well, this drunken rabble isn't going to remember what they drank tonight, let alone how well you did," I said.

Kelly started laughing, and I saw her smile for the first time. I thought her looks were striking. She wore no makeup, had on frumpy sports attire and rarely spoke. I was captivated from that first smile.

I recruited her to play on the co-rec softball team I'd put together. She could field any position and hit a ton. We went thirty-six and four in four seasons. We spent lots of time together, and her company and attention made me feel like a winner. Like all attractive rookies, she was being pursued by several wide-eyed suitors but our implied relationship kept a buffer between her and those other men. Kelly's company went a long way toward curing my loneliness. We went to see the Eagles perform at Tiger Stadium in Detroit. It was the best evening I had spent in a very long time. I was crazy about her, but she preferred a friendship with fun on the side over something more significant. Any time spent with Kelly was worthwhile: she is among that rare and special group of friends that never lets you down.

Moving On

During the third week of March, 1994, I'd gone to a coaches meeting to sign up our co-rec softball team in the U-M Classic League. To celebrate, several of us met at Fraser's Pub, including Kelly Shayne, Joe Brody and Tim D'Andrea. Some nights, officers coming off midnight shift weren't ready to pack it in, even at closing time. Often we'd impose on Joe Brody's hospitality at his apartment. Joe had a cat named for Red Wing Joe Kocur and an extensive assortment of Red Wing souvenirs, but other than that not a stick of furniture.

Brody was a rookie—a very reliable one at that—so we regularly cleaned him out of liquor and beer. That night in March was no exception. We stayed there until nearly 4:00 a.m. Rhonda knew I hung out there, and whenever she called, whether I had been there or not, Joe would tell her "Pete just left." That night, I had a bit of a buzz and got a bit amorous with Kelly. I admired her so much as an officer and thought her such a beautiful person, inside and out.

When we left, Kelly drove beside me across town until we came to the turn into my neighborhood. She rolled her window down and said she wanted to talk for a minute. We pulled onto Henry Street and parked and she hopped into my GMC Jimmy, leaving her car running with the lights on behind us.

She told me how much she liked me and I told her the feeling was mutual. We sat there for an hour bringing the point home. A pair of officers, seeing Kelly's car idling with the lights on, rolled by several times in their patrol car trying to figure out what was up. What was up was Rhonda when I got home. She'd called Joe Brody an hour before and he told her I had just left, which I had. When I told her I'd been talking to Kelly, she threw a fit. She took all my clothes out of our closet and dumped them on the floor of my upstairs study, and pushed my stand-up dresser in there for good measure. She thought she was pushing me out of our bedroom but she had pushed me out of the house. It was the last night I would spend there.

There are two sides to every story and that goes for the conflicts that erode a marriage. Rhonda may have had legitimate reasons for her behavior but I'm not writing this account from her perspective. Her severe mood swings grew tiresome and difficult to handle. I punched my own ticket for the disastrous ride with Marilyn and the emotional fallout that followed: I was wrong to do it and I was a bad sport when I lost. I'm not the first or the last person to self-destruct in that way but I was a wreck and failing as a father. Now I would need to carry on and cushion the fall for William and Jacob because I knew my leaving was going to change them forever, too.

Strangely enough, with all the emotional baggage weighing me down, for the first time, a number of women offered to help me carry it. I'd developed several close personal friendships with a variety of women. Few of them were intimate, but they all helped convince me that I still had something to offer the right woman.

I packed the uniforms and clothing I would need immediately and moved in with Buck Revere. It was St. Patrick's Day, but I didn't feel like celebrating. Rhonda acted quickly. She cashed both federal and state income tax returns and cleaned out all our accounts. Visa had sent me a book of cash advance checks—she redeemed five thousand dollars worth. The check I'd written for the softball league bounced, so I had to scrape up enough to keep us entered. She charged furniture at the Art Van store and at Sears. Overnight, I found myself ten thousand dollars behind. For someone who was seemingly "ambushed" by my abrupt departure, Rhonda's moves felt very calculated. I filed for divorce on April 7, 1994, the anniversary of my mom's passing. Kelly accompanied me to the cemetery that morning to lay flowers on my mother's grave.

Buck was gracious in his hospitality, but I knew I couldn't impose on him for long. He was among the few officers who *would* ride with me for a while. I had become too high-maintenance for most. I couldn't expect Buck to ride with me at work and then look after me at home as well. I answered an ad for a sublet apartment and met my prospective roommate where she worked, the Ann Arbor Art Association.

Lauren Rutledge was an Eastern Michigan graduate and the daughter of University of Michigan academics. Beautiful, bubbly, bright and buxom, I liked her outgoing personality instantly. Lauren was the assistant director of the Art Association and her roommate had moved out, leaving her a spare bedroom in a small apartment on High Street in Ann Arbor. I explained my situation to her, including my volatile wife's unpredictability and the fact that I worked a midnight shift. I also told her my sons would be frequent guests and asked if that would be okay. We met when I was in uniform, so she knew right away I was a cop. She was unperturbed and asked me if it were a problem if she had frequent female company. I told her that if I were welcome, so were her friends. I missed her subliminal hint.

It worked out very well. Lauren was gracious in her hospitality and included me in outings to hear musician friends play open mike nights at the Old Town Bar. Our apartment was underground, so I could easily sleep all day while she was at work. She made me feel right at home. We lived just four blocks from City Hall so it took only a minute to get to and from work. The two of us socialized a lot, and I was impressed with her wisdom and her kindness. William and Jacob liked her, too, and she read them *The Phantom Tollbooth* by Norman Juster when they came to visit.

Maybe I reasoned that insulating myself with women would give me a place to turn if another friendship went south. I didn't have a dime, so their companionship meant something else. I was feeling special and appreciated for the first time in a long time. One girl emerged as the definitive frontrunner in my quest for companionship and our friendship would become among the best-kept secrets in department history.

Gladys Serves Up Some Sanity

When Karen Simpson completed her fourth and final season as an outside hitter on Eastern Michigan's volleyball team, she'd tied the all-time EMU dig record. Being a record setter in digs was worthy of her—saving a spike or a serve requires headfirst determination, skill and courage, three traits she possessed in abundance.

She worked nights part-time at the Dom Bakery on Washtenaw Avenue in Ypsilanti. Midnight Ann Arbor officers had been buying coffee there since our local bakery eliminated overnight hours. Karen and her partner, Sandy, adopted the aliases Gladys and Agnes in an effort to discourage the amorous pursuits of the shop's strange midnight clientele. They were funny, pretty and friendly, and a welcome sight on a shift where most of the people officers encountered were on their worst behavior.

Tall (five-foot eight-inches), fit and athletic, Gladys had a wholesome quality and a ready smile that disarmed one right away. She spent more time in the gym than she did in front of a mirror, and her physique was a frequent topic among officers who patronized Dom Bakery. Her uninhibited candor found some hardened cops blushing, but it was refreshing to hear such brutally honest assessments of people and things. She was not easily intimidated.

I enjoyed her company so much that I invited her to join us on our Thursday night outing one week. Gladys joined us at Aubree's Bar in Depot Town in Ypsilanti. Jack Lee, Tim Laird, Buck Revere and I were there, and Gladys arrived from her nearby apartment.

We wound up in a booth by the jukebox, where she showed me her driver's license to prove that her name really wasn't Gladys. It was the first time we had spoken for more than the few minutes it took to buy coffee at the drive-up window. She was distinctively special and we hit it off right away. Gladys's naiveté struck a chord with me—her simple but direct outlook on life and those living it made me both laugh and think at the same time.

I put some money in the jukebox and played my new anthems: "I Won't Back Down" and "Free Falling" by Tom Petty, and "Move It On Over" by George Thorogood. After we left the bar, we accompanied Tim Laird to Abe's Coney Island to buy him breakfast for his birthday. I left with a great feeling, wondering if my luck had changed.

A few nights later I passed through the drive-up window at Dom's on a night off. Gladys knew I wasn't there for coffee. We decided to see each other and met a few times for beers, and I was so impressed with her refreshing point of view of things. She invited me to join her on a spring break trip and I said yes. At thirty-eight years old, it was to be my first.

We met at my apartment on High Street and drove my '93 Jimmy through the night all the way to Virginia Beach. She played tapes or fiddled with the radio to keep me entertained until she finally dozed off. I had a direct route plotted out and we made great time. She took over when we were nearly there, and drove us to the beach by mid-morning. Gladys had a different notion of accommodations than I did. She suggested we sleep on the beach and slip into various hotels for continental breakfast. I was a middle-aged police officer—that just was not going to work for me.

We found an aging beachfront hotel with rooms at twenty-two dollars a night and on the budget Rhonda left me, it was uncomfortably near my limit. We rented an end room overlooking the beach and settled in. Virginia Beach was a big destination for sailors on shore leave and the crew of a mine tender had taken up nearly a full floor of rooms. We weren't looking for trouble, but it seemed to find us anyway.

Wayne and Tammy were something right out of a reality show. Tammy had been the sixteen-year-old family babysitter when the forty-year-old Wayne swept her away in his new 5.0-liter Mustang. Tammy looked every bit of twenty-one and was built like a swimsuit model dressed as she was in the fluorescent pink bikini for their getaway. The four of us met by chance in the hallway.

Wayne was a prison guard and very proud of his .357 revolver. He carried it everywhere and displayed it with alarming frequency. He was afraid that one of the sailors would try to make off with his Tammy, and he informed me that they had better watch out. I left my sidearm locked in my Jimmy. The four of us rented bikes from a drugstore and rode the length of the impressive boardwalk. When we turned around to head back, Gladys was no longer with us.

Now it was my turn to be worried. It seemed impossible something could have happened because she had been so close behind most of the way. I was wearing swim trunks and she held the room key, the car keys, my wallet and all my money in her backpack. If I needed something I was certainly not eager to prevail on Wayne for any favors.

We headed back to the store where we rented the bikes and found that Gladys had already returned hers and bought some aspirin. My own headache was peaking about the time hers was being relieved. I would tap into this scare and how it all worked out in the coming days at work.

On our last night at the beach, Wayne and Tammy hosted a party in their room and several of the seamen were in attendance. Gladys and Tammy had enhanced the sailors' shore leave wearing all-day bikinis. Gladys had easily fended off several legions of cops at the bakery, so I knew she could hold her own. Tammy, on the other hand, preferred the sailors' attention to that of the sullen Wayne. His mood grew worse the more he drank so Gladys palmed his unattended pistol and passed it to me for safekeeping. Wayne was becoming more and more unpredictable and I kept the rounds and stuffed the gun in his luggage.

Wayne got in such a twist that Tammy ended up taking refuge in our room, snagging Wayne's keys so he wouldn't drive. He threw a fit and tore their room apart searching for both his keys and his gun. When I met him in the hallway he had found his revolver and at gunpoint he demanded to know where Tammy was. I was not impressed and I suggested she might have taken a walk with the sailors. He stormed down the stairs toward the beach and unfortunately for him, he confronted a beach patrol officer who did not know his gun was unloaded. Wayne was summarily body slammed and whisked away in a patrol car, leaving his babysitter behind.

We last saw Tammy driving off in Wayne's Mustang with his wallet and two sailors. Assured we couldn't top those events, Gladys and I packed up and checked out the next morning. Gladys may only have been twenty-two but she was fearless, feisty and fun. She was a born competitor and loved to call someone out with her brutal honesty. The fact that she bent the language to fit her unique meaning merely made her more interesting to listen to. For instance, instead of saying, "Thanks a lot, take care," she'd say, "Thanks, take a lot." I was looking forward to buying all my coffee from her.

When we returned to Ann Arbor, Gladys and I went to the AAA Michigan office on South Main to plan our next trip. We pulled out and headed north on Main Street where there was a patrol car stopped at the red light at Pauline. Marilyn was driving, headed back to the station at the end of her day shift. An Eagle Talon pulled up to the same light driven by Kelly Shayne, who was on her way to her afternoon shift. Then a Buick Grand National rolled up: it was Rhonda. I tried to calculate the unlikely odds of the four women having the most emotional impact on my current life all waiting for the same signal to change. When I pointed out the irony to Gladys, she just shrugged her shoulders and laughed.

Chapter Twenty:
Tucker Williams Takes Me In

Tucker Williams was also an Ann Arbor native, but his formative years weren't spent in military academies or prep schools like mine. Williams lived in a tough neighborhood and attended public schools and he'd played schoolyard football with future NFL and U-M coach Jim Harbaugh. He understood early on that one learned more by listening than talking and when he spoke, it was worth hearing.

Known for his distinctive laugh, Tucker's energetic eyes grew as wide as his arm gestures when telling a story. His accounts of things he'd seen firsthand needed no embellishment. His keen observations put the listener right in his shoes and with his experiences, that was not always a pleasant place to be. He was as generous as he was reliable and, on an early sabbatical from my home with Rhonda, he offered me a place to stay.

Tuck and I were riding patrol together, and he was a fine partner. I had a little better street orientation and did the driving, but Tuck knew precisely how to speak to both victims and suspects alike. He had an assuredness in the way he spoke that you knew his would be the last word in any argument. At that time, I was reliant on Tucker for everything. He kept me safe at work and grounded off duty and this debt is one that you expect you can never repay. That fact always seems to worry you much more than it does your true friends.

I may have worried him a little on one unforgettable night. Tucker and I responded to a domestic disturbance on Fuller Road, near North State Street, where Terry Jarvis was the primary officer. Jack Lee and Boz Gregory, as well as Tuck and I, had been sent for backup. From the hallway we could hear a violent commotion coming from inside—there was slapping, screaming and crashing sounds. Lee and I went to the exterior door to see if we could gain access that way and Boz quickly summoned us inside. A bare-chested subject was on the floor tussling with the other officers. The suspect, Meredith Montgomery, was a big brute. He was able to get his back against the wall and from a prone position use his legs to fend off the officers.

Tucker closed the gap, grabbed Montogmery, and tried twisting him over to get control of an arm. Montgomery suddenly unloaded a series of punches that struck Tuck directly in the face. Tucker's hands were all that held the suspect pinned, so he was unable to defend himself. Lee and I descended on Montgomery, helped flip him over, and got him handcuffed.

Tucker was regaining his composure while Gregory and Lee took the suspect out for transport. I joined Jarvis to check the victim—it looked as if Montgomery had broken every blood vessel in his wife's face after a savage beating. He'd also thrown his infant son across the room onto a tiled floor. Although screaming in terror, the baby was not seriously injured.

For some reason, Boz and Jack Lee thought it more prudent to place the suspect in our patrol car. The barefooted Montgomery wasn't thrilled about getting into any police car and kicked wildly to prevent the back door from closing. The officers' timing was off as the arrestee's big toe was caught in the door when it closed. When I stepped outside, the screams could be heard for a block.

Who knows, perhaps his anger stemmed from his gender-blending first name. His hostility was unlike any I'd ever heard, he was that revved up. I pictured the battered wife and crying baby. I wasn't happy he had just assaulted my partner and friend.

As I turned the car around, Tucker nursed his swelling eye.

Montgomery screamed out from our back seat, telling Tucker how glad he was he got to slug a "nigger." I pulled out of the driveway onto Fuller, and he continued to utter the same epithet. I turned onto North State and he directed "nigger" at Tuck several more times, which finally flipped a switch in me. All the emotion surging through me about my life, my estranged wife, my kids, and the partner who graciously was doing so much to help me suddenly boiled over. In the middle of that brick-lined street, I slammed on the brakes and hopped out of the car.

Gregory and Lee, following right behind us, were forced to stop as well. I flung open the rear passenger door and Montgomery rocked toward me, thinking I was letting him out. I met his face halfway with a closed fist as he reeled back. Incensed, he flung himself toward me again, and once more I punched him as hard as I could. This time the blow knocked him back to the other door.

"What is this?" Montgomery cried.

"It's your beating," Tucker replied. "Get used to it."

An alarmed Gregory grabbed my arm, pointed at two pedestrians across the street, and said, "There are people right there!"

"They're going to have to wait their fucking turn," I said through clenched teeth. I reached in through the door and gave Montgomery an openhanded shove back to allow it to close.

I hopped back in the driver's seat and put the patrol car in gear. The realization of what I had just done hit me as hard as the punches I'd just thrown. It was the first and only time I'd struck a prisoner in handcuffs. We were just a few blocks from the station and certain trouble loomed ahead.

Marty Kozlowski was an old-school sergeant. He could tolerate some deviation from policy when justified but striking a cuffed prisoner was not among those exceptional instances. Montgomery was cussing up a storm in the back seat and I had an idea.

"You can swear at us and call us names all you want," I began, "but please don't antagonize our shift sergeant. He

178

doesn't take criticism very well."

"Fuck him. *And fuck you!*" he spat.

I called dispatch and asked them to have a supervisor meet us in police security. When the overhead garage door opened, I could see Sergeant Kozlowski and a pair of other officers waiting for us.

"There he is. Remember, be cool. Don't piss him off," I pleaded.

Kozlowski whipped open the back car door and Montgomery emerged. He nodded his head toward the sergeant and asked, "Is this him?"

"Yes, it is," I replied.

Montgomery cocked his head back, summoned up some mucus from the back of his throat, and spat it right in Kozlowski's face. "Fuck you!" he screamed.

Kozlowski stood about five-foot-eight-inches and weighed one hundred eighty pounds. He cradled his hand under Montgomery's jaw, thrust him aloft and carried him to the first cell in lockup. "Put him on the ring," he ordered.

The ring was a fixed steel circle embedded in the cinderblock wall of the cell. It was used to secure out of control prisoners. Tucker, Lee, Diane Kingman and I strained to pin him down so we could lock him to the ring but he flopped around with such strength, we couldn't hold him still. The reason became evident when I looked back to see desk officer Andy Michaelson grinding Montgomery's throbbing big toe into the cell floor.

I told him to knock it off and we finally got him secured. Montgomery looked around the room assessing his captors: Tucker, Lee, Diane Kingman, Kozlowski and me. He found a derogatory ethnic slam for each one of us. As I watched the sergeant wipe spittle from his face, I knew my aberrant punching episode was not going to become an issue.

Tucker was still nursing his eye but he was tough as nails and he never complained. We booked Montgomery for assaults on his wife and baby, and he went to jail. He pleaded guilty, and the topic of being slugged by a deranged officer never came up. I regret my conduct, but not the outcome.

The next morning, I left for Yellowstone National Park for a planned trip with sons William and Jacob. I drove out there and back in only a week, just for the opportunity to get some camping in with my boys. We needed a break together.

Tucker Busts a Furtive Move

Good police work is not unlike good fielding in baseball. An outfielder that breaks at the crack of the bat has a good chance to run down well-driven balls. Cops that respond immediately to a dispatched call can find their arrival just as timely.

An alarm at the Hop In on State Street, just south of I-94, found Pittsfield Township without a car to send. Gregory and Lee responded to the robbery while Tucker and I checked the area. Cruising the Motel 6 a block away, Tucker spotted a room curtain quickly close as we rolled by. We ran the license plates of all the cars parked in proximity to the room. Then we checked the rest of the motel and the immediate area, finding nothing else suspicious.

Special Investigations had several suspects in mind for a string of menacing armed robberies that had been taking place around Ann Arbor. Two suspects would physically dominate their targets, which were all commercial businesses. When Detective Jim Wysocki looked at the registrations Tuck and I had run, he recognized one of the names among the vehicle owners. While Tucker and I were off on our leave days, SIU focused surveillance on the new suspect and his companions as they cased several businesses throughout Washtenaw County.

Two straight nights of observation convinced the SIU crew the suspects were about to strike. When Tucker and I returned to work, Sgt. Marty Kozlowski told us we'd been assigned as the uniformed officers for the robbery detail. It appeared their target would be the Arby's Restaurant on Washtenaw Avenue at Glenwood. Tucker and I staged our marked unit in a driveway on Arlington Boulevard.

We listened as plainclothes Detectives Vernon Thomas and Ryan Jazzman monitored the suspects as they debated whether to strike or not. The suspects had parked right next to Thomas, who slid down onto the floor of his car to avoid detection. He whispered over the radio that they were going to hit the restaurant. When he was asked how he knew, he replied, "Because they said so."

The wait made me nervous. We had no one in the restaurant, and no one seemed to have a direct eye on the suspects. Tucker and I were in a marked car and couldn't budge without the risk of being spotted. The most anxious moments of any surveillance operation is allowing the crime to occur. Without the actual act, there is no crime, so we have no choice though innocent civilians can be at risk while a crime is in progress. Tucker and I looked at each other as we wondered what was going on.

Finally Wysocki broke the silence by saying a vehicle had just sped by him, heading down Arlington at high speed. That had to be our guys. I turned north on Arlington and jumped on it. Thomas made contact at the Arby's and confirmed a robbery had indeed occurred. The suspects were making good time, and Wysocki was calling out their route and wondering where his backup was. We crossed the Huron Parkway Bridge and I gunned the patrol car up Geddes Road toward US-23, right through the spot I'd crashed my Belvedere back in December, 1973.

The suspects turned north on Earhart, passing the cemetery where my dad is buried. We were not far behind. As we closed on Glazier Way, we could see their taillights just ahead of us. The suspects rolled down their windows and discarded handguns out either side of the car. I closed the gap near Glacier Hills Retirement Home.

I had an MP5 submachine gun slung and resting in my lap.

Tucker was armed with his pistol. The suspects suddenly stopped in a spot that caught me off guard. I stopped suddenly and hopped out to cover them, neglecting to place the patrol car in park. I had the MP5 trained on the suspect vehicle, one foot on the ground and one foot on the brake pedal. Unable to keep full pressure on the brake, the patrol car inched forward. Mark Fleming and Christopher Sager responded to back us up. Fleming was poised to move up and secure the driver when I asked him to put our car in park.

The suspects surrendered without incident. All the stolen money was recovered as well as the discarded guns, and several armed robberies were solved with those two arrests. The credit went to Joe Randleman for an informant's tip as well as to SIU for their productive surveillance. Only Kozlowski recognized that Tucker Williams had broken the crime spree with his furtive curtain observation. It was for that reason he'd assigned us the uniform detail. But Tuck and I knew, and that was good enough.

Chapter Twenty-One
Fun with Pete & Gladys

The Summer of 1994

The apartment I sublet with Lauren was dank, dark and moldy. I had a solitary bedroom window at the bottom of a window well so deep that a raccoon trapped itself in there on the Fourth of July. It was not an ideal place to entertain guests. Gladys was trying to finish school, switching from nursing to teaching, and I was trying to sort out my female friends. I was attached to several confidants as I slowly emerged from a deep depression.

Annie Brown was a dazzling Fraser's Pub waitress sought after by every male customer she had. A full-time EMU student, she offered an understanding ear and devoted considerable time to keeping me grounded, even riding a patrol shift with me. We spent quality time together after her shifts were done and during the investigation of a personnel complaint, an endorsement she gave me to Lt. Miller Davis impressed him enough to summon me to his office to tell me he was no longer worried about my wellbeing. Her account had prompted him to classify the complaint as unfounded and to tell me my time appeared to be well-spent.

Lisa DeBarra was a bodybuilding musician and artist I'd met while running with Augie at Gallup Park. She was seeking advanced degrees in psychology. She offered intellect, physical therapy and a dose of much needed reality. My roommate Lauren and I spent a lot of time together. She was brilliant and fun and without her, I may have ended up spending my mid-life crisis in a shelter.

Wendy Benet looked like a movie star and worked in the building department. When I was a detective, I would use their records to track down certain suspects. She made me feel right back at home. She transferred to parking enforcement and brought her alluring personality along with her. Kelly Shayne remained a close confidant and friend, but was wisely wary of commitment.

Soon Gladys was due to tour Central America with the Athletes in Action volleyball team. Although it was a missionary trip, Gladys was more free-spirited than spiritual at the time. I liked her a lot. I confided in her with my falling out with Marilyn, my pending divorce from Rhonda and the complex network of close women friends I maintained. I wanted her to know the truth about what I was going through. She shrugged her shoulders and said, "So?"

"I thought you ought to know," I told her.

"Okay, keep your friends. What do you want to do now?" Her reaction floored me. She was completely unaffected and self-assured. My opinion of her soared as my stress level began to subside. Gladys was different from any girl I'd ever met.

I needed a new place to stay as my lease with Lauren was almost up. Fellow STU member and Detective Sergeant George Westwood made me an offer. A two-bedroom unit was available on West Liberty Street that was affordable and convenient. There would be room for the boys to visit and sleep, and George and I had a lot in common, including a love of war movies and beer. Most days, that was enough. Westwood had a pretentious estranged wife, and I had a new girlfriend free of pretension. It was an interesting dynamic.

* * *

It turned out Rhonda wasn't handling my departure very well. I tried hard to avoid her but it wasn't easy.

She stopped by unannounced at the apartment on High Street and a vigilant Lauren made her wait outside. When I returned home to move some furniture out of our house, she stalked my co-workers as they crossed the lawn, cocking her head to one side and offering her unsolicited opinion of my moving out. It was unnerving to be around her.

She arrived on Liberty Street to find Gladys cooking spaghetti while I changed before my midnight shift. It was their first encounter. Rhonda went berserk, stomping into my bedroom and screaming while Gladys waved a spatula with a conductor's flourish all the time laughing in the background.

She may have been amused, but Gladys now understood why I'd tried to keep her insulated. Rhonda was a handful, and potentially dangerous. One night she skidded the car into Mitchell Field after a co-rec softball game with Jacob and William in the back seat of our Grand National. She converged on Gladys with her finger wagging but was restrained by my fellow officers.

One afternoon, Gladys and I sat at Fuller Pool when the PA announced an emergency phone call for me at the office. I picked up the phone and heard Rhonda crying, asking me, "What are you doing at *my* pool?" We packed up immediately and left. We were only a few blocks away when I spotted the Grand National closing on us from behind. Rhonda forced us off the road on Virginia Street, a few blocks short of my apartment. We rolled up the windows and locked the doors while she screamed at us from the outside. I admit to being a bit rattled, trying to figure out what it would cost me if she ran one of my vehicles into the other.

It got worse. Westwood and I pulled into "her" driveway to drop off the boys one afternoon. Rhonda came outside and cracked the windshield with a coffee mug. She stopped by the Liberty Street apartment on a Sunday morning when I was deployed on a SWAT callout and unsuccessful in her attempt to break a window, she bent the screens and pounded on the front door. When Gladys refused to open it, she dented the door on Gladys's car with several kicks and wrote insults on her windshield with lipstick. But she wasn't done.

Rhonda arrived at the station fired up, demanding to see me. I was summoned out of a debriefing to the lobby. We had just disarmed a barricaded gunman from a house on Miller Avenue when Rhonda began screaming and cussing. When Tim De'Andrea opened the door to the secure police area, she pushed past him trying to make her way to the squad room. Nick Stark and Blake Richards moved in to restrain her.

We called Brad Thompson's wife to pick her and the boys up at the station. None of these episodes influenced our "Friend of the Court" worker, who rationalized Rhonda's actions as consistent with a woman under stress. Speeding around the city in a high-performance Grand National with two young boys in the back seat was not my idea of rational.

Gladys was a source of relief with all this craziness. I took her to Michigan Stadium to run the stairs with me. She'd been a competitive athlete her entire life and she wasn't about to allow unfamiliar discomfort make her quit; she and Lee Christiansen became the only friends to run the entire stadium with me without giving up. Gladys was as tough as the look on her face after she finished. We'd throw Frisbees and shoot pool for hours on end. She was good in everything I was great at, and great at things I wasn't. It was a sporting courtship—we had no television or stereo. I found myself wishing my folks could meet her.

Hey Baby, Let's Go to Vegas

My divorce was final, but very costly. I kept my pension and Rhonda got everything else. I'd paid all her debts and my parents' estate had been invested in our Burns Park house. She'd made a clean sweep and I hoped that ultimately, the house would be passed on to the boys. It was odd that the fact she didn't work entitled her to more in the settlement but she sure spent money freely. The whole experience was painful, but it was finally over.

Gladys and I had been dating for a year and a half at that point, as under the radar as we could keep it. She'd had nothing to do with my divorce but Rhonda often jumped to "convenient" conclusions. It was now acceptable to have Gladys at softball games, social functions and around the boys. We planned a July, 1995, camping trip with Jacob and William and my sister Molly, who would join us from Phoenix and camp with us at different spots in Colorado. There was still one pressing issue: my lease with George Westwood was up at the end of that month, and neither Gladys nor I could afford to live alone on the money we had. Gladys's parents were also not going to be thrilled by the prospect of her living with a divorced man sixteen years her senior.

Just before we left, a drunk driver ran a red light and struck Molly's car broadside as she left work. The impact broke her neck and left her in very bad shape. We instantly diverted our destination to Phoenix, nearly driving all the way through. It was one hundred eighteen degrees in the hospital lot when we arrived. Molly was in tremendous pain, but each day she improved, largely by force of will. By the end of a week she was roaming the halls with the assistance of a walker and a mirrored halo.

Gladys, the boys and I stayed at Molly's house, where we walked her dogs and tried to avoid the oppressive heat. Molly wanted us to at least salvage a couple of camping nights before returning home and combining romance with practicality, I proposed to Gladys while we and the boys sat in a Phoenix pizzeria. She said yes! On August 5, 1995, the four of us drove over the Hoover Dam, checked into the Las Vegas Hilton and called A Little White Chapel.

The chapel dispatched a limousine that took us to the city clerk's office for a license. William and Jacob were our official witnesses. The Cadillac then drove us to the chapel where, in the spirit of how we had met, we recited our vows at the drive-through window. We returned to the Hilton, rented a couple of movies for the boys and went down to the lobby to plays slots, trying to win a fortune. We didn't succeed, but we were now husband and wife. That was jackpot enough for me.

We made a brief stop at Molas Lake Campground, between Silverton and Durango, Colorado. Well above the timberline, it is the highest campground in the state. We camped there two nights and headed home, despite not actually having one to return to. I'd signed a lease for an apartment that wouldn't be ready until the end of August. I had to register Gladys with the police department for benefits and the sake of my insurance but aside from Buck Revere and the chief's office, not another soul knew we were married. Her parents didn't, either. When we returned, Gladys immediately left for a scheduled trip back to Colorado, this time with her brother and sister-in-law. Having no other place to go, I moved back in with Buck. He was always one to rely on.

Chapter Twenty-Two
The Adrenaline-Crazed Brutalizer

Buck Revere and I had little in common other than our mutually shared sense of right and wrong. He always preferred to skip the formalities and get right down to the heart of a matter. There was not a phony bone in his body and he had this innate sense of what was right for everybody. His decisions were always made in the best interests of the public and the department but he never appeared to be enjoying work. Rather he performed with a tireless, stoic energy that allowed him to see every job to the end.

Unafraid of paperwork, he would generate as many reports as policy required. Imposing and snappy, his threshold could be thin, and he would bear down on liars, whiners and anyone prone to beating around the bush. Buck's words never came back to haunt him. He didn't talk out of his ass and he left every victim, witness and suspect with the impression that he knew exactly what he was doing. Which he did, of course, and still does. It was evident in the leverage he brought to bear on suspects who attempted to fight or resist him.

Driving down Church Street one night, we saw a guy walking with an open bottle of beer. We pulled up near him and Buck called him over to the car. The guy ignored him. Buck hailed him a second time, and still he acted as if we weren't there. I stopped the car, and Buck got out and approached the twenty-something subject. The guy smashed his bottle at Buck's feet and continued walking away.

Buck grabbed the guy by his jacket. He immediately spun around and took a swing at him, trying to break away. It was a mismatch. Buck grabbed both his shoulders and pivoted toward the patrol car, thrusting the guy onto the hood with a tremendous whomp. The stunned fellow was in handcuffs a moment later and under arrest for failing to obey a lawful order. He was booked and held until he sobered up. He was heard from again in the form of a complaint letter. Along with making allusions to "storm trooper tactics," he characterized Buck as an "adrenaline-crazed brutalizer." Buck was really more of an equalizer.

Some police officers do pick fights. Despite the number of altercations I was involved with, I did not provoke any of them. Neither did Buck. There are some people who simply will not comply. Intoxication, anger, mental defect, or just a flaw in character can account for most cases of noncompliance. When reason and common sense didn't work, Buck and I took control the way we were trained. It happened at lot.

Honor in the Court

Judge Jack Charles was a Washtenaw County circuit court judge recognized for his eccentricities but also known as a tough law and order jurist. In sentencing a man for assaulting an Ypsilanti police officer, he was quoted in *The Ann Arbor News* as saying, "Anyone who assaults a police officer during the performance of his duty is, if he appears before me, going to jail." It was a refreshing thing to hear, as some district court judges were often erratic in dispensing justice, and Washtenaw County juries had long been sympathetic to a sob story, Hester Carlson's and Greg Heschendorf's cases being prime examples.

Just a night or two later, Buck and I were stopped in front of the Nectarine Ballroom on East Liberty Street at closing time. There was a crowd outside, and at one end we saw a subject screaming at a girl while trying to pull her arm. When she resisted, he punched her several times and then spat on her. Before he could strike her again, Buck came up behind him and grabbed his arm. He whirled around swinging, catching Buck off guard. The kid, about twenty-one, was out of control, and was throwing punches wildly as we closed in to get hold of him. I grabbed him in a headlock, and he began kicking. Buck twisted one of his arms, and we spun him to the ground, right in the middle of Liberty Street.

When a suspect is fighting as if for his very life and you're simply trying to handcuff him, it makes for an awkward dynamic. The three of us lay in the street, with the guy between Buck and me. He was thrashing about, kicking and trying to punch each of us. Buck and I eventually had enough. I punched him on his left cheek, turning his face toward Buck. He countered my punch with another. We alternated this Three Stooges-like smackfest for a few seconds. Finally, he gave in and we got him handcuffed.

We got to the station to find our suspect was none other than the son of the Honorable Judge Charles himself. This would put his words to the test. The son faced charges for assaulting his girlfriend, the assault on Buck and resisting arrest. He filed a personnel complaint against us for using excessive force. Buck and I were summoned to the basement to the professional standards section.

Sergeant Shel Phillips was the section's investigator at the time, as well as the department's media spokesperson. A bit of a square, Shel was out of touch and out of step with current police tactics. The first thing he asked is why we hadn't used our batons to subdue Charles in the first place—this in the midst of the trial for the Los Angeles officers charged with beating Rodney King with their PR-24 batons.

We told Shel we preferred to get bloused and get our man than be filmed whacking him. I rarely used my nightstick as a striking instrument, preferring to use it as a crowbar to pry arms tucked underneath a suspect's body, or to pin his legs down. We were issued collapsible tungsten batons but I kept mine in my locker except when I was ordered to carry it, and even then I locked it in my trunk. I much preferred how the look of my battered wooden baton could send an effective message of its own.

Before Phillips could summarize his findings, the younger Charles withdrew his complaint and elected to plead straight up to all charges. It turned out that the judge had been as good as his quote in the paper. A few years later, Charlie James (my former training officer, now a private consultant) contacted Buck and me during the course of a background check on Charles, who'd applied for a job as a Washtenaw County deputy. I had made lots of mistakes in my life and prior to straightening out had several encounters with the Ann Arbor police, but I never punched or spat on a woman, or swung at an officer. Our recommendation was that his application be declined. We later learned he'd found a police job in Texas.

That Dude Was Me

Buck took the job seriously, but he also easily appreciated the comical side of the work. At 3:00 a.m. one February shift, we stopped to check several subjects standing in a Frank's Nursery parking lot at Washtenaw and Yost. We were in the process of getting their ID's when one of them took off running south on Yost. I looked at Buck, who would be left with four subjects if I pursued him. "Go get him," he said.

The guy had a head start, and rounded a corner behind the Ann Arbor Inn and Suites Hotel. By the time I'd cleared a second corner, parallel to US-23, he was just ahead. Oddly enough, when he cleared the third corner, he ran directly back to where Buck stood with his companions. I caught up to him a few steps from our car and tackled him onto the icy parking lot. There were several outstanding warrants for him, and we put him in the back seat. The others were clean, so we cut them loose.

I got behind the wheel of the car and the prisoner, huffing and puffing in the back seat, started giving me a hard time about "fucking cops," this and that. He told me, "You ain't shit," and went on and on about police harassment. Buck climbed in the car in the midst of the guy's tirade. "The only one of you with his shit together is that cop that chased me."

I wasn't sure what he was talking about. Buck turned around and said, "What is your problem?" The guy went on about cops always hassling him and said the only one he respected was "that dude who caught me." Buck explained to him that "that dude" was me.

"Oh man, that was you? Damn man, you're a fast mother-fucker, aren't you?" I just shook my head and smiled. We were inbound on Washtenaw, on our way to the station, going about thirty-five in a thirty mph zone. Cruising through a green light at Observatory, a southbound car ran the red light and headed right for us. I spun to the left and we came to a stop, side by side with the other car. Only an inch or two separated us. The wide-eyed driver just sat there with his mouth open, looking at an angry Officer Revere.

Our prisoner was even more animated than before. "Oh man, you're a motherfuckin' stunt driver man! You're not only fast, man, you know how to drive!" By that time, I was out of the car and confronting the errant motorist to see if he was drunk. Fortunately, he was not. Our prisoner told us that there was no hurry: "Write that dude a ticket, man." We did. I think it was a good thing that Buck was unable to open his door for a few minutes. The errant driver would have preferred the citation to the lecture Buck would have delivered. We also got a rare hazardous ticket out of the close call.

I thought dispatchers sent me on an inordinate number of

suicidal subject calls but maybe it just seemed that way. I was pretty effective with them. I'd explain the unrelenting torment suffered by those left behind, and that now that I was invested in their cause, their death would add to what pain lingered for me after my mom's suicide. It almost always worked, with one notable exception.

On an otherwise quiet night, Buck and I were sent to the Liberty Square (Tally Hall) parking structure on a report of a man poised to leap off the roof. A city parking employee was keeping an eye on him when we arrived. Buck and I spoke to the potential jumper for a few minutes and were able to coax him down. His name was Richard Bolt and he'd been lured to Ann Arbor in the early sixties for an aerospace engineering job with Bendix. Time and takeovers found Bendix absorbed into other companies and left many of their employees out of a job.

Mr. Bolt was clearly brilliant, but unable to adapt to a different kind of work. He lived alone in an apartment house full of other isolated tenants. We spoke at length and his mouth was so dry that as he repeatedly flicked his tongue a white crust formed on the corners of his lips. He was so deeply depressed that he seemed immune to either humor or hope. The hospital kept him under observation as long as policy permitted and at that point I had a spotless record of bringing afflicted people back from the literal edge. A year later, he stepped in front of a train in the U-M Arboretum.

Patrol partners have a lot of time to think and talk in an eight-hour shift. Sometimes they even devise plans related to work. Two suspects—one white, one black, robbed a series of gas stations and grocery stores over a three-day spree. They were armed and intense, threatening employees and customers alike. They drove a dark-colored Honda Civic and an odd thing was that, in all their service station robberies, they had not once filled up with gas.

Buck and I were discussing the random nature of their blitz, and where they might be headed next. We reasoned that they might be running low on fuel. Buck and I began checking every gas station in town and we notified other units, including Tim Laird and his partner. Shortly before the end of our shift, at the only station we had not yet checked, there they were, pushing their empty Honda up to a pump. We ordered the suspects face down at gunpoint. Laird arrived a moment later, and we scooped them up. They'd used all their stolen money on drugs and had neglected to fill up with gas at a station they didn't rob. When it finally dawned on us what to look for, it turned out our timing had been perfect.

The Hikone Bandit

The Hikone housing complex was just south of Packard Road, across from Buhr Park. Although its name had been an homage to a sister city in Japan, its residents didn't always exemplify a spirit of brotherly love. Tucker Williams was a notable exception, and I'm sure he could cite several neighbors and friends who emerged from the neighborhood a success. But I largely dreaded calls in that area and thought of it as a hostile environment.

Derek Hayes had taken a breaking and entering call there one frigid January where the suspect or suspects had taken the clubhouse television and supplies purchased for the neighborhood Super Bowl party. Buck and I spotted a truck matching the description we'd been given pull into the church driveway next door. We followed it into the lot to investigate. The lone male drove to the far end and spun the pickup around. The surface was treacherous as black ice covered the lot. The temperature hovered at about zero. I could see a television partially concealed on the jump seat from the passenger side and signaled to Buck.

He ordered the driver out and was immediately attacked. The suspect was huge, six-foot-three, two hundred forty plus pounds, and was wearing a heavy coat. I worked my way around to Buck's side, but the skating rink conditions made moving difficult. All three of us were on the ground within seconds. There was simply no footing. It was as tough a battle as Buck and I'd ever had. I radioed for assistance because I wasn't sure we could get the man secured by ourselves. It was the only fight we ever engaged in while crawling around on our hands and knees.

Buck had hold of the suspect from behind as I tried to solve the puzzle of controlling him head-to-head. I wrapped him in a headlock trying to flatten him so we could cuff him but he chomped down on my forearm, clamping his teeth through my four layers of clothing. Now I was pissed. I recoiled my arm and punched his face with my gloved fist several times in succession. He was supporting his weight with both hands so he absorbed the best blows I could land to no discernible effect. The moment he picked one arm up to hit me back, I was on him and he went down flat. The backup unit arrived and the two officers just watched us in detached curiosity as we flailed about. Some cops had an aversion to physical contact but what we needed was assistance, not an audience.

At least Buck and I now had the suspect where we could control him. It just took some doing for Buck to apply the handcuffs around the guy's thick coat cuffs and gloves. We sat there panting for a few minutes while I motioned to the backup guys that we could use a hand getting the burglar to his feet. We were well past the end of the shift booking him, logging in the evidence and impounding his pickup.

My arm bore the imprint of his teeth for a couple of days afterward. Fortunately, I was up to date on all my shots. We made a special provision to record the evidence and return the television and components to restore the Hikone Super Bowl party. When we arrived at court we learned the management company for the complex had dropped the charges on our chronic offender. He merely pled to resisting and obstructing an officer. It was typical of the way in which an officer's most hard-fought work is often dismissed. I had to say I found those punches to the suspect's face more satisfying than the final disposition.

Here's Looking Out for You, Kid

If Buck has a sensitive side, he suppresses it well. But he listens, and offers frank, unemotional and unfiltered advice. In my first stage of depression, I burdened my friends with nonstop ramblings about how things might have been if only this or only that. On a slow night in a patrol car, one can jettison a great deal of emotional baggage. When I bottomed out, Buck was the one absorbing more than anyone else. There's one moment that tells you everything you need to know about him.

On a night I was off, several officers were eating at Drake's Sandwich Shop. Diane Kingman and Nick Stark were discussing my current state of madness and wondering aloud, "What are we going to do about Pete?"

Buck looked up from making a sandwich and said, "I can tell you one thing, you're not going to do him any good talking behind his back."

Diane came up to me the next night I worked and apologized. When I asked her what she was sorry for, she related that story. She wanted to tell me before Buck did. She needn't have worried. He would never have said a word.

Chapter Twenty-Three
Point Man Stryker

My first SWAT assignment had been to cover LAWNET (Livingston and Washtenaw Narcotics Enforcement Team) officers on a buy/bust at the McDonald's on West Stadium. The Special Tactics Unit (STU) stayed plenty busy but that was one of our very public operations. I was proficient with an MP5 submachine gun but the STU team was stocked with cops possessing a mastery of every weapons system. The team had expert riflemen and pistol shooters, and a number of others as good or better than I was with the MP5.

Bob LeGrange assigned me to the entry team from the very start, partly because I could run stairs all day and had demonstrated a modicum of common sense. I remained the STU point man for the remainder of my days at the police department. In addition to fine shooters, we had some very strong fellows over the years. Breeching doors fell to them while I covered our entry point. Being the first in the door and up the stairs or to the back of a house exposed me to some interesting people.

On a drug raid at Pinelake Village Cooperative, I bounded upstairs where a single male was watching a *Cops*-like reality show. On the program, officers were busting into a bedroom the moment I burst into his—a bizarre instance of reality TV meeting actual reality. I ordered the man to the floor, but he wasn't wearing a stitch of clothing. We had to put some clothes on him before we led him toward the stairway. He continually glanced back at the television screen to see if *his* arrest was being broadcast.

We served another LAWNET warrant on Sunset Road. I studied the floor plan and was assigned the rear bathroom in the event suspects tried to flush evidence. I encountered no less than six subjects on the way, ordering all of them to the floor. When I reached the bathroom, I could hear the toilet running, as if it hadn't cycled. I threw back the shower curtain, and a very tall teenager cowered in the corner. I ordered him down and covered him while awaiting someone from the arrest team.

Oddly enough, I saw plastic bags containing what appeared to be crack cocaine lying in the tub. I glanced back at the toilet and saw a stack of large bills spinning around as water kept running. In his haste, the suspect had confused flushing the drugs and holding on to the money. He was one of twelve suspects arrested in the raid.

A few months later the same guy was at a call where several subjects were arguing. I recognized him right away, in part due to his outsized height. This time he was running his mouth, giving us a ration of shit to impress his companions. I said, "Hey, aren't you the guy who flushes the money and gets caught with the dope?" All of his friends started laughing. He clammed right up. Some calls have a way of taking care of themselves.

On February 5, 1992, a court employee attempted to serve an eviction notice on Randy Banks at 125 West Hoover Street. Banks told the court employee he would "blow the place up" if she tried to evict him, and he had nailed his door shut. STU was called along with the hostage negotiation team (HNT). Banks appeared to be alone but regardless, his surrender was preferable to an armed encounter.

Captain Fiske was inside with us but he deferred to Ted Randall, Seth Connery and me to make a plan for the entry. We rehearsed a scenario where Connery would ram the door and I would lead the team through. In the meantime, Banks was talking to negotiator Vic Mitchell. He hung up on him several times but gradually Vic wore him down and was ultimately able to talk him out.

This turned out to be a very good thing. Unbeknownst to us, Banks had a booby-trap crossbow setup that would have impaled the first officer through the door. I had a renewed respect for negotiators. The next day was a training day where Tim Beamon tested our vest against his crossbow. We had a heavy strike plate we could insert but we never did. When the crossbow bolt hit the vest without it, the results weren't good and it failed miserably.

Gone But Not Forgotten

Not every SWAT assignment involved a stranger or turned out with a sigh of relief. Danny Sager was a Vietnam veteran turned chef who cooked at a couple of U-M sororities and senior living facilities. When he wasn't working, he could frequently be found sipping coffee at the Washtenaw Dairy.

I talked to him a lot and he treated me as an equal, not in the condescending way some veterans viewed civilian police officers. His stories were often filled with regret. He missed the friends he'd made in Vietnam. Danny frequented a trading post in northern Michigan and once he bought POW/MIA license plates for Bob Beaufort and me. That plate has adorned the front of my trucks ever since.

One night our SWAT team was training with the county on North Campus when we received a call of a barricaded gunman on South Main. Turns out it was Danny. His estranged wife had arrived at the senior facility and made some demands that set him off emotionally. He asked her to leave and when she refused, he retrieved a pistol from his office and fired a round into the wall for emphasis. While their son swept her away, Danny discharged another round and closed himself up in the room. I listened to this information while I drove the SWAT van to the facility and was glad I would be the one to get the chance to talk him out.

We staged in the dining room, outside of Danny's kitchen and Lt. Tony Herrera set up a command post in the lobby. Chief Stan Coates wandered away from Tony's briefing and suddenly appeared between our entry team and the kitchen doors we had targeted. He was like an NFL team owner, wandering onto the playing field to watch a crucial play and the lieutenant physically dragged him out of harm's way. All the while Danny was refusing to answer his phone and would not respond to any of my attempts to talk. He had classic rock blaring through the kitchen's sophisticated sound system.

I led the entry team into his spotless kitchen. The chrome gleamed and you could have eaten off the floor without worrying. The door to Danny's office was closed and we moved into position to confront him. I was no longer glad to be there. The prospect of exchanging rounds with my friend made my mouth go dry. I pleaded with him once more to surrender as I thought of all the animated talks we'd had and how much I personally liked this haunted veteran—but there was nothing. We used a passkey to get the door open. Danny was sitting there with his gun in his hand. He had used it on himself, finding a way to rejoin his missing friends.

I sat through the station debriefing in a daze. I walked out to my truck, saw the POW/MIA plate on the front, and wept all the way home. Danny Sager had succumbed to wounds inflicted thirty years earlier. He'd done his best to adjust to civilian life but it was clear his heart belonged to his unit. Every time I see the silhouette on that plate, it's his face I see. He is gone now but hardly forgotten.

Fishing on the Bridge with Boaz Gregory

Police officers aren't supposed to get lulled into complacency or let their guard down, but it happens. Sergeant Boaz Gregory and I had driven to Lansing on an errand to pick up tactical cold-weather gear from the Michigan State Police warehouse. We drove all that way only to find the gear had been picked clean by another agency just moments before we arrived.

Boaz and I headed back toward I-96. It was just before noon, and traffic was congested. Construction work on the freeway and the bridge made matters worse, and I had trouble figuring out which lane to be in to get back on I-96. The bridge overpass was snarled. I crept forward, eyeing the entrance ramp signs when he said: "Hey look, they're fishing off the bridge." I had no idea what he was talking about and didn't care. Traffic had ground to a halt.

Someone suddenly pounded on his window. We both jumped about a foot. A woman motioned frantically and Boaz rolled the window down. "There's a woman jumping off the bridge! *Do* something!" she screamed. Boaz picked up the radio mic, but we were about thirty miles out of range. The only sound was static. We were in uniform, in a fully marked patrol car, but out of patrol awareness mode. We went from condition white to condition red in a matter of seconds.

The situation couldn't have been much worse. Seventy miles out of our jurisdiction, on a bridge jammed with lunch hour traffic, while bystanders gawked at a diminutive Asian woman perched precariously on the bridge railing. I-96, about thirty feet below, stretched with motorists as far as the eye could see. She balanced directly across from our patrol car. How Boaz mistook her for a fisherman was beyond me. We took a few steps toward her and then split up, silently motioning to the crowd to move way back.

Boaz started speaking to her as she faced the empty lanes of eastbound 96. She turned her head around toward him in an eerie, trance-like, slow motion. She looked to be in her sixties but was not feeble by any means and certainly looked like she knew what she was doing. I sure didn't. Boaz had a knack for some things and talking was one of them. As I've mentioned before, addressing suicidal subjects is delicate business. I don't recall exactly what he said, but had her listening. He moved to a spot where she was forced to crane her neck to see him, and he offered his help. This allowed me to get in a position directly behind her where I couldn't be seen.

We had an audience of over one hundred people. It was strangely quiet, except for sirens in the distance. Gridlock prevented any local first responder from arriving quickly. Construction workers had stopped freeway traffic in both directions, closing the lanes below. I inched closer to where she perched, making sure I stayed out of her peripheral vision. She never adjusted her footing. She was cool, like an aerialist on a rounded railing. With no margin for error, I could very easily push her off myself if she didn't leap before I reached her. Boaz kept spinning, emphasizing the great outcomes of just stepping down.

A Lansing patrol car pulled up at the far end of the bridge beyond her and opposite of me. A stocky officer moved Boaz's way while his partner redirected traffic. The woman's attention shifted between Boaz and the approaching officer. This was my chance. I skirted the concrete wall of the bridge and sprinted up behind her as fast and as quietly as I could.

I thrust my left arm beyond the railing and over the freeway, preparing to scoop her inward. The Lansing cop started running toward us, and Boaz stepped back and yelled, riveting her focus directly at him. His timing was perfect. I wrapped my arm around her waist as I leaned inward, trying to change my momentum.

We both landed on the roadway with her partially on top of me, just as the Lansing uniform arrived. He grabbed her and called her by name while Boaz helped me up. She gave me the most quizzical look as she was handcuffed, canting her head to one side as if I were a curious specimen of some sort. The Lansing officer led her back to his car without even asking who we were.

I was numb. Boaz and I got back in the patrol car and my hand shook so much that I could scarcely put the key in the ignition. "Fishing on the bridge?" I asked. We both broke out in uncontrollable fits of laughter. We said nothing, but shared intermittent looks at each other, sparking more hysterics. I was so wired I could barely drive. Boaz pointed to an exit with a Big Boy restaurant and we plopped down in a booth just staring at each other. The waitress came up and asked what we wanted. We both burst out laughing once again. Her annoyed look made it worse. Boaz waved her away and asked for a few minutes.

Finally we ordered lunch. The waitress must have thought we were on experimental drugs or somethinig. She tossed our food and bill on the table and stormed off. We decompressed on the way back to Ann Arbor, where Lt. Shel Phillips scolded us for being late when we arrived. We never heard another word about the incident. Eventually Boaz Gregory retired as a deputy chief, never receiving due credit for his extraordinary job of diversion.

Chapter Twenty-Four
The Ann Arbor Serial Rapist

When Officer Mel Haynes was dispatched to check the victim of a brutal sexual assault in Eberwhite Woods Park in September, 1992, neither he nor anyone else realized we were looking at the beginning of a long nightmare for the community and the Ann Arbor Police Department.

For the next several months there came savage attacks on women that some veteran detectives thought were random crimes. But Marilyn Kelly believed she'd detected a pattern. She had worked on an inordinate number of CSC (Criminal Sexual Conduct) reports and had become recognized as something of a departmental expert. With innate skill and much experience, she believed we were seeing the work of a serial rapist and reported this to Detective Joe Hazard after an assault she'd taken on Miller Road. He wasn't convinced.

An apparent breakthrough came after a nighttime attack on West Liberty Street near the Eberwhite Woods on September 3, 1993. The victim could only describe her assailant as a black man and a K9 track by Greg Stockton and his dog Homer led directly to a residence on Carolina Street. The occupant claimed he had been out picking up videos at the time of the assault but his alibi sounded contrived, especially to Christopher Sager. The Hollywood Video store on West Stadium Boulevard was closed by then, preventing us from either confirming or refuting his story and the uniformed officers present remained skeptical.

Dispatch called the lead investigator in the Eberwhite Woods assault, Detective Matt Schubert, at home. Aloof and obsessively organized, he was considered one of the top dogs of the major crimes unit. Matt treated anyone with less seniority as if they lacked the mental capacity to absorb what he knew, so he tended not to share very much. During my in-service detective training, Schubert had been in charge of the investigative photography block of training. He showed me how to use various cameras and told me to walk throughout the building and take pictures of all the attractive women I knew. I'm afraid I disappointed him and he wound up with a lot of building and vehicle photos instead.

On the night dispatch called him, Schubert's message to us on the Carolina Street track was to advise the suspect, Samuel Irving, to come see him during business hours. Irving was given a polygraph, which he passed. A criminal check showed he'd pled guilty to an assault charge in Inkster, Michigan, but Schubert, compulsive about the neatness of his desk and files, showed only a passing interest in the likely suspect.

This was unfortunate. A little more digging would have disclosed that Irving's original charge in Inkster had been for *sexual* assault and the reduced charge was the result of suppressed evidence due to a tainted search. Irving's DNA sample was still on file with the Michigan State Police but a comparison wasn't requested. Schubert essentially eliminated Irving due to the polygraph and granting Samuel Irving's freedom would be costly. Christopher Sager would monitor him in the coming months, but the continuing attacks were so sporadic, Sager could not synchronize with them.

A Grim Discovery

On May 7, 1994, the husband of Claudia Gallagher reported

her missing and overdue at home. Gallagher was a member of the undergraduate admissions staff at U-M. Alex Pritula had taken the initial report on the afternoon shift and mentioned the odd nature of her disappearance to Sergeant Henry Jasperson. When Andy Michaelson and I reported to our midnight shift, Jasperson sent us to Gallagher's apartment to retrieve photos to pass out to officers.

The Gallagher home was filled with well-meaning friends and family, but the atmosphere was chaotic. Mr. Gallagher and I stepped into another room so he could brief me on the day's events. Claudia had placed a pot of beans on the stove before running to the store for a couple of items while her husband lay down for a nap. When he awoke a few hours later, the over-heated beans had scorched the smoking pan and his wife hadn't yet returned. Mrs. Gallagher's coat and umbrella were also gone; a cold rain had persisted all day.

Gallagher handed me a stack of pictures of his wife, but I thought we ought to look for her before returning to the station. Alex Pritula hadn't had time to search and I thought his hunch that this was an urgent call was right—Claudia would have been home had she been able. It was clear the group crowding in their apartment was making Mr. Gallagher anxious and I asked whether he'd prefer to be doing something other than sitting around. He jumped at the offer.

He and I set out on foot. With Michaelson monitoring our route from the patrol car, I asked him to show me the likely way his wife would have taken to the drugstore at West Stadium and Liberty Street. The most direct route ran through their apartment complex and right down Stadium. As we were walking, I told him of the trip that Gladys and I had just taken to Virginia Beach and how on that bike ride with another couple she'd fallen behind, leaving me anxious and worried.

I explained how Gladys had fallen ill during the ride and had simply pedaled back to the store where we'd rented the bikes to get some aspirin. He appeared a little relieved that these frantic moments worrying about his wife could turn out to be just a simple mix-up but I wished I was more convinced this story was heading the same way. A walk to the store on that route revealed nothing, and by that hour the drugstore had closed. I asked if there was another way she might have taken and he told me they sometimes cut through the Boulevard Plaza behind the post office on Stadium.

The miserable rain continued. Many of the stores in Boulevard Plaza had been shuttered up for some time, and the lot as well as the path heading south were dark and desolate. Michaelson pulled onto Commerce Drive at the other end of the path to wait for us near their apartment building. As I was walking ahead on the narrow trail with my flashlight, something caught my eye off the path to the left. I shined my light over that way and Mr. Gallagher said, "Oh my *God*, that's her stuff!"

A red umbrella lay open on the ground alongside a backpack and two-liter bottle of soda. It was an ominous sign. To spare him the shock of seeing more, I took him the length of the path to our patrol car and placed him inside with the police radio turned off. I told Michaelson what we'd found and called Sergeant Jasperson to come meet us on the path. He was already on his way and arrived in just moments. We went back to where the items lay and shone our flashlights along both sides of the trail. Michaelson had a Super Magnum light that found something under a clump of bushes. "There she is," he said.

Claudia Gallagher lay twisted but face up in the rain. Her slacks and underwear had been pulled down to her ankles. There was no sign of life remaining in her thirty-two-year-old body. We called dispatch and asked them to call in a department chaplain to meet Michaelson and Mr. Gallagher at the station. Jasperson posted me on the trail with Mrs. Gallagher while a full detective division callout was conducted. If this was the work of our serial rapist, he had just escalated to murder.

A steady, bone-chilling drizzle settled on Claudia Gallagher's last path. It was the first time the nature of a call or the presence of a victim had given me shivers from the inside out. We'd transitioned to short-sleeves on May 1st and the rain continued to fall on my hat cover and thin poncho. Because it was a crime scene, I was confined to a specific scope of movement to ensure its preservation. I wanted so much to cover her exposed body but I couldn't.

I thumbed through the stack of photos her husband had given me. She was smiling and enjoying the spirit of living in all of them. Police officers get a sense about people they meet and those they just hear about. I got that Mrs. Gallagher was as genuinely nice as she was portrayed and guarding her body bonded me to her like few other victims of any crime. The wait for the detectives was interminable.

When Officers Matt Fontaine and Bruno Stevenson arrived, they summoned me to the Boulevard Plaza end of the trail. Fontaine's window went down, and he extended a tall, capped Styrofoam cup of hot coffee—they had just left Gladys at Dom Bakery and she'd sent me a personal cup of Joe. It was the best-tasting and timeliest cup of coffee I'd ever had.

This was a Saturday night and several detectives were attending a party. It took forever before they arrived and among the first to reach the scene was Sergeant Ron Lindsey. I escorted him up the path, showed him the umbrella and the groceries—the point of the initial attack—and where Claudia Gallagher had been dragged several yards away. Having completed my in-service detective training, I was ready to help process the homicide scene but Lindsey produced a clipboard and paper from his car and instructed me to keep a log. I was to note the time and names of the personnel entering or exiting the designated crime scene area.

At first I thought he was kidding. It was our diligence that had prevented the victim from being discovered by an innocent passerby. It was our call and our crime scene. Holding a clipboard seemed like such a dismissive assignment. I was seething. Lindsey told me that my job was as critical as any he'd assign that night.

It was a full-blown detective division callout but a few of them arrived showing the effects of the party they'd attended. Lindsey assigned them accordingly. Those not showing one hundred percent effectiveness were given administrative tasks, not evidence collection duties. It turned into a very long night, and when dawn broke they sent a day shift car to assist me in a thorough search of the area beyond the immediate scene perimeter. We hoped the suspect had discarded or dropped something that would reveal his identity but we found nothing we could link to anyone. I was numb from the cold, damp rain and the grim image of the scene was embedded in my mind.

The murder sent a rippling wave of fear through the community. The anonymity of the previous sexual assault victims had placed some distance between them and the general public but the killing of Claudia Gallagher put a face as well as a name on a victim. The reality that there was a predator among us prompted many women to take proactive steps to protect themselves. Self-defense class enrollment skyrocketed, as did handgun sales.

A multiple-agency task force was formed to process the tips the department was counting on. So far no victim had gotten more than a furtive glance of the man. He was described as a black male, twenty-five to thirty-five years old, five-foot-seven-inches to six-foot-two-inchues tall. The severity of injuries he'd inflicted on his victims suggested a degree of strength while the savagery of the attacks spoke to his depravity.

An FBI profile did little to illuminate the suspect. I spent a good deal of my own time compiling clues. My hunch was that he lived in the geographic area where most of the assaults took place, possibly as a renter. It was likely that he worked at manual labor or, as so many suspects we dealt with did, in a restaurant. His obvious contempt for women made it logical that he had been a domestic assault suspect at one time or another. The attacks revealed we were dealing with a very angry man.

My suggestion to the task force was to interview owners of

rental property and landlords in that geographical boundary to see if our vague description rang any bells about their tenants. I knew that building department files were complete and up to date and since many landlords owned multiple buildings, using these would make the prospect of contacting each one less daunting. It seemed like an easy way to narrow the search to a manageable number of suspects but the task force rejected my idea. They didn't want to use outside resources.

Ron Lindsey had another idea. In the mid-1980s, a pair of rapes and murders that occurred three years apart baffled police in an English village. The DNA found on both victims matched but they had no physical description of the suspect. Police had the novel idea of gathering blood samples from men and teenage boys from not only their village but neighboring ones. Although nothing was found initially, co-workers advised police that a subject had falsified his identity in an attempt to avoid giving the blood sample. His DNA turned out to be a perfect match.

Lindsey read a book on the subject of blood samples. He suggested the task force launch a similar campaign to eliminate suspects. The theory of the English police was that no innocent person would object to helping solve such heinous crimes. The general description of the Ann Arbor serial rapist fit about one thousand African-American men in the community but unlike the willing English villagers, they took their presumption of innocence seriously. They felt no compulsion to aid a police department that had maintained a dubious relationship with them for many years.

The task force kept regular hours and drank gallons of coffee but the job of soliciting the blood of these men of color fell primarily to the road patrol. As hard as it was to justify in our own minds that such measures were warranted, it was significantly harder to sell it to our clients. The absurdity of the initiative had a peculiar irony for my partner, Tucker Williams. Had he not been a police officer, he would have been a likely candidate to provide a sample himself.

In our briefing, we were routinely given names of men they wanted brought involuntarily. The ability to broker compliance had always been one of my strengths but my creativity and ingenuity were severely taxed when trying to summon up a good reason for men to submit to the needle. The friction of this task eroded what little credibility we enjoyed with these men.

One night, several weeks into the search, Tucker and I were told to bring in B. D. Holden, a frequent customer of the AAPD. That night, we stopped him on the west side in a car with several women. Evidently, they were all current girlfriends. We asked him to step out of the car so we could talk. He was well aware of what was going on and he extended his arm toward the car full of women and asked us, "Does it look like I need to knock women unconscious to have them?"

It really didn't. Tucker and I looked at each other, shaking our heads. I told Holden he was free to go, but asked him to contact the task force the next day to submit a sample and get crossed off their list. He did just that. The entire patrol division was fed up with the indiscriminate nature of the search. The situation was compounded by the multiple police contacts that each man was subjected to after he had already complied. They were understandably angry, and they vented it on those of us who dealt with them on a daily basis.

The Michigan State Police Crime Laboratory retained the samples of those eliminated as suspects. They reasoned that such samples could solve an infinite number of future crimes. That logic would prompt a lawsuit from a random sampler, who ended up losing his job during the investigation. The fact was that we already had a sample from the true culprit; it just had not been compared to the DNA recovered from the victims. Finally that mystery was about to be solved, on the annual day of miracles.

Early on Christmas Eve, 1994, a man attempted to grab a

woman's purse and then attacked her on the west side of Ann Arbor. Responding Officers Scott Hardin and Bob Beaufort thought the actions of the suspect matched those of the serial rapist. Communications Operator Kendra Johnson called area cab companies to give them a thorough description, calling him a man of maniacal strength, distinctive also in that he wore a dark jacket and white gloves.

This was another typical Christmas Eve night, with holiday double-time stocking the two midnight shifts with officers. As was my custom, I brought in several movies to run in the squad room while officers rotated through, helping themselves to food brought in by holiday-spirited citizens. Riding with Tucker, we went to assist Officer Jay Edwards on a burglary call on North University Court. We checked five apartments and found several of them had been broken into, so we split up the reports and hunkered down to do the follow up.

Then early on Christmas morning, a Yellow Cab driver called to report a subject matching the description from the night before. Lindsey Guyer dispatched the call of a black male walking north across the Broadway Bridge, wearing a dark jacket and white gloves. He also carried a brick. Officers scarfing food in the squad room streamed out the back door and into their cars.

Officers Larry Stevens and Tim Laird won the race to the Broadway Bridge. The suspect surrendered without a struggle and it was none other than Samuel Irving. He was transported to the station where the upper echelon of the detective division descended. When Officer Mack Sinclair exited security I didn't yet know the suspect's identity and I asked, "Is this the guy?"

"I think so," he said. He was right.

I regretted being mired in paperwork while the arrest of a career was spending his last few moments of freedom walking just a quarter mile away. But it gave Tim Laird and Larry Stevens a different kind Christmas story to tell their grandchildren in years to come.

The Trial of Samuel Irving

As it turned out, we'd had the right suspect back in September, 1993, after all. Detectives often dismiss the impulsive notions of patrol officers because they're paid a premium wage and are supposed to be smarter than the rest of us. But sometimes the best ideas come at a bargain price. Several officers had a feeling about Irving but the assigned detective came up a step short by deciding not to verify their hunches. Instead the department checked the DNA of hundreds of random men and ignored the suspect that should have been first in line. Irving must have wondered why he was passed over.

He went on trial in March of 1995. The best evidence against him had been gathered at the scene of Claudia Gallagher's murder. Ron Lindsey may have misjudged the effectiveness of the large net we cast to draw blood samples, but he'd made no mistake protecting the homicide crime scene and preserving that evidence. That clipboard I'd manned made me an important witness. It also helped refresh the memories of several detectives and supervisors.

District Attorney Ryan Nichols handled this high-profile case personally. Eccentric and seemingly self-absorbed, Nichols had never said more than a passing "hi" to me. He was often seen walking with his eyes to the ground, scavenging for lost coins around parking meters. By all accounts he was a brilliant lawyer, as I was soon to find out. Nichols summoned me to his office for a pre-trial briefing and we went over my report thoroughly. I had relived the events of that time during many sleepless nights and all of it was etched into my mind. Nichols was satisfied that I was ready.

The insolent Irving appeared detached in court. He coveted the media frenzy the trial brought him and he did not look at all worried. His court-appointed attorney, Kevin Barnhart, did not appear as confident. I'd dealt with Barnhart when I was working in the detective bureau and I thought he was sharp and easy to get along with. He was an honorable attorney with a loathsome client and he had his work cut out for him.

In the hallway outside the courtroom, I ran into Mr. Gallagher. It was the first time I'd seen him since we found his wife's umbrella and groceries two years before. The corridor was packed with witnesses and media, so I invited him to join me for a cup of coffee in the courthouse café. He'd remarried and I was happy to see he looked like he was doing okay. He told me how vividly he recalled my story about Gladys disappearing when we were on vacation and how many times he'd wished for a similar outcome to his own story. He was grateful to have taken part in finding his wife, though. He felt as if he had at least done something, contributed. I understood this.

Irving was charged with five assaults, beginning with the jogger in Eberwhite Woods that Mel Haynes handled, and ending with the assault and robbery of the woman on Dexter Avenue on December 24, 1994. My testimony focused strictly on Claudia Gallagher. Prosecutor Nichols asked me to recount the events that led to her discovery. He asked me to describe, in detail, the scene as David Gallagher and I had found it.

Irving stared right at me as I testified to the site description, the location of Mrs. Gallagher's items, and the position of her body. I saw him scribbling on a legal pad next to his attorney. He wrote something down and pushed it over for Barnhart to read. Barnhart never changed expression as I continued testifying. Then Nichols placed the crime scene photographs on the table attached to the witness stand.

It was the first time I had ever seen them. A *Michigan Daily* photographer snapped a picture at the moment I looked at them and my reaction said more than any caption ever could. It was a stark reminder of the grim image I had been trying to expel from my memory since that night. I looked through the stack and testified that the photos were an accurate depiction of what we had found. Barnhart waived cross-examination.

Later that very day, a retirement party for a veteran officer was held at the Zal Gaz Grotto Club on Ann Arbor's west side. I was standing in the front room when Kevin Barnhart walked in. It took some grit for him to appear. Suspects and their defense attorneys are often linked in the eyes of police officers and his current client was among the worst. I for one was glad to see him as I walked over, shook his hand, and asked the question that had nagged me all day.

"Kevin, what was it that Irving wrote on that pad and showed you while I was testifying?"

"It said you were lying," he replied.

I thought for a second. "I wasn't, but even so, how would he know if he hadn't been present at the scene himself?"

"That is precisely what I wondered," he said.

Samuel Irving was convicted on all counts. He wasn't going to escape the truth. He could practice his icy glare on his cell-mate as he spent the rest of his life locked up as a predator. His surviving victims could rest assured that he was gone.

Chapter Twenty-Five
Out On a Limb, Alone

"Community oriented policing" (COP) was a national trend in law enforcement that followed our new Police Chief from Minneapolis. It was designed to empower citizens and break down barriers between communities and their police. As charismatic as Chief Thomas Jones was, I didn't share his optimism for a program geared at community engagement. Calling the police was one thing; inviting them to your barbeque was quite another.

Ann Arbor was divided into four districts and a coordinator was assigned to each one. My shift lieutenant asked if I'd consider taking the downtown coordinator spot and he schmoozed me by saying that once an officer with my reputation got on board, it would legitimize the entire program.

As I approached my fortieth birthday, I had a much-needed, three-week vacation planned. I still wasn't sold on the COP concept. The lieutenant added that as a coordinator I would attend the weekly crime meetings and may be able to influence how patrol officers were deployed in the COP program. I much preferred effecting change to complaining, so I finally agreed. I'd have a patrol car and could largely freelance calls but first the first three weeks of that assignment were spent in Florida with Gladys.

During my stint as Adam district coordinator, I attended all the requisite meetings and luncheons. I also managed to lead the gas team in a full-scale riot response at City Hall following an appearance by the Ku Klux Klan. The event was widely reported in the national media and while clearing the street in the aftermath I was struck in the head by a cinder block. My Kevlar helmet saved my life.

I also made an off-duty arrest of a juvenile who'd assaulted my wife Gladys while she rollerbladed in Burns Park near my old elementary school. While leading the suspect to a summoned patrol car, I was confronted by former mayor and current state representative Bev Slater, who insisted I release the boy immediately.

A small crowd of curious bystanders gathered, and Gladys explained what had happened as Representative Slater eavesdropped. When she heard Gladys had been assaulted she turned to me and said, "I didn't know."

"That's never stopped you before," I said.

Slater was notorious for butting into the middle of Ann Arbor officers taking action without her knowing the circumstances. Later, after pleas by his attorney for leniency were rebuffed, the suspect pled straight up.

But the most memorable experience as a coordinator occurred on the grounds of another school I'd attended. It was an ambush I would have never expected.

Huron High Homecoming

I spent three years at the Ann Arbor Huron High School and excelled only in writing, PE and anonymity. I didn't care for school when I attended and a call twenty-two years later did little to enhance my memory of the old alma mater. What began as a request for help disintegrated into a small-scale riot.

Matthew Caswell was one in a long line of liaison officers at Huron High School. It was a job I couldn't imagine doing. On Wednesday, October 23, 1996, a student witnessed a drug transaction go down in a school restroom. A staffer escorted one kid involved to the office when they passed the primary suspect. He refused to cooperate, and Caswell was summoned. He called for assistance, so I responded from the district office downtown.

When I pulled up, Matthew was following a lanky kid across the driveway and into a parking lot. Caswell was in plainclothes; I was uniformed. There was a crowd of about thirty kids behind Caswell, presumably agitated over his pursuit. I cut the kid off between two cars, and he tried to bull rush right through me. He continued to be aggressive and I spun and threw him face down on the ground, but he was wiry and evaded my attempts to cuff him. Caswell joined me on my right, and together we had him pinned. But before we could control his wrists, the crowd descended on us.

One guy tried pulling my gun from its holster, while another repeatedly punched me in the back of the head. A very large girl, later identified as Tiana Daniels, kicked me repeatedly in the left temple with the toe of her boot. School principal William Arthur and two assistants stood facing us to prevent an attack from that side, but they were also taking punches and swipes. It was all I could do to keep a hand on the suspect while retaining my holstered sidearm. At one point, one of Daniels' kicks snapped my shoulder mic from my sweater epaulette. I couldn't grasp my dangling microphone so I hit my emergency button.

Daniel Arguello and I had ridden together a lot on day shift. Daniel knew me well enough to know that if my emergency button was activated I really needed help. He broadcast a ten-thirteen (officer needs emergency assistance). The fight continued, and the crowd around us swelled as word spread around the high school. I was able to get good looks at the guy trying to snatch my gun, the subject punching me from behind and, of course, the distinctive Tiana Daniels. She stood about five-foot-eight-inches and weighed two hundred fifty pounds. It felt like a considerable amount of that was brought to bear in her foot.

Help arrived shortly, and lots of it. Ron Russell, who seem-ingly did nothing but complain about the department and show up when I needed help, was among the first. We handcuffed the guy I'd initially tackled and stuffed him in a patrol car. Russell looked at me shaking my woozy head and asked, "Who else do you want?" My assailants had tried to slink back into the crowd, but their images were seared into my aching head. I walked around the crowd and pointed them out to Ron one at a time. Ron Russell was a buzz-cut, two hundred sixty-pound martial artist who always wore black gloves, even in short-sleeve weather. No one interfered with him.

Russell snagged the three wide-eyed suspects, and they too were cuffed and placed in waiting patrol cars. The entire shift, as well as a large contingent from the station, had responded to my call including our first female deputy chief. Administrators didn't often leave their office to assist on anything and I was grateful for the rapid arrival. Matthew Caswell was taken to the hospital for treatment, but I refused to leave the site. Rumors circulated that there would be a disturbance after school, and I wasn't going to miss it. We staged for an hour in Gallup Park, across from the school, but nothing else happened.

I came in the next day to complete my reports but Deputy Chief Jerry Lane sent me home. I was suffering some memory lapses and had trouble concentrating. I sat down in our living room with a glass of ice water, only to see I already had three more on the table next to me. I had a weeklong headache and was sent for a CAT scan. As I suspected, they found nothing. It was my fifth or sixth concussion, I believed, but I'd lost track.

Tiana Daniels spent nearly a year in the Washtenaw County Juvenile Detention Center and was convicted on aggravated assault charges. Guilty as she was, her defense attorney didn't help her much. The public defender's first question when I took the stand was, "Officer Stipe, exactly when did you realize you were in full uniform the day you arrested my client?"

"Um, when I got dressed?" I wasn't grasping where he was

going unless he was suggesting Tiana didn't know I was a cop when it was obviously the reason she'd targeted me. I requested to be reinstated to the road the next week. Administrative positions were much too stressful.

Months later, another officer and I stopped a car in which Tiana Daniels' older brother was a passenger. The driver was giving the other officer a ration of shit. I asked the Daniels kid, "If I were on the ground, you wouldn't kick me in the head, would you?" It suddenly dawned on him who I was. His jaw dropped and he shook his head in a definitive no. He slapped the driver's arm and told him to shut up and cooperate, which he did. There was a powerful psychology in suggesting what someone wouldn't do.

You Can't Make This Stuff Up

Arriving first on calls was a natural instinct for me. It made me anxious to think of anyone out there waiting for help or assistance, and they weren't going to wait long if I could help it. There were definitely times when I'd found myself feeling alone, even when a partner was present, and those made for some anxious moments. A lot of the action was to be found on midnight shifts but there were plenty of hair-raising episodes that took place in broad daylight. Some of the fights we faced were struggles for life or death and over the course of my career I'd found myself in a few of them.

Point Blank

Joe Faulkner was a community mental health (CMH) professional working for Washtenaw County. In the winter of 1997, he and his partner brought a petition for committal to the Ann Arbor Police Department for immediate service. What he might have thought was a routine commitment turned out to be any-thing but.

Willis Portman was a seventy-seven-year-old World War II veteran living in a low-income senior citizens' high-rise. His war experiences in the Pacific left him embittered toward anyone of Asian descent. War wounds left him with a disability and pronounced limp in his leg that required the use of a cane. He used that cane to assault two Asian doctors who tried treating his mental infirmities at the VA Hospital. This prompted them to sign the petition.

On the day we served it, I was riding with a police recruit whose training officer was off that day. Normally two full-fledged officers would handle such a call but Shift Lieutenant Shel Phillips was shorthanded. Weren't we always? The department estab-lished policies on staffing certain calls for a reason and we'd be reminded why shortly.

Willis Portman may have been seventy-seven years old, but he was well over six feet tall and weighed one hundred ninety plus pounds. He lived in Miller Manor, a regular stop for west side patrols. I informed him of the purpose of our visit, and that we needed to give him a ride to the hospital. It was bitterly cold outside and he asked if he could put on some shoes.

Willis was likely leaving home for the last time. Extending the courtesy befitting a disabled vet, I agreed to let him put on some shoes. The condition of his leg required him to sit on the couch to tie the laces and as he did he fretted about two disability checks he didn't want to leave behind. He was worried about someone he characterized as a thieving neighbor. A stack of letters was piled on the cushion next to him and he muttered about his checks as he sorted through them. Then, with the subtlety of a cardsharp, he tucked his hand behind the seat cushion and I knew my trust had been betrayed.

I drew my sidearm and closed the distance as he revealed what he was holding: a dark, two-inch revolver. At gunpoint I ordered him to drop the weapon. He brought it up and directed it at me. We were a mere two feet apart. Once again I ordered him to drop his gun, inserting assorted expletives for effect. He did not respond. I parried his gun with my left hand as I jumped on his lap, pinning his legs with my right knee and shin. I held his arm against him and pressed my pistol against his chest, ordering him to drop the gun.

I'd been in many armed encounters, some where shots were fired, but I'd never been in one where I could smell the breath of my adversary. His eyes showed neither resignation nor fear and I think he wanted me to shoot him. I honestly pictured tomorrow's headline: Police Officer Shoots Elderly, Disabled, Mentally Ill Black War Veteran! There was a technique I'd just learned in a dignitary protection course I could use to strip the gun out of his grip. It worked, and I secured his pistol, holstered my weapon, and whipped a handcuff around his left wrist. The fight was on.

Willis was someone who was used to doing what he wanted, and at the moment he did not want to be cuffed. He was the strong, silent type and I needed the timely assistance of CMH's Joe Faulkner, who weighed in once the guns were out of the picture. The new recruit had sought cover in the bedroom but emerged to assist Joe and I in finally getting Portman secured. I offered Willis an unsolicited rant about his actions and I think Joe considered a second petition request before I finally calmed down. My emotions and my adrenaline dump had left me shaking.

We drove Willis to the VA Hospital and returned to the station where Lt. Phillips lectured me for exposing the rookie to such a close call. The incident was discussed in the weekly crime meeting being held in the squad room, which brought significant criticism for my failing to handcuff Portman immediately. My shift sergeant, Ted Randall jumped to my defense, noting that the policy of assigning two experienced officers and not just one had not been followed. Ted also commended my quick action and restraint and his support meant a lot. It was all I got on this call.

I took Willis's revolver to the property section to log it into evidence and got my first good look at it. It was a starter pistol.

Bus Stop

As district coordinator, I had no assigned calls and could respond to whatever I wanted to. When I switched back to road patrol, I found little had changed. My mind was sometimes more conditioned than my body but helping others was the reason I was out there. But there were sometimes I needed more help than the citizen who called in the first place.

One such call came in late 1997 when a snow removal employee from Detroit suddenly bolted his crew and hopped on an Ann Arbor Transit Authority bus on Eisenhower Parkway. He walked toward the rear seats, popped the roof hatch, and climbed into the frigid air atop the moving vehicle. The frantic driver called his dispatcher and they in turn dialed 911.

Afraid to stop and challenge the subject, the driver continued downtown to the main terminal with the man pacing the rooftop, screaming at passersby. I arrived on Fourth Avenue when the bus did. The subject was pointing at passengers waiting at the terminal while I hopped aboard and headed to the open hatch. I climbed onto the roof, and the fight was on. The blustery wind and slick surface made it nearly impossible to stand. The crazed man was determined to push me off onto what looked like a very distant street below.

As we struggled, I swept him off his feet and dragged him toward the open hatch. Help arrived in the form of beat man Jim McCoy, who popped out of the opening and snatched the guy down into the bus like a vacuum. The man had simply snapped. He was raving as we led him off the bus and into a waiting patrol car. There are certain times when you feel your life is hanging in the balance; when backup arrives to pull you back, you are eternally grateful. This was one of those times.

Randy & Andy and the Martial Arts

I rose in seniority as the retirement ranks grew. I took Fridays and Saturdays as my leave days so I could spend more time with sons William and Jacob. Sundays were usually pretty quiet, at least in the morning, and my shift ended at 2:30 p.m. Stress fractures in my feet had become a constant problem, however, and I wasn't running as much as I once had. I paid the price for my lack of conditioning one sunny Sunday afternoon.

Gerald Kung was a twenty-seven-year-old Ford Motor Company engineer on a medical leave of absence due to a mental disorder. He'd been harassing customers at the McDonald's restaurant in the Galleria Mall at Forest and South University avenues for weeks. He'd hover around innocent diners, lunging at them with his car keys and acting strangely. There had been several previous calls, but I had yet to deal with the guy. I was in front of my old house, talking to my boys, when the call came in that the troublemaker was back. Dispatch had sent two cars but I wasn't far away, so I responded, too. It was still my habit to arrive first, which only meant something if the assigned units actually showed up. In this instance, I was not only first, but I was alone.

The property manager pointed out an Asian male seated at a table in the Galleria lobby. He'd frightened away all the customers from the neighboring businesses, as well as an employee who had simply been monitoring his behavior. The property owners wanted the trespass statute read to him in an attempt to keep him from returning.

He looked at me and walked out to the South U sidewalk. As I followed after, he spun around, cocking his arm back as if to throw a full-size drink on me. I pivoted behind him, grasping his forearm to prevent him from drenching me and told him that he needed to produce some identification. He bent forward, thrusting his right foot back and kicking me in the shin. He then spun around and punched me in the mouth.

Kung leaped into a martial arts fighting stance and proceeded to go berserk. He launched a series of blows and kicks at me that I deflected with varying degrees of success. He was extremely fast and landed several body blows, also nailing me with more of those kicks in my shins. I drew my nightstick and was able to block his next series of attacks, but I was done with the fist-of-fury treatment. Kung lunged at me again, and this time I threw my left arm over his head, secured him in a headlock, and threw him to the ground.

I still held my nightstick in my right hand, which made it impossible for me to gain control of either of his wrists. I laid it aside to free both hands and he grabbed it and began jabbing me in the back with it. He raised it up over my head, and I knew I had to get better leverage. I pushed forward and pinned Kung against the wall of the building.

He still held the baton aloft but now he was unable to effectively use it. The property manager stepped forward and ripped it out of Kung's hand. I had him where he couldn't move, but at that point I was too gassed to cuff him. I was not in my customary shape and I was sucking wind. We'd been fighting for several long minutes and I wondered why the other cars hadn't arrived yet.

I listened to the radio traffic. Warren Meyer, the downtown beat officer, had gone to the wrong location and seeing no one there, advised dispatch that Kung must be gone. The double car that had been sent drove right by without seeing our fight because we were on the sidewalk behind a line of parked cars. I would have thought the crowd gathered around us would have caught their attention. Anyway, I was on my own. Kung was a good six feet tall and one hundred eighty pounds—not supersized, but he seemed bent on destroying me; I'd never absorbed so many blows. We continued to struggle for control. He later admitted to Sgt. Roy Frazier that he was trying to kill me, but he hadn't been able to get a good strike at my head.

Several citizens called 911 to report the struggle, and they broadcasted the fight. Rob Innes responded all the way from the west-side office, and I was grateful for his arrival. He helped me flip Kung over and get one handcuff on him. But Kung continued to struggle, and we needed the assistance of Rick Rakowitz to apply a second set of cuffs so we could link them together. As Innes transported him to security, Kung tried kicking the windows out of his patrol car.

I was spent, and my adrenaline dump left me shaky. I was also pissed at Meyer, who never seemed to be where you needed him when you needed him. For some, being late is a chronic affliction. I was so tired after that arrest. I pledged to never again let my conditioning slide and leave myself vulnerable to to that kind of struggle. That had been more than enough. Kung was not only charged with assault but with disarming a police officer, a felony.

This incident shook me up in a couple of ways. Tiana Daniels' heavy boots had added to my list of concussions and now Kung had delivered more blows and kicks than I'd ever taken at one time. My standard takedown move often involved absorbing some hits, but this had been more like going through a twelve-round fight with a bonus round. Had Kung succeeded in killing me, he might never have gone on to create the "Randy & Andy Panda" children's book series, teaching kids to speak Chinese. Maybe it was a lucky break for both of us that I lived.

Always On Duty

For a number of years, I commuted to and from work in uniform. It saved me having to dress between the relative widebodies of Benny Dyer and Ron Russell, whose lockers flanked mine. Stopped at a red light at Division and William streets on my way to work one evening, a car pulled up in the lane to my left, with a passenger pointing a pistol at me. I drew my gun and pointed it back, recognizing his as a .177 caliber pellet gun. His eyes widened seeing my uniform and Sig Sauer, and he shouted to the driver to take off. They turned against a red light onto William, and I holstered my weapon.

Detective Jim Wysocki pulled up in an unmarked car where they had been just a moment before and asked what had happened. Before I could say anything more than they'd pulled a gun on me he took off in pursuit. He called for a marked car to make a traffic stop, and the occupants of the car were arrested.

I put my gear in the squad room to get ready for briefing and poked my head into security in time to hear the passenger deny he had pointed his gun at anyone. I stepped into the doorway of the interview room and his shoulders sank in resignation; he'd been exposed and he knew it. Reminded by Wysocki that I might have shot him, he gave up a full confession.

Looking for a Bargain at Payless Shoes

On an afternoon off, I went to Payless shoes in Arborland to find some running shoes. The store was divided into three main aisles, separated by display racks. A man of Middle Eastern descent who looked to be about forty was browsing for shoes with his young daughter. I was seated with my back to that side of the store when I heard him raise his voice: "You did that on purpose." Someone had bumped into him deliberately. I stood and turned to see he was speaking to a late-teenaged skinhead in the company of a girl and another guy dressed like him. The younger man swore at the father and told him if he didn't shut his face, he would kick the father's ass.

The daughter recoiled in fear. The group of three passed through my aisle to the other side of the store.

I went up to the tough guy and told him very quietly, "The most dangerous opponent you can choose is a father in the presence of his children. Many will sacrifice their lives to retain their dignity. You may think you have the advantage with your friend over there. But in this instance that dad has me to back him up, and take my word for it, you'd regret that."

"He bumped into me," he whined.

"Not likely," I said. "You frightened his daughter. Go apologize."

The sight of that frightened girl had me wound up. I wanted to throttle this kid and his smirking friend. I think the skinhead sensed my total investment in the matter. He walked over to within a few feet of the dad and daughter and said, "Hey, I'm sorry."

I sat back down to resume trying on shoes when the father came over. I stood to meet him. "I appreciate whatever it was you said to that kid," he said.

"It's nothing," I replied. "I just told him that calling you out in front of your daughter was a very dangerous thing to do. I also told him that although you didn't look like you needed backup, if you had, I was more than willing to pitch in."

His look of genuine gratitude made me feel great. Payless employees had watched the entire scenario unfold without summoning security or making any effort to intervene. They made out okay for themselves when our random trio of customers all made purchases.

The Pow Wow Baby

Ann Arbor hosted an annual Dance for Mother Earth Pow Wow, organized by the Native American Student Organization, like the one held in January, 2003. Several ceremonial events were scheduled at varying Ann Arbor sites over a selected weekend and many of the attending families roomed at the declining Ann Arbor Inn and Suites hotel.

A Native American couple had been up late celebrating with friends after returning from the pow wow. They'd gone to bed at about 3:00 a.m., placing their infant son on the mattress between them. When the mother woke up she found the boy unresponsive. I was just about a minute away and was the first unit to arrive. Their hotel room was packed with grim-faced, heavyset Indians. The mother sat on the edge of the double bed, cradling and rocking the child. I asked to see him, but she just stared at me and sobbed, refusing to give up her baby. Firefighters and paramedics arrived and there was a commotion at the entry door between them and the sentries posted there.

I ordered everyone but the father and a female firefighter into the hallway and enlisted their help in getting a look at the baby. The mother was catatonic. "Can we both hold him?" I asked. I put my hands on the boy and could feel he was stiff. We had a momentary tug of war as I wrestled him out of her grip. There was no breathing and no pulse. I tried to pass the baby to the firefighter, but the mother screamed and flailed her arms at her. "You hold him!" she told me. The firefighter summoned an HVA paramedic and they both examined the boy while I held him.

Gladys and I had welcomed a son into the world the previous March, and we'd named him Bronce—this boy was almost the exact same age and my heart was breaking. The paramedic looked up and confirmed the boy was dead. The mother insisted I not give her baby to anyone else and I called for a supervisor, a detective and the medical examiner. It was excruciating to hold the lifeless boy while they made their way to the eastern outskirts of town. If I tried setting him down, the mother would go into hysterics. I'd worked with the firefighter on several south side calls and she recognized my discomfort. "I'll stay with you," she promised.

The parents were both big people. Their bodies wouldn't have left much space between them in the room's double bed. They appeared bleary-eyed and wrought out from a combination of drinking and grief. The coroner never informed me whether we had a case of sudden infant death syndrome or if it was an accidental asphyxiation—it didn't matter. The situation was so bleak and depressing and I was especially thankful for my children's good health.

Years before, I had been dispatched to a "baby not breathing" call on Hemlock Street in Ann Arbor. I'd arrived far ahead of the fire department and Huron Valley Ambulance. The hysterical mother thrust the unresponsive infant in my arms and I covered her nose and mouth with my own, and gave her a series of quick puffs. Within just a moment or two she came around.

I offered her back to her mom, but she shook her head and began heaving and sobbing. The baby in turn, seeing her mother in distress, began to cry. That emotional moment was then interrupted by the arrival of the girl's aunt, who marched directly over to me, snatched the infant from my arms and snapped, "Give me that baby. You're making her cry." The mother silently shook her head, but her eyes expressed appreciation. Better a crying baby than one at eternal rest.

A Day Shift Reunion

There was a reason I wound up working days. I suppose I thought I'd meet a better class of people out on calls. One night, a disengaged partner and I were sent to a fight on Hemlock Drive on the south side. Two rival girl gangs filled the street, punching, kicking, ripping hair and throwing bottles. I wrestled with one of the principals for a few moments and finally got her cuffed.

My partner stood by as the suspect's adversary drilled a bottle at us. I put my hand up to block it, shattering the glass, and the resulting cut required both stitches and a tetanus shot. Was this the last straw, making me want to shift to days? Yeah, it was. I was particular about whom I rode with and Buck Revere and I had just enough seniority to secure the last two-day shift spots. Months later I saw the girl I'd arrested and she apologized for getting me hurt and was grateful I had blocked the bottle. It wasn't all her fault— my partner had been too slow to react.

I was assigned to the south side, along with Marilyn Kelly—

my former best friend—and Daniel Arguello. At first she was a little prickly with me: she probably thought I was going to get weird on her, but I'd come a long way since our past together. We had the good fortune of alternating our rides with Daniel, who was a constant beacon of calm in an often turbulent department. He served as the perfect buffer for the two of us.

I brought something of a wound-up midnight mentality to day shift. I liked getting suspects cuffed immediately—I'd chased far too many through darkened alleys and backyards. Daniel and I were sent to several businesses to serve warrants or arrest suspects for one crime or another. I was a little nervous when Daniel wanted to escort them out of their work area and to the car before handcuffing them. He didn't want to unnecessarily humiliate them in front of co-workers or customers. It took me a while to get used to this form of discretion.

Daniel had an utter calmness about him, almost a Zen-like composure. His dad was a respected professor and Daniel displayed the same kind of scholarly patience. I don't recall ever once hearing him raise his voice. He was among the department's most senior officers, having been on the road since 1971. As a dispatcher he was unflappable, clear and cool under pressure. If he had any sense there was tension between Marilyn and me, he never let on. I was even able to have some fun at her expense, alluding to my sudden brush-off a number of times.

Only a handful of officers and administrators knew about my marriage to Gladys and I realized how well off I was with her. She let me be myself and she didn't see any of my baggage as a burden. I was in a good place, and Marilyn was, too.

Marilyn always liked gossip when someone else was the topic. One time I intrigued her by mentioning that I'd found out one of the dispatchers was married only when she'd answered the door at a towing company with shampoo in her hair; she and the company owner were living quietly in an apartment over the garage.

"There's another officer with a marriage you don't know about," I told her casually.

She was hooked.

I wouldn't tell her who it was and I made her guess by going through a standard process of police elimination, and although she narrowed it down she couldn't figure it out. When I finally told her she was looking at him, her jaw dropped like an oven door. She hadn't had the slightest idea. That was a sublime moment for me and it made me interesting to her again. I rationed more information little by little over the course of a few weeks. It took the edge off our relationship and any concerns she'd had about the two of us vanished. She'd always enjoyed my sense of humor and now I had that back.

I came to both like and respect her husband Mark, too. He declined a promotion to sergeant, preferring to take on a tough job as liaison officer at Pioneer High School instead. The next time I went to assist a high school officer, the results were much better.

One day while picking up lunch at Busch's Market I heard Mark Kelly call for assistance at Pioneer, just two blocks away. Two guys were scrapping on the ground, and Mark was making contact just when I arrived. We picked up the bigger and more aggressive of the two and started to lead him to my patrol car. As the suspect began struggling to escape, I did a leg sweep, which slammed him hard, face down on the ground. That took the fight out of him. As I resumed leading him to the car, I looked to see my son Jacob watching. I saw him turn to tell another kid that I was his dad. We got nothing but cooperation from that moment on.

Marilyn and I teamed up for several felony arrests on that shift. One was particularly gratifying as the suspect had just been released from juvenile confinement for a series of sex crimes. Somehow he got off his bus and wound up in one of Ann Arbor's most affluent neighborhoods. He knocked on a woman's door off Melrose, asking for directions and wanting to come in. Something about him instinctively made her close the door but he pushed back, trying to force his way inside. He had his hands on her when she screamed, finally prompting him to run.

Daniel Arguello was the dispatcher and Marilyn and I were in separate cars, coming from the south-side office. Something about the inflection in Daniel's voice lent an extra urgency to the call and we flew up to the neighborhood of sprawling estates and luxury homes. I saw the suspect running to the rear of a house on Devonshire at Londonderry Road and I screamed up the driveway, sliding to a stop on the side lawn, leaving twenty feet of skid marks in the grass.

I chased him to the rear and onto Vinewood Boulevard, where I tackled and cuffed him. Marilyn was right there with her car and transported him downtown. He was a big kid, a six-foot-two-inch, two hundred-pound nineteen-year-old, but he had run a long way. A very large veteran officer once advocated "staying with the Motorola" (the patrol car) as long as possible before bailing out. It allowed the suspects to expend more energy. As I got older, that advice made more and more sense when I was chasing down kids twenty-five years younger than me.

It turned out the victim in this case was the wife of an old Granger Avenue neighbor. Their gratitude and our renewed teamwork made it a very satisfying effort. The kid was convicted at trial and sent back to jail. Marilyn and I had been in perfect sync as to where we needed to be and the result was a great day shift arrest.

Chapter Twenty-Six
Instinct vs. Policy

The Detroit Police Academy never discussed racial profiling. Our tactical officer and sergeant were both black and they would address the volatile nature of police/minority encounters and emphasize discretion in what one said and did. The issue was also never mentioned in the Ann Arbor Police Department in-house academy. It just wasn't something we consciously thought about. We stopped people who we believed were up to something. We didn't target African-Americans, Hispanics or hillbillies.

We didn't need a contrived excuse to check someone out. Moving violations gave us all we needed to pull someone over. If there wasn't a moving or equipment violation, an officer relied on factors that, based on experience, added up to suspicious activity. The location, time of day, absence of other traffic, subject behavior, patterns of crimes and suspect descriptions all combined to arouse suspicion. If we believed someone posed a legitimate threat, we patted them down for weapons. The U.S. Supreme Court upheld the legitimacy of those instincts in Terry v. Ohio, 1966.

The New Jersey State Police had been routinely seizing large quantities of drugs and cash en route from Florida to New York using their drug interdiction training program. The concept was simple: stop particular new or rental cars and see what they have. There was a list of indicators that suggested which cars should be stopped but the driver profiles tended to be consistently Hispanic or black males. Unfortunately, the Ann Arbor Police Department made the misguided decision to invest in this sort of interdiction training. Like many agencies, they had been tempted by the promise of large returns.

I suppose the AAPD was envisioning an influx of cash from drug dealers they could use to buy equipment and fund additional training. One large bust by Anthony Herrera and his LAWNET crew—made after a thorough, unbiased investigation—netted a storage unit that contained several hundred thousand dollars. That money paid for the department's first K9 tracking dog. But doing interdictions like the New Jersey troopers would have required officers to prowl I-94 and US-23 at the expense of being able to respond in the city of Ann Arbor itself.

The New Jersey program came under intense scrutiny when the Middlesex County public defender's office claimed a disparity in the ethnicity of out-of-state motorist stops. All such programs were suddenly stopped, and various agencies scrambled to conduct damage control. Ann Arbor initiated racial profiling forms we used to document every single driver encountered on traffic stops.

We'd gone through a series of "sensitivity training" sessions where African-American scholars scolded us for carrying on longstanding traditions of institutional racism. Officers were often sent there as discipline for a founded personnel complaint, which was probably a formula for failure. It seemed that a far more logical solution could be to have the training instructors accompany officers on a ride along in order to gain their perspective and see what the officer saw. Then they'd be in a better position to deliver their lecture. I was in favor of anything that would help solve the problem. I'd lost my mom as a casualty of the civil rights movement and I was not the one standing in its way.

A Washtenaw County Sheriff's Department "specialist" offered training to "deprogram" Ann Arbor officers from their perceived ethnic discrimination practices. Their agency was no less culpable for the credibility gap with our constituency and his haughty tone came across as hypocritical. As for his program, I was equally unimpressed.

I'd been groomed in an era when officers used their instincts to make investigatory stops. When Chief Justice Earl Warren rendered the majority opinion in Terry v. Ohio, he called those feelings we'd get about certain cars and people, their actions, and what we were seeing "routine habits of observation." Race and gender had little to do with it. But now, regardless of cause, every motorist contact was being closely scrutinized. Police critics were seeking a pattern that simply didn't exist everywhere.

The tally numbers from the submitted profile forms suggested little other than the wide ethnic blend of Ann Arbor residents and University of Michigan students. Still, the spotlight was on, and the implied message was clear: don't rock the boat. Aside from simple moving violations, officers refrained from stopping persons of color unless they had specific information about a certain subject.

Road patrol officers disengaged in checking suspicious behavior unless the department received a call from a verified source. Descriptions of suspects had to be detailed and specific. Instincts were set aside, unloaded and placed in a display case along with antiquated weapons and processes. It changed us all. I became so cautious and conscious of the constant micromanaging I let it interfere with my better judgment.

On July 16, 2003, the TCF Bank on Plymouth Road was robbed of $17,527 by two heavily armed men. A witness advised 911 operators that two black suspects had entered the back seat of a dark-colored Lincoln driven by a black female before fleeing the bank lot. Marilyn Kelly and I responded and positioned our patrol car on the entrance ramp to southbound US-23 at Washtenaw Avenue. We saw a dark blue Town Car pass by and got only a glimpse of a woman driver.

We stopped the car at the I-94 interchange. I carried a G-36

.223 caliber assault rifle slung over my shoulder, and Marilyn had her pistol drawn as we flanked the vehicle. There were no passengers inside, and the driver was a white girl of about twenty years. Carla Renfrew obviously wasn't black and we thought we must have the wrong car. A Pittsfield township officer had all southbound lanes of US-23 blocked and traffic stretched back toward Washtenaw Avenue. I recall thinking about the professional standards lieutenant and what he would think if we searched a car driven by a black woman if the driver had been described as white. I applied the same standard to the reverse scenario and we released Renfrew and returned to our spot.

A few minutes later we stopped a second Lincoln, this one driven by a middle-aged white woman. She, too, was let go. Eventually, at the end of our shift, we left and began an Ann Arbor Art Fair assignment patrolling downtown on foot. Partway through our detail we got a message to call Detective Lesley Brooks. She asked us for details of the first Lincoln we'd pulled over earlier and told us that we actually had stopped the robbery suspects. The witness who had provided the initial description left the scene and had to be tracked down. When she clarified her account, she said two black males climbed into the *trunk* of a Lincoln driven by a *white* female.

Robbery suspects Walter Leonard and Cal Phillips had been lying in wait if we'd ordered Carla Renfrew to open the trunk. Marilyn and I felt sick to our stomachs. We'd done everything right by being in the right spot and stopping the right car, but then we immediately disengaged when the racial disparity in the description arose. It is okay for witnesses to be mistaken, it's quite another for the police to be.

It is hard to say just what would have occurred had we tactically opened that trunk. The sure-shot Marilyn had been armed with her 9mm, and I had the high-capacity G-36, but Leonard and Phillips were also armed and keyed up from their takedown robbery. The exchange may have turned out ugly. We will never know.

The vehicle was registered to Leonard (a white Taurus decoy car driven by robbery mastermind John Gregory was following the Lincoln in the traffic backed up on US-23). When it was traced to their hideout in Detroit that afternoon, the money was recovered and the suspects taken into custody. Our stop made the identification, arrest and recovery possible.

But it was little consolation and something of an embarrassing episode with just seven months to go before retirement. Letting armed suspects go like that gnawed at me. I'd been trained to be one hundred percent sure of racial impartiality. The new policy left no gray area allowing for witness fallibility. We wouldn't detain a black motorist for a suspect described as white—it would be an outrage. Did that theory not apply in reverse? In the old days, I would have allowed for witness error, inspected that car thoroughly and justified my hunch with time, proximity and experience. Had we been wrong we would have cleared the car and apologized for any intrusion.

It was the first time I'd felt hindered and my performance negatively affected by political correctness. My citizen complaint record was nearly spotless. Every officer receives complaints of targeting African-Americans; this was a common strategy by some suspects for sidestepping responsibility in criminal or civil actions. It's true that had they never been unjustly harassed, the tactic wouldn't work, but it wasn't the way we did business. And in this case, Marilyn deferred to me and I'd let the armed bank robbers go.

After I retired, FBI Special Agent Joseph Hanrahan subpoenaed me to testify when the case was heard in federal district court in Detroit. Hanrahan never hinted at our misstep; on the contrary, he commended our stop as being the pivotal step in bringing an active robbery ring to justice. John Gregory's gang had struck several banks throughout southeast Michigan. The agent also reminded me that opening that trunk would have likely resulted in a dangerous shootout. He said he preferred it the way it was. Marilyn accompanied me to court for support and to refresh my memory. But what happened still bothers me to this day. It could be that God was just ensuring that the shift we worked in July, 2003, wasn't my last.

Chapter Twenty-Seven:
A Who's Who and a
Conversation with Gregory Peck

I had a few celebrity encounters in twenty-five years of city service. Future First Lady and First Mother Barbara Bush came up behind me, massaged my shoulders and announced her husband's candidacy as I sat at my building department desk typing in late 1979. She was quite unforgettable.

I'd trained two notable former Michigan athletes, Mel Haynes and Bobby Hodges. Haynes soared to five blocked kick attempts in a single season for the Wolverines before fulfilling a lifelong ambition to become a police officer. He combined a child-like curiosity with superhero athleticism to become one of the department's finest. His combination of street sense, good humor and speed helped acclimate him quickly. He and former Notre Dame cornerback Larry Stevens made for an effective neighborhood tandem.

Haynes' character was best exemplified by his courageous battle against cancer. He was as puzzled as anyone as to its random nature, but that didn't diminish his resolve to face it head on. The twenty-year veteran continued to serve his community in limited duty, and offered more support than he accepted. He passed away in 2011. I was riding with him the first time he called his badge number 155 into service, and wept at his grave-side when the dispatcher called him out for a final time. Few men have displayed such grace and dignity either in life or in death. He is missed very much.

Bobby Hodges was a forty-year-old rookie when he joined the Ann Arbor Police Department. Born in Canada, he'd acquired American citizenship and attended the police academy after an eleven-year NHL career and a stint at Domino's Pizza. His lean playing physique had bulked up into a stocky frame that, combined with his hardened look, lent him an imposing presence.

It was easy to see why Bobby had been so successful in every endeavor he'd undertaken. He had a talent for grasping the nature of complex situations immediately. As a defenseman in the NHL he'd earned three Stanley Cup rings, including two with the legendary Wayne Gretzky on what's considered the greatest team in league history. Bobby adapted just as quickly to defensive tactics in the streets, becoming one of AAPD's finest instructors. He was particularly adept at practical demonstrations.

A ticket scalper fled from us one football Saturday but Hodges caught him several blocks away. When the suspect resisted efforts to seat him in the patrol car, Bobby delivered a knee strike to the common peroneal nerve in his leg. It wasn't serious but he ceased resisting. Three weeks later, at the next home football game, we saw the same subject in the same spot. He turned for a moment as if to run, but the pronounced limp in his right leg made him reconsider. Bobby Hodges knew how to deliver a blow.

Sparky and Dutch and the Man on the Moon

As a National Hockey League champion, Hodges had long been exposed to luminaries, once sipping an after-dinner scotch with Gerald Ford, a fellow Michigan alum. He considered it his pinnacle moment. Bobby's wife was an editor at Sleeping Bear Press. They launched their company with a series of books spotlighting local personalities and they invited Gladys and me to several book publication parties. Among them were events for radio personality J. P. McCarthy's biography and Detroit Tigers manager Sparky Anderson's autobiography.

At the Sparky event I was introduced to writer Elmore "Dutch" Leonard. I'd long been an admirer and *Get Shorty* was about to be released amid much anticipation. I told Dutch how much I liked *Mr. Majestyk* and *Hombre* and he shared his writing ritual with me. He wrote every day, getting up early with coffee and usually writing from 9:30 a.m. to 6:00 p.m. He had his "10 Rules of Writing," the best of which was number ten: "Leave out the parts readers tend to skip." He hand wrote his manuscripts on yellow legal pads and then typed them up on an electric typewriter. No editing was necessary. "That's what I went to college for," he said. Honestly, I was more thrilled meeting him than I was Sparky Anderson.

Hodges and I once had a chance encounter after stopping a Lincoln Town Car that made a prohibited turn at Huron and Main. The four men inside were dressed in pinstripe suits and the driver explaining that they'd gotten lost coming from an Allen Ginsberg benefit at Hill Auditorium. Backseat passenger and REM lead singer Michael Stipe leaned over to remark, "Officer, we share the same last name."

I recognized him right away but acted like I didn't, just to mess with him for a moment. A month earlier, after an REM concert at Crisler Center, he'd hosted sons Jacob and William in his backstage dressing room. He and bandmate Mike Mills signed shirts and posed for pictures. My two boys had been through a lot with my divorce and it was a timely and generous gesture on Stipe's part. I thanked him again for his kindness and got the car reoriented. His driver was visibly relieved.

* * *

Knowing my affinity for film, Bobby Hodges once asked me what celebrity I would most like to meet. My first choices would have been Jimmy Stewart and Robert Mitchum, but they died a day apart in July, 1997. In June, 1999, the No. 3 guy on my list came to town as a stop for his speaking tour. Gregory Peck got the idea from the reclusive Cary Grant, who had strictly limited his post-retirement public appearances to similar events for decades. "A Conversation with Gregory Peck" would open with a handpicked montage of film clips, after which Peck would engage the audience with personal anecdotes. This would be followed by a one-on-one question and answer session. When I saw the ad for his appearance at the Power Center in Ann Arbor, I immediately called Deke Bernard.

Hunter Bernard's older brother Deke, or "DK," started working for the University of Michigan right after graduating from Eastern Michigan as an accountant on the medical service plan. He ultimately became the business manager and administrator for the University Music Society (UMS) and helped rescue them from financial disaster. He oversaw the thirty-five million dollar restoration of Hill Auditorium and revived the Ann Arbor Summer Festival.

I asked DK if it was possible to simply meet Peck after his show. For me, Gregory Peck epitomized strength, integrity and restraint on screen. His Atticus Finch was voted the top father figure in cinema history and the American Film Institute's list of Top 20 Actors of All Time had just been published—Peck was ranked twelfth. He was one of only three members of the list still living and he was the one I most wanted to meet. DK called back and asked, "How would you like to have dinner with him?" That would be the ultimate. "Tickets are seven hundred dollars a plate... but I can get you and Gladys in for one hundred." Deke Bernard's gesture was one I will always remember.

* * *

Pete & Gladys and Gregory

We were going to dinner with Gregory Peck. I was wound up and worried about what to wear, what to say and how to act. I'd watched Peck's films since they first aired on television, and he was a bigger than life figure to me. *Twelve O'Clock High* was my favorite. His General Savage was just the kind of boss I liked working for, and I'd had some great ones that were much like him. We spent the week leading up to the event at the Wolf Lake cottage owned by Gladys's grandparents. I was trying to come up with a strategy for not making a fool of myself.

I figured Peck would be hounded by autograph seekers and the last thing I wanted to do was impose on him. I decided to give him something instead, something very important to me. When the Ann Arbor Police awarded me the Medal of Valor and two Distinguished Service medals, I was also bestowed with three *Ann Arbor News* Awards. Those six medals were the most prestigious recognition I'd ever received and they validated the bona fide effort I put into being the best cop I could be. I decided to give Gregory Peck one of my medals as a token of the influence his humble characters had on me. They related to the qualities needed to be an effective law enforcement officer.

I composed an accompanying note:

> Some people watch movies simply to be entertained. But those of us who draw inspiration, strength, and self-confidence from the role models in films have been enriched by your portrayals for a lifetime.
>
> Surviving a crisis takes training and experience. It also helps to see it done. Your poise and composure in any number of roles has served as an example to me. I want to thank you for bringing something extra into my life—in some ways, even life itself.

I was all set for my big moment with the legendary film star. The question I had was if an opportunity to present my gift would materialize. June 19, 1999, arrived and the day ticked away slowly. Our daughter Darby was born May 8th, the month before, and would be watched by next-door neighbors while we attended the event. I put on the dark suit I wore for circuit court appearances and Gladys dressed in a black-on-black pantsuit. In a small satchel we packed the medal, my note and *Life* magazine's *Twelve O'Clock High* issue from February, 1950, with Peck on the cover—just in case an autograph was offered.

We sat on the main floor of the Power Center while the lights dimmed and the screen flickered with a montage of vintage Gregory Peck moments. Clips from *The Big Country, Spellbound, Twelve O'Clock High, Roman Holiday, Duel in the Sun, To Kill a Mockingbird* and dozens of others flashed by. The curtain rose and the tall, distinguished figure of Gregory Peck stepped into the spotlight to thunderous applause. He, too, wore a dark suit with a blue shirt and tie. Although his long hair was gray, his eyebrows were black above a salt and pepper beard. He looked like the legendary figure he was. He sat in a wooden studio chair and held court for nearly two hours.

Peck answered a number of questions posed by audience members. I was too nervous to ask one myself, and couldn't summon up one worthy of his time. After the program ended a white stretch limo awaited us outside on Fletcher Street. Carole Holmes, wife of Indy racer and Jiffy Mix heir Howdy Holmes, joined Gladys and me. Carole cranked the air conditioner down to sub-zero for the ten-block ride to dinner.

A canopied red carpet extended from U-M's School of Education outdoor courtyard to where we were dropped off on East University Street. A string trio played while bartenders filled glasses of Chardonnay and we awaited Peck's arrival. I placed my satchel by our table and met Gladys at the bar. Mayor Elsa

Hammond and her husband, Paul, soon arrived and joined us. I asked her where she was sitting and she sheepishly answered, "At the main table."

"Um, of course," I said. We killed time chatting about children, greyhounds and public speaking.

With no announcement at all, Gregory Peck suddenly appeared. He extended his large hand to me as I stammered to introduce Gladys to him and his wife, Veronique. Here he was! This was my big chance to present him with my medal and... I'd left it at our table. I looked beyond him at the satchel, which sat at the far end of the giant dinner tent. He was engaging me in a personal, one on one conversation, and inside I was panicking. Other dinner guests were descending on our private talk and I saw my opportunity evaporating. I don't even recall what we spoke about.

Dinner guests who had paid full price to rub shoulders with Atticus Finch quickly surrounded us. He graciously greeted each one and I scurried to our table to retrieve the box holding the 1989 *Ann Arbor News* Award. When I returned, some pillar of Ann Arbor society was dominating Mr. Peck's time and personal space. She went on and on, or so it felt, punctuating her rant with animated gestures. I tapped my foot, waiting for just one more second of his time, but the wait staff came and coaxed us to our respective tables—the moment was gone.

Our tablemates owned a local printing company and we were all enjoying the Chardonnay immensely, but I restricted myself to one glass in the event another chance arose to speak to the guest of honor. The seven-course meal included entrées of roast vegetable strudel, sesame salmon and roast venison loin. While waiting for the main course to be served, Gladys removed the *Life* magazine from the bag to show our companions. The black and white photograph of Peck in a black bomber jacket and goggles was impressive.

"You'd better get that signed in a hurry," our table mate said. "He's eighty-three years old. How many courses do you think he'll live through?" Questionable humor aside, Gladys sprang up from her chair, snatched the magazine, and walked over to the main table. She knelt down between the mayor and Gregory Peck, wrapping her arm around his shoulder. They paused their conversation and Gladys dropped the magazine down between them saying, "Can you sign this for me?" He stared at the magazine for a moment, as if he'd never seen it before. The others seated at the table rose up far enough to get a better glimpse of it.

"Where did you get such a rarity?" Mayor Hammond asked.

"In an antique shop," Gladys said, and the table roared with laughter.

"I wish you hadn't said that!" Peck said.

Gladys offered, "It was the best-looking picture there." More laughter.

"What is your name?" he asked Gladys. She said "Karen," offering him a Sharpie pen we'd brought, just in case. He signed it: "For Karen – Gregory Peck."

She returned to the table beaming, and looked at me. "Sorry your name isn't on it. I thought I'd asked too much already."

"It's alright," I said, happy for her. But time was running out on my big plan.

I tried one last gambit. I approached festival promoter Marti Stasiak and told her of the gift I had brought. She said there would be a toast, followed by an announcement of dessert, and I should look for my opening then. Anxious and clutching the blue velvet case containing the medal, I moved off and found a spot slightly behind and to the right of Peck. He was absorbed in conversation with the mayor, and I waited for her to notice me there.

She saw me and stopped speaking. I stepped forward and extended my hand. He took it in a firm handshake grip and just as I was about to speak, Marti came up behind me, put her arm around my back, and said, "Mr. Peck, this is Peter Stipe. He is the most highly decorated officer in the history of the Ann Arbor

Police Department. He would like to present you with something." He quickly rose to his feet and turned to look directly at
me.

I opened the box revealing a bare-breasted Lady Justice,
leaning on the handle of her huge sword. I said, "Mr. Peck, I
received this medal ten years ago. It means a lot to me, but it
would mean even more if you would accept it as a gift. You and
your characters have been an inspiration to me, and I want you
to accept this as a token of my appreciation."

Mayor Hammond added, "Peter is one of my finest officers."
I felt the blood surge to my face and head.

Gregory Peck looked at the medal and then at me, saying, "I
am deeply honored. Are you sure you want to part with this?"

"I know you've been honored by many great institutions and
have received many awards, but this one represents law enforcement and your influence on my success. I want you to have it."

"This is the greatest I have ever received," he said. "I am
deeply grateful."

Veronique Peck motioned to an open space between his chair
and the mayor's and said, "Get him a chair."

"Yes, by all means, sit down," he said.

I snatched an empty seat from a nearby table as the mayor
sprang up offering her own to me. I declined, placing the one I'd
grabbed next to him. His finely crafted wooden cane lay on the
grass between us. We engaged in the most exhilarating talk I
have ever had. I handed him the envelope containing the note
putting the gift in perspective. He opened it, partially removing
the contents, and asked, "Is your address in here?" I assured
him it was. The lighting was dim, and he folded the envelope
closed and slipped it into his coat pocket.

I told him his characters from *Pork Chop Hill*, *Twelve
O'Clock High* and *To Kill a Mockingbird* convinced me he
must possess the qualities of courage and restraint he portrayed
so convincingly. He explained he was working on his book of
film and life anecdotes and was about forty pages along.

Four months of the year they lived in France among sixty-five acres of olive trees, three mules and a goat. Every morning the goat barged into his open-ended kitchen and munched on his Kellogg's All-Bran or Post Toasties cereal. While he struggled to come up with a book title, it suddenly dawned on him that he saw it every morning: *The Goat Is in the Kitchen.*

During the Q & A part of his appearance, one woman had posed a political question about "justice in America." He asked me how I thought he handled that question and added this was supposed to be a fun night, not a controversial one. I told him his answer was concise and smoothly deflective, making it clear questions of that nature were off topic.

He thanked me again for the medal and said he was deeply honored to receive it. "It is the finest award I have ever received," he said. I was well aware it wasn't, but I appreciated his generosity just the same. Marti Stasiak snapped a photograph of the two of us talking, then she asked if he wanted to pose for a picture with Gladys and me. Gladys slipped in between us, leaving a gap on either side. He wrapped his arm around her and said, "Get in here!" The resulting image makes it appear as if she is his date.

With that, the dinner wound down and we shook hands for the last time. Marti promised copies of the pictures, and each pair of guests received an autographed copy of *To Kill a Mockingbird.* Souvenirs were the last things on our minds as we floated home on a cloud illuminated by a yellow gold halfmoon that night. We packed a copy of *Twelve O'Clock High* along with our other items for a return trip to the Wolf Lake cottage. Gladys's parents and grandparents basked in the afterglow of our evening while we relived it with them the next afternoon at a lakeside barbecue.

A few weeks later, a typed letter awaited me in the day shift briefing mail at work. The return address was North Carolwood Drive, Los Angeles, California. I was so nervous I was afraid to open it and tear the envelope. I asked a civilian employee to do it for me and sure enough, it was from Gregory Peck, dated July 8, 1999. It read:

> Dear Pete Stipe,
>   Thank you for your remarks at the Ann Arbor reception on June 19th, for your note to me, and especially for presenting me with your Justice Medal from The City of Ann Arbor.
>   I am honored by your sentiments, and I will cherish and guard the medal.
> With warm regards, Gregory Peck

The note was typed but bore his distinctive signature stretching from one margin to the other. It was the icing on the cake for me. I had it framed along with the photo of us talking together. Aside from the birth of my children and my union with Gladys, that meeting was the greatest moment of my life. Movies had always been my particular refuge as the youngest child in my family. They consumed many extended hours of being alone both before and after my parents' deaths. Gregory Peck may not have always delivered an Oscar-worthy performance, but his characters as he portrayed them in countless roles sustained me. To be able to discuss those films with him in person lent authority to my homegrown movie expertise. It enhanced every viewing of his films.

In 2006, we built a cottage high on a hill overlooking a lake in the Michigan countryside. We fittingly called it *"Twelve O'Clock High."* The framed letter and photo of Gregory Peck and I hangs on a wall in the study. Gladys's autographed *Life* magazine cover is shadow boxed and occupies an honored place on the front wall. Peck's Brigadier General Frank Savage looks over my shoulder as I write these words.

Chapter Twenty-Eight
Calling It a Day

I'd come a long way from Culver Military Academy. My citizenship had evolved, as had my sense of responsibility. Like at Culver, the AAPD's qualities of leadership and dependable loyalty had emerged in me enough to make my stay worthwhile. My one real regret was that my father had missed my transformation.

A lot changed at the Ann Arbor Police Department since I was sworn. The old guard was now gone. Marilyn and I were the remnants of a bygone era of revolvers, call boxes and handwritten reports. We both began at the city on January 22, 1979, and we were eligible to retire as partners on the same day twenty-five years, five Presidents, lots of chiefs and too many calls to catalogue later.

I was no longer as fast or durable as I once was. I was forty-seven-years-old and weary from fighting the same people and mediating the same disputes day after day. I would be the first to retire from both the SWAT unit and the department at the same time. My fifteen years made me the longest running operator in team history, though I would be capably replaced—and ultimately eclipsed—by Hardy Cooper and then Scott Hardin. Training with them made me a harder target for opponents.

Marilyn had also set a standard for durability. She had been a uniformed road patrol officer longer than any woman in Washtenaw County history. It was an impressive record. Her sometimes high-maintenance partner must have made a tough job more challenging, but she had steadied my pace.

Before my final exit, I took William and Jacob on patrol, as well as some trusted friends and neighbors. I shared after-shift beers with Buck Revere, Bobby Hodges and Jay Edwards and Jennifer McBride—four cops who understood me well. I was surely going to miss the camaraderie and watching dawn break from a patrol car with a cup of black coffee in my hand.

Ann Arbor News feature writer and Burns Park native Dave Markham wrote an elegant column about my retirement. He titled it "A Great Cop Decides to Call It a Day." He's a fine writer and I appreciated his thoughts.

January 22, 2004 — The Last Shift

On my last day Gladys followed me into work and documented my morning ritual on video. She followed me to the police garage as I loaded the car for the last time and gave a ceremonial briefing with Marilyn to a standing room only crowd. It was hard. I'd been an irreverent wiseguy in briefing for years, dropping spontaneous punch lines in response to bulletins, messages and announcements, but I wasn't very clever without a setup line. None were forthcoming.

Before we went on the road, Sgt. Jay Edwards told Marilyn and I to be careful, not to get involved in anything, and to come in early. He was not going to be responsible for something happening to us on our last day. We stopped for coffee at our usual spot for the final time. The same stoned-faced but friendly barista had served us coffee for twenty-five years.

We had an exhaustive list of stops to make, checking in with every city department to ensure we had no outstanding business to conduct. It was something that could have all been done over the course of several weeks, but policy dictated we fill out a last-minute waiver in one office after another.

The longest ordeal was in the property section, where the property officer insisted we account for equipment we'd either turned in or discarded long ago. Sergeant Ted Randall stopped in to bid us farewell and asked to look at our check-off lists. He initialed almost every stop remaining on our sheets. He told us if anyone asked, he'd deal with it. He saved us hours of needless tedium.

It's difficult to absorb the last day at a job one has worked at more than half their life. The great memories suppress the bad ones, and there's an overwhelming feeling of dread about your last chance to speak to this or that friend or to be in that certain spot just one more time. After all those exhausting hours working and driving it seems the day you're finished will never come. Then suddenly it arrives and time has run out.

Marilyn and I were summoned into Deputy Chief Cary O'Grady's office along with newly promoted Deputy Chief Boaz Gregory for an exit interview. It was about 1:40 p.m. on our last day. My coffee hour was scheduled for 2:00 p.m.—two of the sharpest guys in the building showed an amazing lack of forethought with their timing. They wanted to know what Marilyn and I thought the department's most pressing needs were. Really?

Soliciting our input in the last twenty minutes of our employment after twenty-five years of service struck both of us as odd. Although they'd both maintained their friends after they were promoted, neither one of them seemed truly in touch with what was currently going on with department morale or efficiency. They weren't unsympathetic, but they were otherwise occupied with current Chief Stan Coates' chaotic agenda, which left little time to bear down on details.

We had been offering our opinion of the operation every morning at briefing for years. We hardly knew where to start. There were a dozen different uniform options, projecting the image of a department that didn't know what to wear. The report writing system was cumbersome, time consuming and hard to access. The front desk was a nightmare; citizens had to air their dirty laundry in a public lobby, and it was increasingly rare to have an actual human being answer the phone. The new computer-aided dispatch system displayed calls waiting for service on patrol car screens but no one volunteered to take them. Units were often driving in the opposite direction, so the dispatcher would assign calls to someone else. There was little or no space to park patrol cars—officers pressed for time would park in public spots, displacing citizens who came to City Hall on legitimate business.

The list was limitless but we had a new chief who seemed focused on enhancing his resume and the department's profile as opposed to improving its efficiency. O'Grady and Gregory sincerely meant well, but administrators were left juggling too many balls to worry about the spin on any one issue.

Gregory served as deputy chief until his retirement in 2016. He did an admirable job of making common sense decisions, often under the scrutiny of some dubious bosses. He never forgot where he came from, nor did he lose his sense of humor.

Cary O'Grady became interim chief when Stan Coates left for Aurora, Colorado. He'd earned his law degree while working as an Ann Arbor officer and detective full-time. He was of the finest sort, as an officer and a man. We'd combined his thoughtful, wise decisions with the presence of my MP5 to disarm some truly desperate men.

He went on to become head of the Eastern Michigan University Department of Public Safety. He took several fine Ann Arbor police retirees with him, Joe Randleman, Terry Johnson and Oh-Two-Three Hayes among them. Cary had a quiet, private way about him. He was a great listener who seemed to absorb everything going on around him.

In the end, he may have taken on too much. On the day before Christmas, 2011, he ended his life. In a profession where jaded veterans and entitled rookies gripe about everything and everyone, Cary O'Grady was among those rare officers who were universally liked and admired for his talent and his optimism. His passing snatched a slice of certainty and life from all who survived him.

Marilyn wanted to leave quietly. I wanted to have a last word and share the moment with my family, friends and co-workers. The city council chambers were full of food, friends and lots of emotion. Best of all was the presence of Gladys; sons William, Jacob, and Bronce; and daughter Darby. I started by literally saluting the officers who were present, in all directions.

First I thanked all my partners: Marilyn, Nick Stark, Buck Revere, Bobby Hodges, Joe Randleman, Tucker Williams and Daniel Arguello. I acknowledged former roommate and intrepid friend George Westwood and my "female support group," Kelly Shayne, Jennifer McBride and Joanna Mitchell. I also thanked Jay Edwards, who knew how to blend supervision and common sense in a uniquely pleasant way.

The kinship I feel with cops continues to this day. I'd immersed myself in the profession at considerable expense, but it rewarded me with a sense of satisfaction and purpose I don't think I could have achieved doing anything else.

I presented Marilyn with a letter from Michigan Governor Jennifer Granholm recognizing her service. Several officers as well as the mayor stepped up to speak on my behalf. I posed for pictures with the family, holding two-year-old Bronce aloft for my last photo in uniform.

After addressing everyone I could, I went down to the empty locker room to change out of uniform for the final time. On my way out, I stopped at property to turn in my gun and my key to the building. When I stepped into the afternoon sun as an unarmed civilian, I no longer had any law enforcement authority. It was hard to believe it was all over.

* * *

Postscript: The Party

Gladys organized the retirement party to end all retirement parties. She rented a spacious hall down the road from our house. She arranged for Ray Reynolds and his band to entertain. Gladys's brothers freely dispensed cases of liquor to a crowd stacked four deep. She screened a PowerPoint presentation using theme songs from the movies *The Sons of Katie Elder*, *Silverado* and *The Commancheros*. There were photos of softball and SWAT teams, family and friends that included nearly everyone in attendance. I heard Paul Ocklander whisper to his children, "There I am," as a photo of him and I in an Ann Arbor Tire Co. ad flashed by.

Nick Stark showed up and reunited with Buck, Joe Randleman and me. Nick had left a department in turmoil a couple of years before while it was in the midst of a contentious search for a new chief. He found a new home as a regional FedEx investigator. No three cops ever had a more profound impact on public safety than those guys. It was an emotional night.

Max Burleson drove down from the Upper Peninsula to attend. Vic Mitchell told me Max's presence alone made the event significant. He was the legend by which all others were measured. I was overwhelmed. Most of the invited guests came, as well as several who crashed. They were all welcome. One way or another, each one had played a part in my survival. When it came time to vacate the hall, we moved the party to our house.

As we stepped outside, the temperature was minus-sixteen degrees. The weather was so frigid the ice sculpture of my badge Gladys had ordered stayed intact in our front yard for a month after the party. Guests stayed until dawn. I was sorry to see them go. It took me several days to compose thank you notes for all the gifts I'd received: books on writing, journals, several bottles of scotch, and many, many thoughtful cards. I was officially retired.

* * *

Reflections and the Aftermath

In late 1972, my dad began to plan for his retirement. He and his third wife Deb were happy and he was ready to pass his tire business on. We planned a motorhome trip out west. One day the three of us sat in the study while they sipped Bloody Marys and discussed the itinerary. Our targeted departure was in one year— my dad never made it. He was diagnosed with cancer of the lymph nodes and cobalt treatments drew the life right out of him. He died a tired fifty-eight in November of 1973.

My grandfather was kicked in the chest by a horse at age fifty-two and also died before his time. In 2004 I was forty-seven and weary from all I'd absorbed as a cop. Stress fractures in my feet still caused chronic pain and I had lost count of my concussions. I was done.

Hypervigilance had wrung me out. So many fights, so much internal departmental strife, and so many gruesome, tragic and sudden deaths loitered in a darkened alley of my memory. Now that I had stopped pressing forward, those ghosts and others began to close in.

I have vivid dreams. Armed encounters and shootouts are portrayed with startling realism. Under fire or not, I always converge on my adversary—some training runs deep. There have been dreams of fights I seem neither to win or lose. Going to sleep isn't a problem; it's going back to sleep after some of these episodes that isn't easy.

The mounting toll of officers killed in the line of duty makes me wonder if I wasn't lucky just to escape with my life. I should have died many times. I am especially grateful to those whose training helped me to survive and those who showed up when I needed them most. That list alone could fill a volume.

I extend my sincere thanks to my family and friends for being there for me. Any omissions are due to story compression, not lack of gratitude. Airing out the most painful and personal episodes of one's life and career doesn't resolve them all, but at least they no longer stalk me. I sought to dispel some myths, apply due credit and set the record straight.

Police officers are being assailed from all sides for their use of force. The conduct of a few sullies the reputation of all good cops.

There is a contentious history between law enforcement officers and people of color in this country. It's documented quite clearly and police bear much responsibility for the atmosphere that currently exists. Distrust of authority is a hard heritage to resolve.

About one hundred fifty law enforcement officers are killed in the line of duty each year. Officers rely on their own experiences to draw conclusions in the field. They too are exposed to an inordinate amount of ill treatment, sometimes at the hands of people of color. Until we all bear our share of the blame, that dynamic will continue to plague us. When leadership fails, it is up to line officers and citizens to close that gap, one encounter at a time.

The dynamics that justify the use of force are too complex to discuss here. There might be a Thin Blue Line but there is no Code of Silence. The officer's job is to take action to resolve or diffuse issues, not engage in public debate about them. Departments designate spokespersons to do so. There may be corrupt police departments out there, but the Ann Arbor Police Department isn't among them. Few jobs are more difficult. Few agencies do it better.

Brad Thompson, Hunter Bernard and other longtime friends enlisted me in their "Northern Exposure" golf weekends in upper Lower Michigan. We tour the finest courses Michigan offers. The bonfire evenings on the shore of Lake Charlevoix are unlike any other outing, a mark of achievement and friendship rolled into one. Single malt scotch and bourbon were aged to toast those who've passed before us and to celebrate the friends we still have.

Gladys and I designed and built a lakeside cottage. Nestled atop a hill, it overlooks magnificent sunsets on shimmering water every evening. I have five children, and my youngest son Chance is a constant companion. I am immensely proud of them all. I've been given the opportunity to make up for the field trips and events I missed with the older boys. I took up photography and thoroughly cover every vacation and every game. I'm now home for the holidays.

I taught tactical classes to recruits, using police videos and numerous film clips to bring survival tips home. There was John Wayne giving Ron Howard a shooting lesson in *The Shootist,* Paul Newman refusing to give up while boxing George Kennedy in *Cool Hand Luke,* and Sean Connery dispensing the best advice ever to Kevin Costner in *The Untouchables.*

Jennifer McBride gave me an engraved photo album full of pictures on my retirement. It bore Connery's quote from *The Untouchables,* written by David Mamet:

> "You just fulfilled the first rule of law enforcement. Make sure when your shift is over you go home alive. Here endeth the lesson."

ACKNOWLEDGMENTS

Editors:

Rick Ollerman   Andrew Gulli
Gretchen Kennard   Heather Hughes
Darby Stipe   Karen Stipe

Special Thanks To:
Brad Thompson   John B. Kennard
William E. Brown IV   Diane Augustus
Peter Maupin   Dave Kennard
Rick Stern   Pat Codere
Bernard Tucker   Dennis Aguirre
Pat Hughes   Tom Seyfried
Michelle Lance
The Officers and Dispatchers of the
Ann Arbor Police Department

My Role Models:
Writers, Teachers, Mentors, Bosses, Partners and Characters

David Niven, Irving Boim, John Rebel Tucker, Coach Loren
Carswell, John Nordlinger, Bob Winkle, Chet Brown, George
Gardner, Bill Yadlosky, Larry Pickel, Tim Gilbert, Chief William
J. Corbett, Lt. G. Miller, Byrl Racine, Jim Stimac, Jim Stephenson
Jim Ghent, Gordie Steers and Sgt. Saunders

Photo Credit Leisa Thompson Photography

PETER STIPE retired from the Ann Arbor Police Department in 2004 as its most highly decorated officer. His assignments included the Special Tactics Unit, Detective Division, Field Training Officer and District Coordinator. A writer and film noir buff, he now resides in Michigan's Irish Hills.

BOOKS

On the following pages are a few
more great titles from the
Down & Out Books publishing family.

For a complete list of books and to
sign up for our newsletter,
go to DownAndOutBooks.com.

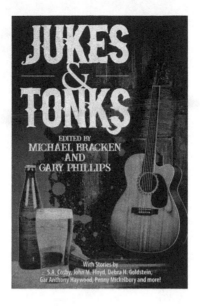

Jukes & Tonks
Crime Fiction Inspired by Music
in the Dark and Suspect Choices
Michael Bracken and Gary Phillips, editors

Down & Out Books
April 2021
978-1-64396-184-2

The stories in *Jukes & Tonks* introduce sinners and saints, love begun and love gone wrong, and all manner of unsavory criminal endeavors.

What they have in common is that they plop you down in worlds where the music pulsating from the stage provides the backbeat for tales that are unsparing, heartbreaking, twisty, and a few are as dark as the night.

Radicals
Nik Korpon

Down & Out Books
May 2021
978-1-64396-185-9

When a mysterious cyber-terrorist organization begins erasing Americans' medical debt, enigmatic FBI cybercrimes agent Jay Brodsky must focus on an attack threatening to destabilize the US economy.

But when the trail leads to his own family, Jay will be forced to confront everything he never knew about his parents and his long-missing sister and decide where his true loyalties lie.

Dead-End Jobs
A Hitman Anthology
Andy Rausch, Editor

All Due Respect, an imprint of
Down & Out Books
June 2021
978-1-64396-212-2

A collection of eighteen short stories about contract killers by some of the hottest crime writers in the business.

"An incredible collection of powerful and haunting stories that exist in that shadowy realm between tragedy, nihilism and noir." —S.A. Cosby, author of *Blacktop Wasteland*

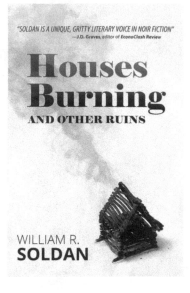

Houses Burning and Other Ruins
William R. Soldan

Shotgun Honey, an imprint of
Down & Out Books
May 2021
978-1-64396-115-6

Desperation. Violence. Broken homes and broken hearts. Fathers, junkies, and thieves.

In this gritty new collection, one bad choice begets another, and redemption is a twisted mirage. The troubled characters that inhabit the streets and alleys of these stories continually find themselves at the mercy of a cold, indifferent world as they hurtle downward and grapple for hard-won second chances in a life that seldom grants them.

CPSIA information can be obtained
at www.ICGtesting.com
Printed in the USA
JSHW030921160621
15945JS00004B/15